Civilization is a System of Abusive Control

Adrian Ellis

Copyright © 2022 Adrian Ellis

Cover Design by Adrian Ellis

www.adrianellis.uk

All rights reserved.

ISBN: 979-8-4059-2676-6

For Everyone

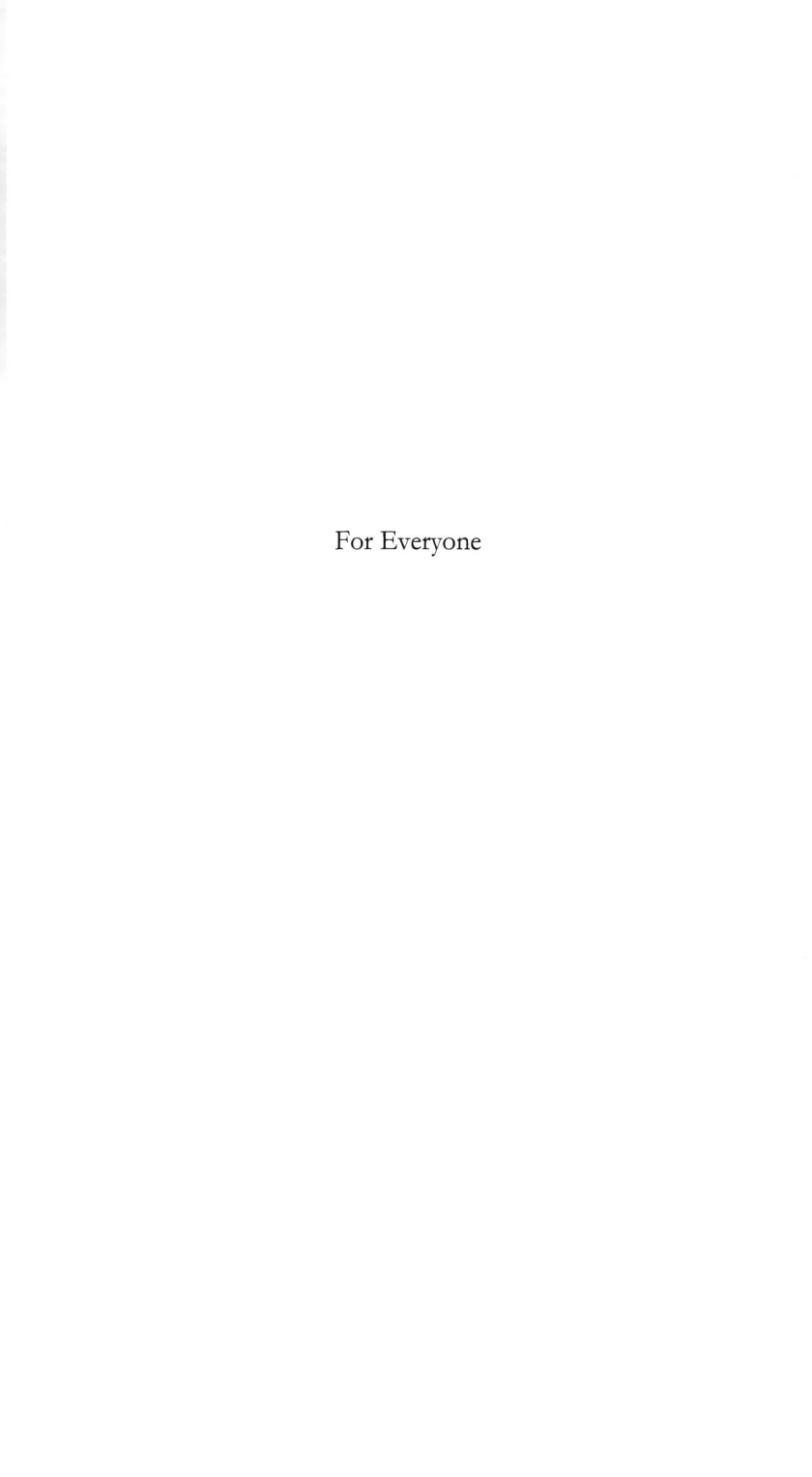

CONTENTS

Part 1: The Bread and Butter of Civilization, *and what it does to our bodies.* — Pg 1

Part 2: The Controllers of Civilization, *and what they do to our minds.* — Pg 59

Part 3: The Gods, *who they were, and what they did to us.* — Pg 169

Part 4: Bio-robots; *how we're not biological machines, but the gods were.* — Pg 229

Part 5: The Way Out; *how we can make something better.* — Pg 319

Part 1: The Bread and Butter of Civilization

Introduction

The title of this book – *Civilization is a system of abusive control* - may seem strange. Many of us have been told, from a young age, that civilization has been an enormous step forward for us. Before civilization began, which officially started in around 4,000 BC in Mesopotamia, we, as a species, lived in a state of barbarism. In that primitive state, we foraged, hunted game and lived from hand to mouth. We spent our time forever in fear of predators. We knew little of the world outside our range of activity. Our lives, to quote the philosopher Thomas Hobbes, were nasty, brutal and short. We had very little culture, primitive technology and were functioning at a level only slightly above those of animals. Civilization rescued us from this primitive state.

The process of humanity's transition from hunter-gathering to civilization is said to have occurred slowly, over many thousands of years. This process began soon after the end of our last ice-age, in around

8,000 BC, and for the next four thousand years, gradually gathered pace. During this time, in the Fertile Crescent area of the Near East and Persia, small, tribal groups learned, adapted, experimented, and communicated skills and knowledge until they had assembled a host of abilities: irrigation, animal husbandry, pottery, writing, metalworking, selective animal breeding and so on. These skills, together, created civilization and produced the first city-states, kingdoms, and theocracies. To quote Wikipedia, civilisation is:

> "...any complex society characterized by urban development, social stratification, a form of government and symbolic systems of communication such as writing. Civilizations are intimately associated with and often further defined by other socio-politico-economic characteristics, including centralization, the domestication of both humans and other organisms (livestock), specialization of labour, culturally ingrained ideologies of progress and supremacism, monumental architecture, taxation, societal dependence upon farming and expansionism."

Officially, thanks to civilization, we have become a far better species. We live safer, healthier, happier and more culturally enriched lives than our primitive forebears. We have expanded our knowledge and broadened our horizons, but in recent decades, several scientists, archaeologists, historians, and other academics have pointed out that civilization may have not been an entirely good thing. For example, the

American historian and writer Jared Diamond pointed out, in the Discovery Magazine article, *The Worst Mistake in the History of the Human Race* (May 1st 1999), that the official view of civilization, and our civilized selves as a pinnacle of development, may be seriously wrong:

> 'To science we owe dramatic changes in our smug self-image. Astronomy taught us that our earth isn't the center of the universe but merely one of billions of heavenly bodies. From biology we learned that we weren't specially created by God but evolved along with millions of other species. Now archaeology is demolishing another sacred belief: that human history over the past million years has been a long tale of progress. In particular, recent discoveries suggest that the adoption of agriculture, supposedly our most decisive step toward a better life, was in many ways a catastrophe from which we have never recovered.'

During the rest of the article, Diamond supports this idea by referencing the latest scientific evidence, which we'll look at in this book. This idea, that civilization hasn't been an entirely good step forward, has been thought about by many people, not just academics. Perceptive writers have spotted that we, as civilized humans, aren't entirely lovely. What's more, many of us aren't happy, many of us lead miserable lives, and collectively, we are now only a whisker away from destroying ourselves, through nuclear war or a bio-weapon or through the destruction of our environment. Something is seriously wrong.

The British comedy science-fiction writer Douglas Adams touched on this matter in his book, *The Hitchhiker's Guide to the Galaxy*. To quote from his book:

> "Man had always assumed that he was more intelligent than the dolphins because he had achieved so much - the wheel, New York, wars and so on - whilst all the dolphins had ever done was muck about in the water having a good time. But conversely, the dolphins had always believed that they were far more intelligent than man, for precisely the same reasons."

In other words, civilization is supposed to have been a massive step forward, but have we just replaced harvesting clams, and sitting in the sunshine, with 72-hour weeks and carpet-bombing?

This book will study what civilization has brought us, and assess what it's done to us, particularly in relation to the world of the hunter-gatherers. It'll then examine a darker idea, that many of the negative aspects of civilization, elements that have made us malnourished, exhausted, repressed, ignorant, deluded, stressed and fearful, were not an accident of history. Instead, the people who created civilization deliberately chose these facets to keep us in a subjugated state. To understand the nature of this subjugation and suppression, it's worth studying something a dark episode took place in New Zealand, in the 1980's.

The Monster of Mangatiti

> "Heather was a teenager in New Zealand when she got the job of tutor to the son of William 'Bill' Cornelius. She was taken to his hut in the Mangatiti Valley, leaving Murumuru Rd on a vehicle track through 12km of dense bush. From the road end it is at least another 40km to Raetihi. Cornelius was charming and treated her "incredibly well" at first but then came rapes, starvation, and threats of torture and death. The young woman became pregnant, but miscarried. Finally, she escaped by stealing a utility while Cornelius and a friend were out hunting."

This is a quote from the New Zealand Herald article *Victim of sex attacks relives ordeal*. It describes the traumatic experience of Heather Walsh when she made the fateful mistake of answer a job advert in 1985 to work at a remote farmhouse in the Mangatiti Valley. Her experience is the source material for the documentary *the Monster of Mangatiti*. The article goes on to say:

> "When she heard how Cornelius had kept women captive, Ms de Lacey (the programme's executive producer) wondered how such a thing could happen in New Zealand. The isolation of the place was one answer. 'It allowed him to hold those women in a very vulnerable position. It was an environment that he controlled,' she explained. 'Another was the effect of psychological abuse. What really intrigued me

> about this case is that it explores the psychological breakdown of a victim - he was a master manipulator. You could ask why she didn't just leave, but it's not that simple. We've got a massive issue with domestic violence in New Zealand.' The film, hopefully, goes some way to explain it from a victim's point of view."

Walsh's experience mirrors the experiences of many women who have suffered at the hands of an abusive man. In some cases, the man is fully aware of the abuse he's inflicting, but in other cases, he does it unconsciously, or instinctively. For example, in the Guardian article, '*It's like you go to abuse school: how domestic violence always follows the same script*', which draws on material from the book *See what you made me do*, by Jess Hill, one abuser, identified as Rob, is toxically controlling his his female partner. He doesn't realise that he is being abusive, as he isn't being physically violent with his wife. Instead, he tries to control her through abusive psychological tactics. He is locked into his own toxic attitude. To quote from the article:

> "Rob wasn't physically violent, but he behaved like a typical perpetrator: he constantly criticised and bullied his wife, tried to stop her from working, made it hard for her to see family and friends, and kept total control over their bank accounts. The bullying and criticism weren't always overt; sometimes Rob would use humour to demean Deb. But it was always sending the same message: he was more important than her, and she was there to serve him. The only thing that wasn't typical

about Rob was that he had sought counselling without being forced."

Rob's unconscious and habitual, negative behaviour was psychologically damaging his partner, and yet he still seemed to care about her. It was as if his behaviour had been trained into him, at a low level. This possibility reflects something noticed by many female survivors of abuse. When they gather together in support groups, and discuss their experiences, they are often shocked at the similarity of the tactics used by their male, abusive partners. To quote one woman, 'it's as if they'd been to abuse school'. In other words, the methods that abusive controllers use seem to be the same, over and over again. It's as if a standard method of abusive control exists in our civilization and permeates it at a deep level. The facets of this abuse-control system are relatively straightforward, and perhaps mundane, but their power is shockingly effective, so effective in fact that they have been mistaken for a far more notorious system of control: brainwashing.

Brainwashing

In the 1950's, the American public was shocked when many U.S. prisoners-of-war in Korea, taken captive by the Maoist communists, began confessing to outlandish crimes against the enemy forces. By February 1953, highly ranked soldiers such as the pilot Colonel Frank Schwable, who was shot down over Korea, had falsely confessed to using germ warfare against the Koreans, dropping everything from anthrax to the plague on unsuspecting civilians.

In total, 5,000 of those 7,200 U.S. POWs either petitioned the U.S. government to end the war, or signed confessions of their alleged crimes. A final blow to U.S. morale came when 21 American soldiers, who were freed, refused repatriation. According to one report, after being given the opportunity of returning to the United States, they turned around and joined the Communist forces. The people of the United States found this behaviour almost impossible to believe. Instead, many members of the American public became convinced that the soldiers had been brainwashed. This term had gain prominence in America after the article, *Brain-washing Tactics Force Chinese Into Ranks of Communist Party*, written by the journalist Edward Hunter, was published in the Miami Daily News in September 1950. Hunter explained in his article that Mao Zedong's Red Army had used terrifying ancient techniques to turn the Chinese people into mindless, Communist automatons. He called this hypnotic process "brainwashing," a word-for-word translation from xi-nao, the Mandarin words for wash (xi) and brain (nao). Hunter warned about its dangerous applications. To quote, the process was meant to "change a mind radically so that its owner becomes a living puppet—a human robot—without the atrocity being visible from the outside." Hunter's article sounded ominous and scientifically knowledgeable but in truth, the Communist forces in Korea had not used exotic or advanced techniques to 'brainwash' captured U.S. servicemen. Instead, they had used more mundane but highly effective methods.

Korean POWs (Wikipedia commons - Staff Sgt. Ken Scar)

Albert Biderman, a social scientist with the US Air Force, was given the job of investigating what had happened to these captured servicemen. He interviewed defectors and released prisoners and learned of their experiences. He concluded that they had not been brainwashed. Instead, he explained that their captors had inflicted a well-coordinated but seemingly simple programme of abuse. Biderman explained his findings in his article *Communist attempts to elicit false confessions from air force prisoners of war*. Biderman states:

> "The finding of our studies, which should be greeted as most new and spectacular, is that essentially there was <u>nothing new or spectacular</u> about the events we studied." (my underline) We found, as did other studies such as those of Hinkle and Wolf, that human behavior could be manipulated within a certain range by controlled environments. We

found that the Chinese Communists used methods of coercing behavior from our men in their hands which Communists of other countries had employed for decades and which police and inquisitors had employed for centuries. The Chinese interrogators succeeded or failed to influence the behavior of their victims roughly to the extent that the skill and persistence of the personnel they employed matched those of practitioners in other places and times. While their initial attempts were generally inept and unsuccessful, their success tripled with experience.

Biderman goes on to say:

"The methods they used to shape compliance into the now familiar pattern of the forced confession, we believe, can be understood as essentially a teaching procedure; teaching the prisoner how to comply. It was a complex teaching procedure, however. Its complexities were due to the elaborate and complex behavior which was sought, as well as to the fact that this behavior was so alien and offensive to the prisoner. It was further complicated by irrational aspects of the system within which the Communist interrogator operated. The system required him to teach without making his lessons explicit."

Biderman, in his article, lists the elements in this process of forced compliance of the prisoner by his or her captors. They are as follows:

1. <u>Isolate the prisoner</u>: Remove social support - Make the prisoner dependent on his/her captor.
2. <u>Monopolise the prisoner's attention</u>: Force the prisoner to mentally focus on his/her predicament. - Remove other sources of distraction, interest or focus through monotonising food, limiting stimulus and making the environment barren.
3. <u>Debilitate the prisoner</u>: Semi-starvation or malnutrition. - Exposure. - Sleep deprivation. - Over exertion. - Prolonged constraint.
1. <u>Threats of Death</u>: endless isolation, vague threats, threats against family. - Mysterious Changes of Treatment.
2. <u>Occasional indulgences</u>: Indulgences provide positive motivation for compliance. - Indulgences prevent the prisoner habituating to their deprived situation. - Promises of rewards for partial compliance.
3. <u>Demonstrations of omnipotence and omniscience</u>: Make the futility of resistance clear. - Enact confrontations. - Pretend complete control over the victim's fate.
4. <u>Degradation</u>: Make costs of resistance appear more damaging to the victim's

self-esteem than capitulation. - Reduce prisoner to "Animal Level" concerns. - Prevent personal hygiene. - Make surroundings filthy. - Perform demeaning punishments. - Insult the prisoner. - Taunt the prisoner. - Deny the prisoner privacy.

5. <u>Enforce trivial demands</u>: Enforcement of Meaningless rules. - Enforcement of Meaningless actions.

Biderman's article concludes:

"Among the Air Force prisoners pressured for false confessions in North Korea and in Communist China, there are cases of simply incredible heroism, fortitude and attachment to principle in the face of particularly intensive Communist coercion. There are also cases - far fewer in number although far more publicized - of a surprising inability to withstand coercion. Nonetheless, depending upon how one chooses to draw the line, it is impossible for us to say truthfully that all who were really involved fully resisted, or that all fully complied, for in truth the behavior of all involved, at some point, was a mixture of compliance and resistance. In almost all, resistance was the dominant ingredient."

"The one remaining question is why the Communists proceeded in this strange way. It is not, I am convinced, because they were guided by some esoteric knowledge and rationale which gives them an unprecedented ability to bend people to their will, insofar as "confessions" for propaganda use are concerned, for these could have been elicited much more quickly and easily by coupling the standard measures for inducing compliance with very explicit demands for the false statements that they required. False confessions were in fact extorted from Air Force personnel more quickly and economically by North Koreans who apparently had not yet learned the Communist way of doing things. This self-castigation and ideological ranting which the Communists sought, and at which almost all of our people balked, I would think, detracts rather than adds to whatever propaganda value "confessions" might have. All this assumes that some purpose as rational as propaganda is always the major reason for extorting "confessions," and this appears quite definitely not the case. The mystery associated with the things I have discussed stems not from the captors' rationality but from their irrationality. Unlike the cynical Nazis who merely perpetrated the Big Lie, the Chinese Communist personnel, whom our prisoners encountered in Korea, were required to live the Big Lie."

Biderman's closing comments touch on an important aspect to the experience of the U.S. Korean prisoners. Primarily, they were being abused by their Communist captors in order to make them betray their homeland, but they were also being abused by their captors, to make the U.S. prisoners agree with their captors' *own* irrational, state-induced behaviour, which they themselves been trained to follow from an early age. In other words, the captors were themselves prisoners of an abusive, irrational regime and they were doing their best to make the U.S. servicemen join their mad, abused mindset. The prisoners, and their captors, were both agreeing to irrational views to reduce their levels of suffering.

It's worth studying Biderman's list again because its elements will crop up repeatedly in this book. As Biderman explained, the abuse-control system he investigated is relatively simple, yet devastatingly effective. It contains the following elements of reducing the victim to a willing follower, acolyte or slave: Isolation, Removal of support, Creation of Dependency, Monopolisation of attention, Removal of other interests, Monotony of food, Limitation of stimuli, Barrenness of Environment, Malnutrition, Sleep deprivation, Overwork, Prolonged Constraints, Threats of Death, Continual Fear/Anxiety, Mysterious Changes of Treatment, Occasional indulgences for greater compliance, Promises of Rewards for partial compliance, Demonstrations of Omnipotence and Omniscience, Degradation, Prevention of Personal Hygiene, Performing Demeaning Punishments, Denial of privacy, Enforcement of Trivial Demands, and Enforcement of Meaningless rules and actions.

Some readers, as they work through this list, may spot that these elements are present in a lot more situations than just Korean War interrogations. In fact, these elements seem to be present in aspects of our daily lives. To understand how far this goes, it's worth taking a fresh, clear-eyed view of what civilization has brought to humanity, using the latest scientific evidence. To start with, we can look at one of its key features: farming.

Farming

According to the history books, our species gradually shifted from hunter-gathering to farming over many thousands of years, particularly in the Fertile Crescent of the Near East, from around 8,000 BC to 4,000 BC. This explanation neatly explains how the first civilization on Earth began; it was a consequence of progressive, intelligent hunter-gatherers using their skills, curiosity and efforts to better themselves and improve their lives. By switching to ploughing fields, sowing crops and harvesting grains, they had taken a big step forward. The only problem with this theory is that it makes no sense. Hunter-gatherers live a very different life to farmers. They do not work at all, in the normal sense, since they are simply hunting and gathering what has naturally grown by itself. This approach to obtaining food requires a complex understanding of the natural environment: what foods are edible, when they can be harvested and so on. A hunter-gatherer's diet is therefore highly varied, and shifts with the seasons, but it works extremely well. Since the food grows by itself, once the hunter-gatherer knows enough about his or her environment, he or she simply travels around, picking it up. According to many anthropologists, hunter-gatherers only 'work' for about four hours a day, depending on the day, after which they relax, play and create. They do face threats, dangers, and disasters but no more than any human being in history, right up until the present day. In many ways, they lived an idyllic existence. It is therefore extremely difficult to understand why any of them would switch from that life to one of agriculture, or farming. Why would any of them shift from gathering foods to the arduous work of clearing fields, ploughing up the soil and planting a particular grass, such as wheat, to ground up its seeds into a flour? Why would they switch to such a backbreaking form of subsistence? In 1963, the anthropologist Richard Lee asked this very question to a !Kung Bushman in Botswana. The Bushman replied:

> "Why should we plant, when there are so many mongongo nuts in the world?"

Why indeed?

The Bushman's critical comment about switching to ploughing, sowing and harvesting grains is supported by the latest research into the effect of farming on our ancient forebears. For example, the science article *Dawn of agriculture took toll on health*, published in the Science Daily magazine, reports on studies on how early civilized humans fared, compared to the hunter-gatherers of that period. Its summary states:

> "When populations around the globe started turning to agriculture around 10,000 years ago, regardless of their locations and type of crops, a similar trend occurred: the height and health of the people declined. The pattern holds up across standardized studies of whole skeletons in populations, say researchers in

the first comprehensive, global review of the literature regarding stature and health during the agriculture transition."

Amanda Mummert, an Emory graduate student in anthropology, explains in the article:

"This broad and consistent pattern [of a decline in health in civilized humans] holds up when you look at standardized studies of whole skeletons in populations," says Amanda Mummert, an Emory graduate student in anthropology. Mummert led the first comprehensive, global review of the literature regarding stature and health during the agriculture transition, to be published by the journal Economics and Human Biology. "Many people have this image of the rise of agriculture and the dawn of modern civilization, and they just assume that a more stable food source makes you healthier, but early agriculturalists experienced nutritional deficiencies and had a harder time adapting to stress, probably because they became dependent on particular food crops, rather than having a more significantly diverse diet." She adds that growth in population density spurred by agriculture settlements led to an increase in infectious diseases, likely exacerbated by problems of sanitation and the proximity to domesticated animals and other novel disease vectors."

As Mummert makes clear, those humans who switched from hunter-gathering to farming, and keeping of livestock, suffered. They weren't the only victims. The wild animals they domesticated also suffered. As the Wikipedia page on Animal Husbandry explains:

> "David Nibert, professor of sociology at Wittenberg University, posits that, based on contemporary scholarship by ethologists and biologists about the sentience and intelligence of other animals, "we can assume that, for the most part, the other animals' experience of capture, enslavement, use, and slaying was one of suffering and violence." Much of this involved direct physical violence, but also structural violence as their systemic oppression and enslavement, "resulted in their inability to meet their basic needs, the loss of self-determination, and the loss of opportunity to live in a natural way." He says that the remains of domesticated animals from thousands of years ago found during archaeological excavations revealed numerous bone pathologies, which provide evidence of extreme suffering: 'Excavations from 8500 BCE revealed bone deformities in enslaved goats and cows and provided 'some indication of stress, presumably due to the conditions in which these early domestic animals were kept.' Remains of sheep and goats from the early Bronze Age show a marked decrease in bone thickness, reflecting calcium deficiencies "resulting from the combined effects of poor nutrition and intensive milking.'"

We can see, already, that civilization brought many elements of the abuse-control system into play. It introduced physical exhaustion and overwork, malnutrition, poor hygiene and continual constraint (because of the high-population density of an urban environment), a monotonous diet and regular sickness from disease incubating in the penned livestock. None of these elements were present in the world of the hunter-gatherers.

Fortunately, nowadays, for many of us, some of these elements are no longer an issue. The mechanisation of farming has reduced the backbreaking aspect of ploughing, sowing and harvesting. Modern sanitation and antibiotics have reduced the dangers of infectious diseases but this, perhaps, has hidden more subtle problems of our switch to a civilized diet. To understand what they are, we need to draw upon the latest nutritional research and use them to study the staple foods of civilization, and what they do to us. To start with, let's examine wheat.

Wheat

Wheat is the most popular staple food in the Western world. To quote from Wikipedia:

> "Wheat is grown on more land area than any other food crop (220.4 million hectares, 2014). World trade in wheat is greater than for all other crops combined. In 2017, world production of wheat was 772 million tonnes, with a forecast of 2019 production at 766 million tonnes, making it the second most-produced cereal after maize. Since 1960,

> world production of wheat and other grain crops has tripled and is expected to grow further through the middle of the 21st century. Global demand for wheat is increasing due to the unique viscoelastic and adhesive properties of gluten proteins, which facilitate the production of processed foods, whose consumption is increasing, as a result of the worldwide industrialization process and the westernization of the diet."

These figures show how important wheat is to us. It has been a staple part of civilization, from its very beginning, and little has changed. Many people wouldn't want to live without wheat. What's more, many of us couldn't even believe that we *could* live happily without wheat, and yet the latest scientific studies of that crop, and how it affects our bodies, might give these people second thought.

In 2014, Dr David Perlmutter published a book, *Grain Brain*. In the book's introduction, he explains that many of the ailments that plague our old age, in the modern world, such as Alzheimer's and dementia, are not inevitable. They are not an intrinsic part of human ageing. To quote from page 4 of his book:

> "There are plenty of perpetual myths about the basket of brain-degenerating maladies that includes Alzheimer's: *It's in the genes, it's inevitable with age,* and *it's a given if you live into your eighties and beyond*. Not so fast. I'm here to tell you that the fate of your brain is not in your genes. It's not inevitable. And if you're someone who suffers from another type of brain disorder, such as chronic

headaches, depression, epilepsy, or extreme moodiness, the culprit may not be encoded in your DNA. It's in the food you eat. Yes, you read that right: Brain dysfunction starts in your daily bread..."

In the next 300 pages, Dr Perlmutter explains, in great detail, how wheat damages our brains through inflammation. Many people already know that sugar damages our bodies, by causing diabetes, but Dr Perlmutter's latest research shows that all carbohydrates and starches can cause inflammation. What's more, wheat contains compounds that affect our hormone signalling, in particular the molecule leptin. For example, when we eat wheat, it suppresses leptin signalling in our body, a hormone that tells us when we're full. In other words, eating wheat makes us overeat.

Wheat also has another trick up its sleeve. The gluten in wheat breaks down into peptides in the stomach. These peptides travel to the brain and bind to opiate-type receptors in our brains. In other words, while wheat is causing inflammation in your body, spiking up your blood-sugar levels, and turning off your 'full feeling' it's also giving you a morphine-like pleasurable high. As a foodstuff, it might keep you alive but it's a nutritional and health disaster zone.

Dr Perlmutter recommends, in his book, that we follow a very different diet to the carbs/ wheat/ sugar/ fruits intake many of us currently consume. He explains that natural fats, such as those found in nuts, olives, seeds, avocados, coconuts, eggs and other foods, create a far healthier brain and body. Not only do these natural foods produce less inflammation, they also change our body's hormone-signalling system, stopping the food-craving peckishness. We also lose abdominal fat because our body is no longer desperately turning blood-sugar into far, to get it out of our blood systems. If we consume a diet high in natural, healthy fats, then we feel full sooner, we stay feeling full longer, and we don't have the wild swings of blood-sugar levels. Paradoxically, by consuming a diet higher in natural fats, we become slimmer. This diet is very similar to hunter-gatherer diets, which explains why hunter-gatherers, even now, are almost never obese.

Therefore, wheat, may be the most famous food in the civilized West, but from a health & nutrition point of view, it's an abusive charmer. It drugs us with its gluten-peptides, inflames our bodies and leaves us brain-fogged, sluggish, diabetic and overweight. As a staple food, it's a disaster.

Let's now look at another key foodstuff that we've gained in civilization: milk.

Milk

Milk seems, on the surface, to be an excellent foodstuff. It contains fats, proteins, and sugars. This is understandable, since cows make it to give to their growing calves. The problem with milk is that it *is* for baby cows; it's not designed for humans. We don't possess the same digestive enzymes as calves. Because of this, we can't digest milk in the same way. The New Scientist article, *Guzzling milk might boost your risk of breaking bones* (October 2014) highlights this problem; it explains that there are big drawbacks when you consume another species' milk. It reports that a health study, carried out on tens of thousands of people in Sweden, which ran for over 20 years, found the following:

> "The study, which tracked 61,433 women aged 39 to 74 over 20 years, and 45,339 men of similar age for 11 years, found that the more milk people drank, the more likely they were to die or experience a bone fracture during the study period."

The study found that women who reported that they drank three-or-more glasses of milk a day had almost double the risk of dying during the study period as those who reported only drinking one glass.

At first glance, the study's result makes little sense. Milk, according to our media and governments, is a healthy food. In particular, it contains a lot of calcium, which our body needs to maintain healthy bones. Herein lies the twist. Cows' milk does contain a lot of calcium, but we lack the enzymes to digest that calcium, or the milk itself, to some degree. As a result, the milk isn't fully broken down in our gut. As a result, its proteins and its other constituent molecular parts enter our bloodstream where they can create an acidic environment. The ph-balance of our blood – the balance between acid and alkali – must be maintained in our body within tight values for our organs to function. Our body therefore must rectify this acidic imbalance, caused by the milk proteins. It does that by drawing calcium from our bones, thus neutralising the acid excess. The bizarre result of this biological process is that drinking milk can actually cause us to lose calcium from our bones, not gain it. A far better source of calcium, for human beings, comes from leafy vegetables, such as greens and spinach, since we have the enzymes to break these foodstuffs down and absorb their calcium content.

The problem of milk paradoxically producing calcium deficiency is known in the milk industry. For example, here is an article published by the U.S. Mid Atlantic Dairy association on the issue of blood acidity and calcium loss:

> "When protein intake is very high, this causes an excess of acid production in the body; an excess protein intake is considered "acid-forming." Body chemistry is very sensitive to what is called pH, or the acid/base relationship. The body's chemistry cannot work well unless the pH balance is maintained within very strict limits. What this means is that if what you eat is acidic or generates acidity, then your body has to neutralize the blood to keep the pH balance where it needs to be. Calcium is used to neutralize the extra acid that is formed in the body, and this calcium is coming out of your bones. When blood is too acidic, calcium inside the bones is released into circulation to neutralize the excess acidity and to maintain a healthy pH level. When calcium intake is not adequate, a high-acid diet can lead to bone loss over time."

Milk is therefore deceptive. On the surface, it seems to be an ideal foodstuff, and yet the latest science shows that one of its key benefits to us – that it is a source of calcium – may be wrong. In its defence, milk is also a source of protein, fat and sugar in the form of lactose, but these elements in our diet can be sourced from nuts, vegetables, pulses and seeds. Fundamentally, cows' milk is for baby cows; for us, it's an alien concoction. The domestication of cattle at the beginning of civilization may have given us easy access to cow's milk, but from a health point of view, we should only use it in desperation, which is probably how it *was* chosen, all that time ago.

The temptation to drink cows' milk was an inevitable consequence of domesticating cattle, but that result is likely to have been a side-issue. The main use of domesticated cattle has always been as an easy, plentiful supply of meat. Unfortunately, like milk, this boon also possesses a dark side.

Meat

Before civilization began, hunter-gatherers ate meat – the 'hunter' aspect of hunter-gathering – but for many hunter-gatherers, eating wild game was only part of their diet. Hunting and killing game isn't easy; it requires lengthy effort and can be very dangerous. By comparison, collecting eggs, nuts and seeds is far less risky, and they are also rich in protein and fat. As a result, hunter-gatherers would have steered, if possible, towards a foraging diet. They certainly did eat meat, but it would have been wild, very fresh and consumed intermittently.

Civilization radically changed humans' meat-eating situation. Once cattle had been domesticated, selectively bred to be docile, and kept in pens, it was relatively easy to kill them and thus eat meat on a daily basis. The problem with this plan has always been that cattle require *a lot* of grain or grass to feed themselves. As a result, for much of the history of civilization, only the elite were able to eat meat regularly. To quote from the Wikipedia page on medieval cuisine:

> "Barley, oats and rye were eaten by the poor. Wheat was for the governing classes. These were consumed as bread, porridge, gruel, and pasta by all of society's members… Meat was more expensive and therefore more prestigious. Game, a form of meat acquired from hunting, was common only on the nobility's tables. The most prevalent butcher's meats were pork, chicken and other domestic fowl; beef, which required greater investment in land, was less common."

In recent times, the availability of meat has increased to most areas of society. Modern farming technology, the clearing of forest en masse, and the production of high-protein crops such as soya bean, has enabled a large percentage of people in the developed world to regularly eat meat. For example, in 2017, the U.S. Department of Agriculture reported that Americans consume, on average, 274 pounds of meat per year. This is nearly a pound of meat, or half a kilogramme per day, per person. This is roughly ten times the nutritional requirement. Hunter-gatherers would have found it been extremely difficult, if nigh-on impossible to hunt, process and store this much meat in their daily lives.

The reasons many of us eat such large amounts of meat is only partly to do with enjoyment and little to do with nutritional requirements. Meat-eating, in most of the developed world, is a statement of success and of affluence. Nowadays, this applies even in countries that have a tradition of vegetarianism. For example, India is famous for its religious vegetarians but, as its GDP has increased in recent decades, and wealth has come to large numbers of its citizens, meat-eating in India has shot up, in clear defiance of the religious rules of many of its citizens. As the following Forbes article, *Demand For Meat Is Growing Rapidly in India. This Could Impact All Of Us* (Dec 17th 2017) states:

> "India is projected to be one of the largest growth areas for consumption in chicken, beef, and mutton. And while vegetarianism is often believed to be widespread in India, influenced by religion and other factors, the data seems to suggest otherwise. According to the sample registration system (SRS) baseline survey 2014 released by the registrar general of India, 71 percent of Indians over the age of 15 are non-vegetarian. While that means 330 million of India's 1.2 billion people are vegetarian, it obscures the fact that many are rapidly abandoning their vegetarian diet due to an increased desire for meat. Higher meat consumption in India is not entirely surprising, as meat-heavy diets are often correlated with an increase in wealth. As the emerging market countries like India gain a larger share of the economic pie, the trend is likely to continue."

The mass consumption of meat in the developed world might be enjoyable and a sign of success, but there is evidence that such a large amount of meat-eating may be causing us extensive damage. Eating factory meat doesn't just condemn large numbers of animals to a life of incarceration and slaughter, it is also a danger to those who consume it. Recent scientific studies report that a diet high in cooked meat can cause a string of serious illnesses, including heart disease, arteriosclerosis, stroke and cancer. For example, the science paper *Dietary protein, growth factors, and cancer*, by T Colin Campbell, published in *The American Journal of Clinical Nutrition*, states:

> "My research group worked for many years on the hypothesis that dietary protein in excess of ≈10% of calories is a risk factor for cancer. Our work began after an observation of an association between primary liver cancer and animal protein consumption in Filipino children, which coincided with the findings of a highly supportive experimental animal study in India. This led to a series of experimental research investigations and publications over the next 30 years concerning the association of animal protein consumption with primary liver cancer, its mechanisms, and its implications for human cancer at many sites. We showed that tumor growth in rats was greatly enhanced by diets containing >10% animal protein (casein) and was completely repressed with either 5% animal protein or >20% plant protein (4, 5). This protein effect depressed the activity of the major enzyme complex responsible for carcinogen activation."

In other words, if we eat too much meat, it seems to stimulate the creation of cancers in our body, possibly through the creation of rogue hormones. As the article comments, there is, 'a correlation between circulating IGF-1 (Insulin-like growth factor) and risk of certain cancers.' The opposite is also true; scientific studies have also shown that a diet low in animal protein can make us healthier in the long-term. For example, the New Scientist article, *Healthy living can turn our cells' clock back* (16th Sept 2013) reports on a study in California that aimed to see if diet and lifestyle could reduce or revert cell-ageing in 10 men in their early sixties with prostate cancer. To quote:

> "The test subjects were asked to follow a strict healthy-living regime rather than take a course of drugs. They ate a meat-free diet, did exercise and yoga daily and went to weekly group therapies. After five years, the telomeres on a type of white blood cell were 10% longer on average in these men. In contrast, 25 men with the same condition who kept to their usual lifestyles saw the telomeres on these cells shrink by an average of 3% over the same period."

Telomeres are our cell's biological clocks. They sit at the end of the chromosomes in our nuclei - the DNA sections that hold information on how our cells should function. These telomeres shorten in length as our cells age. According to scientific studies, there is evidence that people with short or truncated telomeres are more likely to contract several major diseases – heart disease, dementia, and cancer – and live shorter lives.

This worrying connection between a diet high in animal protein and a host of serious illnesses is the central message in a popular and inspiring documentary: *Forks over Knives*. The documentary shows, by reporting on major scientific studies and personal stories, that reducing one's meat intake can have a transformative effect on one's health. *Forks over Knives* is an excellent example of how a documentary can get a scientific issue across to a general audience. By reporting on human stories and real-world effects, the documentary's message becomes meaningful to people who find dry, academic papers abstract, complex and divorced from the real world.

Meat, according to a lot of scientific evidence, can therefore be a danger to our health, especially if we eat a lot of it. It may taste great, and be a sign of success, and help save our lives if we're starving, but it can be a poison to us in the long-term. As the *Forks over Knives* documentary explains, a high-meat diet can cripple the body, damage our arteries, veins, and organs, and stimulate the growth of cancers.

There is also a problem with meat that isn't a slow

effect – damaging us over years and decades – but one that can act in literally an hour. It is rarely mentioned in any literature and yet it could be blighting the lives of literally millions of people in the developed world. The problem comes from the act of preserving meat, so that it can be eaten days, weeks or months later. This preservation might be useful, but if we lack one crucial enzyme, eating preserved meat can be a fast trip to depression, anger, and violence.

Preserved Meat

A while back, a friend of mine told me that her ten-year-old son was having behavioural problems at school. He'd become increasingly irritable, moody, tearful and sensitive. The problem had become so acute that he'd had a fight with a classmate. It was a worrying development since, normally, he was a friendly, relaxed, cheerful child. At their house, while thinking on the problem, I noticed that my friend was giving her son more ice-cream than before. I pointed this out to her. She explained that since her son's infant food allergies were gone, he was enjoying the ability to eat dairy. I asked her what he'd been eating on the day he'd had the fight. She said they'd had garlic sausage for lunch. Her reply made me wonder; were these foodstuffs connected to his problem behaviour? He'd been severely allergic to milk and egg when he was an infant. Was this related to his mood problems? After some research, I discovered an intriguing connection.

We humans are good at eating and digesting a wide range of food. We're omnivores, from 'omni' meaning 'all' and 'vorare' meaning 'devour' as in 'voracious'. Being omnivorous is a useful ability, but our bodies need to be careful what they let into our bloodstreams. If certain food molecules enter our bloodstreams, they can cause us a host of problems, especially in our brain. One of these problem groups are amines. There are many types of amines in nature and our bodies use a subset of this class of molecules for a variety of tasks. In particular, our brain uses certain amines in its functioning. For example, it uses a tryptamine, serotonin, to keep us in an awake and positive state of mind. It also uses melatonin to put us in a comfortable sleeping state of mind. Other tryptamines can give us hallucinogenic 'trips', such as DMT, psilocybin and LSD. DMT is an interesting tryptamine because it's actually made by our body. It is only when there's more than a certain amount of it in our brain that we experience hallucinations. Another amine that our brain uses is dopamine, a famous reward or pleasure chemical. As we can see, it's very important that we do have amines in our brain, but it's also clear that these amines have a powerful effect on our mental state. It's therefore important that our bodies keep out any unwanted amines.

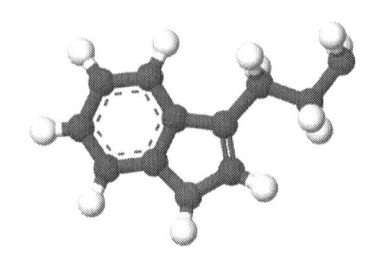

The tryptamine molecule (Wikipedia – Sbrools)

DMT and LSD are rare in nature, and so pose little

problem to us, but there are other amines that can turn up in our foods which we *definitely* want to keep out of our brains. For example, when animal proteins such as meat or milk decay and break down, they form amines such as putrescine, meaning 'rotting', cadaverine, as in cadavers or dead bodies, and histamine, an amine used by your body to trigger swelling (for example when you get an insect bite). These amines don't just sound nasty, they can have a nasty effect on our state of mind. If they get into our bloodstream, they will then travel from there to our brains, passing through the blood-brain barrier, and affect the functioning of our brain-cells. The article, *Biogenic Amines: Signals Between Commensal Microbiota and Gut Physiology*, published in *Frontiers in Endocrinology*, makes this point:

> "There is increasing interest in the interactions among the gut microbiota, gut, and brain, which is often referred to as the "microbiota-gut-brain" axis. Biogenic amines including dopamine, norepinephrine, serotonin, and histamines are all generated by commensal gut microorganisms and are suggested to play roles as signaling molecules mediating the function of the "microbiota-gut-brain" axis. In addition, such amines generated in the gut have attracted attention in terms of possible clues into the etiologies of depression, anxiety, and even psychosis. This review covers the latest research related to the potential role of microbe-derived amines such as catecholamine, serotonin, histamine, as well as other trace amines, in modulating

> not only gut physiology but also brain function of the host. Further attention in this field can offer not only insight into expanding the fundamental roles and impacts of the human microbiome, but also further offer new therapeutic strategies for psychological disorders based on regulating the balance of resident bacteria."

In other words, the amines swirling around in our gut can have a big effect on our state of mind.

To stop problem amines entering our bloodstream and affecting our body and brain, our stomach and intestines possess a special enzyme that breaks down amines. This enzyme is called mono-amine oxidase or MAO. The 'oxidase' part is because the enzyme neutralises the bad amines by oxidising them (the same process as something burning). As a result, many people can eat food that does contain problem amines without ill-effect, such as preserved meat and cheese. They can munch away and not become irritable, moody and violent because the MAO in their digestive system is knocking out the problem amines.

But if someone's gut doesn't make enough MAO to break down all the problem amines, then those amines will slip into the person's bloodstream, make their way to the person's brain and liver, skin and other organs and cause all sorts of problems, from itchy skin (the histamine) to bouts of aggression, mood swings and even hallucinations. The effect is a sliding scale, a combination of the person's inherent MAO levels, how much preserved meat and dairy they consume and the state of decay of that preserved food. It's worth noting that all animal proteins break down over time at room temperature. Salt and other traditional preservatives only stop bacterial action, and other natural agents. The only way to stop proteins breaking down into amines – in the short to medium term – is to freeze the food, and even this just slows down the process. The net result is that anyone who is low in MAO should not eat preserved animal proteins, such as cheese, garlic sausage, bratwurst etc. Historically, preserving meats was a vital way to maintain an adequate diet when food was sparse but, like meat in general, it's a very bad idea to keep using it when healthier foods are available.

I explained my findings to my friend. She was very interested, and she immediately changed her son's diet. She limited ice-cream and gave him freshly cooked meat whenever possible. His behaviour at school improved dramatically. At his school's next parents' evening, several of the teachers commented, to my friend, how much more relaxed her son had become. There were no more reports of fighting and it was clear to all concerned that he was a much happier boy.

This story therefore had a positive ending, but it reveals something that may have plagued our society for centuries. One valuable source of information on low MAO levels, and accompanying behavioural problems, comes from research in Australia. There is a possible reason for this. During the 18th and 19th centuries, the ancestors of many Caucasian Australians were poor British people who were transported to the Antipodes for minor crimes, a draconian and cruel policy. A large percentage of these people may have been eating cheap, poorly preserved food and had low MAO levels in their gut.

As a result, they were continually moody, aggressive, and hyper-sensitive. This could have easily led to violence and a life of crime. They would therefore have inevitably ended up in court and punished for their actions. As a result, a whole set of vulnerable people, who had done little more than suffer the consequences of a bad diet, had ended up transported, in miserable conditions, half-way around the world.

There is sound evidence that low MAO in the gut, and bad amines in the diet, is a significant problem, and yet this issue, to my knowledge, has never been mentioned in the mainstream media, or in schools. How many children are getting into trouble simply because their diet is frying their brains? Why don't school kids have a mandatory MAO test? Why isn't this problem in standard literature about improving children's behaviour? Western nations have made huge developments in many aspects of healthcare, but the foodstuffs many people eat, particularly those on low incomes, haven't changed significantly. It is a problem that carries on, year after year, adding to the suffering in our civilized world.

It's worth noting, before we move on to the next gift of civilization, that the problem of poor diet and crime extends beyond the problem of low-MAO. Many low-income individuals suffer from a malnourished diet from an early age. There is evidence that this increases the likelihood of them becoming criminals. As the Guardian newspaper article, *Prison study could show better diet reduces violence* explains:

> "Researchers will look at the levels of violence, drug-related offences and self-harm perpetrated by each individual over the 12-month period when he took the [dietary] supplements. At Aylesbury, they found that those who had the extra nutrients committed on average 26% fewer disciplinary offences than the rest, and 37% fewer violent offences."

Similar studies have shown a marked improvement in inmate behaviour, over time-periods as short as six-months, simply from improving their diet.

We can therefore see that there is a lot of evidence that key foodstuffs, ones of which civilization has given us a plentiful supply, such as wheat, meat, cheese, dairy, sausage etc, are only good for basic survival in the short-term. In the long term, the more we consume them, the worse we'll be and, eventually, they can inflict a crippling, painful, premature death on us. This dietary problem is bad enough by itself, but it is seriously exacerbated by another key gift of civilization: alcohol.

Alcohol

Alcohol is a simple molecule – ethanol – but it rarely exists in the wild. It can form naturally when fruit ripens, rots and ferments, due to the actions of bacteria and fungi. When this happens, wild animals can eat the fruit and become intoxicated. There are anecdotal stories of elephants getting drunk on fermented fruit, but these incidents are rare. These animals would also need to eat a lot of fruit to ingest a significant amount of alcohol, since they would need to consume the whole fruit to gain its alcohol content. Such incidents are also rare, as fruit is a seasonal crop. As a result, in the wild, there is no alcohol available of any kind for most of the year. This situation changed dramatically with the arrival of civilization. As we've already seen in this book, grain production was a major element in the development of civilization. Once this grain was sown, grown and harvested, it could then be stored for months on end. This did enable a steady, continuous, all-year-round food production but it also enabled a steady, reliable all-year-round production of alcohol. There was no longer any need to wait for fruit to appear, and then ferment. People in civilization, if they wanted to, could get drunk every day.

It's hard to summarise, or even quantify, the effect that alcohol has had on human beings since it was developed. We know, from the archaeological evidence, that it has been with us since the beginning of civilization. Here is a quote from the Wikipedia page on alcoholic beverages:

> "As early as 7000 BC, chemical analysis of jars from the Neolithic village Jiahu in the Henan province of northern China revealed traces of a mixed fermented beverage. According to a study published in the Proceedings of the National Academy of Sciences in December 2004, chemical analysis of the residue confirmed that a fermented drink made of grapes, hawthorn berries, honey, and rice was being produced in 7000–6650 BC. This is approximately the time when barley beer and grape wine were beginning to be made in the

> Middle East. Evidence of alcoholic beverages has also been found dating from 5400–5000 BC in Hajji Firuz Tepe in Iran, 3150 BC in ancient Egypt, 3000 BC in Babylon, 2000 BC in pre-Hispanic Mexico and 1500 BC in Sudan. According to Guinness, the earliest firm evidence of wine production dates back to 6000 BC in Georgia."

Over the last six-millennia, or more, civilized people have drunk alcohol in large quantities. For example, Jeffrey L. Singman states in his book, *Daily Life in Medieval Europe* (Westport, Connecticut: Greenwood Press, 1999, P. 54 – 55):

> 'A prosperous English peasant in the 14th century would probably consume 2 - 3 pounds of bread, 8 ounces of meat or fish or other protein and 2 -3 pints of ale per day. The bread was usually mean of rye, oats, or barley. Meat was expensive and usually only available on special occasions. Often eggs, butter, or cheese were substituted for meat. Vegetables such as onions, leeks, cabbage, garlic, turnips, parsnips, peans and beans were staples. Fruits were available in season.'

Three pints of ale every day is a substantial habit, which is an interesting coincidence, as much of the ale drunk in Medieval Times was brewed by monks.

'Gin Lane' by William Hogarth (1750)

Over the millennia, people have drunk alcohol to feel good, to drown their sorrows, to celebrate and strengthen social and tribal bonds, to deal with depression, trauma and other mental issues, and they've also done it because they're addicted to alcohol. Alcohol is viewed by many as a fun drink, but it is toxic to the body. Alcohol, to put it simply, is a poison. To quote again from Wikipedia:

> "Excessive alcohol use can damage all organ systems, but it particularly affects the brain, heart, liver, pancreas and immune system. Alcoholism can result in mental illness, delirium tremens, Wernicke–Korsakoff syndrome, irregular heartbeat, an impaired immune response, liver cirrhosis and increased cancer risk."

The general view, that alcohol is mostly just a fun drink, may also be a result of advertising. According to the spiritbusiness.com article *Alcohol ad spend to hit $6bn by 2023*, a lot of money is spent on encouraging people to drink booze. Most alcohol advertising makes out that booze is fun, enjoyable and a key part of successful socialising. Alongside this message, it tells us that drinking booze in moderation is not a cause for concern. For example, the current UK alcohol consumption guidelines are 14 units per week for men and women. The problem with these messages, both commercial and official, is that the latest scientific evidence indicates that *any* consumption of alcohol harms our health. For example, the Guardian newspaper article, *Any amount of alcohol consumption harmful to the brain, finds study* (18th May 2021) explains:

> "There is no safe amount of alcohol consumption for the brain, with even "moderate" drinking adversely affecting nearly every part of it, a study of more than 25,000 people in the UK has found. The study, which is still to be peer-reviewed, suggests that the more alcohol consumed, the lower the brain volume. In effect, the more you drink, the worse off your brain. "There's no threshold drinking for harm – any alcohol is worse. Pretty much the whole brain seems to be affected – not just specific areas, as previously thought," said the lead author, Anya Topiwala, a senior clinical lecturer at the University of Oxford."

Alcohol is a poison. Understandably, therefore, if

you have any of it, you're worse off. In a sense, alcohol is like arsenic, as that chemical also causes numbness, dizziness, dehydration and cancer. The only difference is that you feel good when consuming alcohol, at least in moderate amounts, whereas you never do with arsenic.

Professor David Nutt (Wikipedia - Anon284773943)

The clash between the biological reality of alcohol, and the messages our corporations and governments give us about it, came to a head in 2009, in the UK, when the British Government asked their senior scientific advisor, Professor David Nutt, to report on the most dangerous drugs affecting the British population. The government probably assumed that Professor Nutt would say, 'heroin and cocaine are the worst'. Instead, he reported that alcohol and tobacco were the most dangerous drugs in Britain. The government read his report, assessed its implications and promptly removed him. As the Sky news article,

Professor David Nutt: Former drug tsar says alcohol is most dangerous drug, explains:

> "The professor claimed in a research paper that alcohol and tobacco were more harmful than many illegal drugs including LSD, ecstasy and cannabis. He stands by the claim and believes, "alcohol is the most damaging drug in pretty much every Western country"... He said that, if looking at the UK, alcohol is the most harmful drug overall. He added: "Every family in Britain is damaged to some extent by alcohol. If not in terms of physical or psychological damage, then in terms of the financial damage that excess drinking causes." He said one thing that has become "very clear" over the last 10 years is that "there has been absolutely no action whatsoever on the fact alcohol is the most harmful drug". He also said there was a continued attempt to undermine the harm of alcohol by saying it has health benefits. But, he argued, any health gains from alcohol are limited to consumption of 5g of alcohol per day – the equivalent of sharing one 175ml glass of wine between three people."

Unfortunately, our governments and our corporations do not help us stay healthy when it comes to booze. In some ways, it is little different from the historical approach to arsenic in Britain. In late Victorian times, arsenic was used in wallpapers and paint, due to its lustrous, stable, green colours. To quote from the documentary, *Hidden Killers of the Victorian Home*, a large Victorian drawing room could contain up to 2.5kg of arsenic (5.5lbs)! Germany soon banned arsenic in wallpapers, after public outcry, but the British government did nothing. William Morris, a famous champion of Victorian arts and crafts, and a major wallpaper designer, was fully behind the use of arsenic in wallpapers. This may have had something to do with the fact that he also owned the world's largest arsenic mine: Devon Great Consuls. When Morris was asked to respond to the multiple claims of arsenic poisoning from members of the public, he responded in a letter that the claimants were, 'bitten with witch-fever'. In other words, that they were spouting superstitious hysteria.

William Morris (Wikipedia – Frederick Hollyer)

The tide of opinion only turned fully against arsenic when Queen Victoria became involved. A diplomat, visiting her palace, fell seriously ill after spending the night in one of her rooms wallpapered in a bright, arsenic, 'shield green'. At first, Her Majesty was most unamused that he had stayed in bed, rather than attended the arranged meeting with her, but it soon became apparent what state he was in. She put the pieces of the puzzle together and had all the arsenic furnishings removed. Word got around, and soon everyone was shedding their bright green décor.

The story of arsenic in Victorian homes ends on a bitter note since the Victorian British government never actually banned arsenic. Instead, consumer power ended its use. Victorian consumers refused to buy wallpaper containing it. In response, the wallpaper, carpet, and furnishings manufacturers switched to selling products that were 'arsenic free'.

Nowadays, arsenic use is carefully controlled, as it is a Class 1 carcinogen or cancer-causer... which brings us back to alcohol. By interesting coincidence, acetaldehyde is also a Class 1 carcinogen, and it is produced through the partial oxidation of ethanol by the liver enzyme alcohol dehydrogenase. This is part of an important process, for when you drink booze, the alcohol enters your bloodstream, travels to your liver and your liver uses that enzyme to break it down into something non-toxic. If it didn't, your body would be in a terrible state. Unfortunately, this transformation can only proceed at a certain rate. Therefore, if you drink booze too quickly, it's a lot like making your own arsenic.

Hopefully, this first Part of this book is showing that a lot of the foodstuffs that we've been able to consume, thanks to civilization, have not been good. They might be easily available, in civilization, and a lot of them are pleasurable to consume – more fun than a lettuce, or an olive – but they have a dark side. They are a dietary equivalent of an abusive partner. You might have a pleasurable time with them, but in the long term, they're making you sick, weak, confused, depressed, and internally damaged.

Unfortunately, we haven't even got to perhaps the nastiest foodstuff of all, the one that is full-on pleasure-and-damage: sugar.

Sugar

Civilization, by clearing land, fencing off fields and ploughing them up, has enabled us to grow particular crops in large amounts. These crops can then be harvested, and their seed component stored. We can then refine, mill, bake or preserve this foodstuff and eat it all year around. In order to do this, this harvested crop has to stay intact for weeks or months, and not break down or get eaten by mould, bacteria, insects etc. One way to do this is to remove the components that bacteria, fungi etc want to eat. This is why reducing crops to their starch contents works well, because it's easier to store, as it doesn't rot. Of course, by doing this, you've lost the crop's fibre, vegetable protein, vitamins etc, but you can't have everything. In fact, you can take this process even further by reducing everything to sugar, as it's very stable – almost nothing natural feasts on it – and it's very nice to eat, and calorific. But herein lies the trap. Why don't natural things eat sugar? Why is it as impervious to mould as salt?

For much of human history, we weren't able to grow, harvest and produce sugar, as we didn't have a crop with a high sugar content. This changed in the eighteenth century with the selective breeding of white Silesian sugar beet. Up to that point, crystallised sugar had been so rare that it was only used for sculptures. No one ate pure sugar, unless you Queen Elizabeth I. According to many accounts, she made use of her West Indies contacts to consume a lot of sugar, to the point where many of her teeth fell out, but apart from her indulgence, sugar was thin on the ground, until people began growing white Silesian sugar beet. Soon, a lot of people in Europe could eat sugar, or add it to their foods. This caused a lot consternation in countries that didn't have the climate to grow sugar beet, such as the UK. Britain sorted out their lack of sugar production by setting up Caribbean slave plantations. As a result, thanks to the horrors of the international slave trade, British traders, particularly Scottish merchants, could make enormous fortunes through the sale of sugar. This was then sold to Scottish people, particularly those who'd been pushed into the cities by the forced Highland clearances. The results were disastrous. As the New Internationalist article, *The Taste of Salvation* by Geoffrey Canon (5th January 1990) states:

> "Until the middle of the nineteenth century, the Highland Scots were the tallest and heaviest of the European peoples. The average height of a man was six feet, while seven-foot giants were by no means uncommon. Of 600 crofters evicted from Glen Tilt at the end of the eighteenth century, not one was less than six feet in height or measured less than 17 inches around the calf. People remained active long after their eightieth year, and ages of over a hundred were common. The staple diet of the Highlanders at this time was oatmeal

> porridge, cakes made from barley or stoneground oat-flour, vegetables, milk, butter, eggs and cheese with occasional fish, beef, venison, wild fruits, honey and the famous Scottish soups."

After the Highland Clearances, these Scots were forced to eat an urban diet of, 'white bread and flour, white sugar and fat, some salted meat or fish and pitifully little fresh food'. The poorest often survived on little more than white bread and jam, which was mostly sugar. Not surprisingly, like the humans of civilization, their height, health, strength and longevity declined.

The rise of sugar in Europe, and then North America, took another step forward (of a sort) with the creation of high fructose corn syrup or HFCS in the twentieth century. HFCS, as its name implies, contains fructose sugar rather than glucose sugar. When the two sugars link up, they form sucrose.

Fructose sugar is often produced naturally by fruits to sweeten themselves, so they'll be eaten by animals, and it works well, because it is a very sweet sugar. HFCS global production is now worth around six billion dollars a year. It is also deemed to be a safe foodstuff. According to The United States Food and Drug Administration, HFCS is officially a safe ingredient for food and beverage manufacturing. But fructose, naturally, is bound up in a fruit, along with a lot of fibre and water. What if we remove all that fibre and water and just consume the fructose? If we did that, we'd get a *very* sweet drink, and it'd be natural too, so everything's fine… or perhaps not.

In recent decades, many nutritionists and scientists

have warned about the effects of large amounts of fructose on our health. For example, the nutritionist and biochemist Dr Robert Lustig has researched and written extensively on the worrying connections between fructose and multiple health problems. His science paper, *Fructose: It's "Alcohol Without the Buzz"*, published in Advanced Nutrition (March 2013) states:

> 'What do the Atkins Diet and the traditional Japanese diet have in common? The Atkins Diet is low in carbohydrate and usually high in fat; the Japanese diet is high in carbohydrate and usually low in fat. Yet both work to promote weight loss. One commonality of both diets is that they both eliminate the monosaccharide fructose. Sucrose (table sugar) and its synthetic sister high fructose corn syrup consist of 2 molecules, glucose and fructose. Glucose is the molecule that when polymerized forms starch, which has a high glycemic index, generates an insulin response, and is not particularly sweet. Fructose is found in fruit, does not generate an insulin response, and is very sweet. Fructose consumption has increased worldwide, paralleling the obesity and chronic metabolic disease pandemic. Sugar (i.e., fructose-containing mixtures) has been vilified by nutritionists for ages as a source of "empty calories," no different from any other empty calorie. However, fructose is unlike glucose. In the hypercaloric glycogen-replete state, intermediary metabolites from fructose metabolism overwhelm hepatic mitochondrial

capacity, which promotes de novo lipogenesis and leads to hepatic insulin resistance, which drives chronic metabolic disease. Fructose also promotes reactive oxygen species formation, which leads to cellular dysfunction and aging, and promotes changes in the brain's reward system, which drives excessive consumption. Thus, fructose can exert detrimental health effects beyond its calories and in ways that mimic those of ethanol, its metabolic cousin. Indeed, the only distinction is that because fructose is not metabolized in the central nervous system, it does not exert the acute neuronal depression experienced by those imbibing ethanol. These metabolic and hedonic analogies argue that fructose should be thought of as "alcohol without the buzz."'

In other words, sugar damages us as much as alcohol. The only difference is that we don't get drunk, and it tastes a lot sweeter.

Dr Lustig has also written bestselling books this topic, such as *Fat Chance: The Hidden Truth About Sugar, Obesity and Disease.* Is Dr Lustig right? Unsurprisingly, the food industry disputes the connection between fructose and insulin resistance, aging and excessive consumption, and yet rates of diabetes, Alzheimer's Disease, and obesity do closely track the rise of HCFS in the Western World. Then again, it could be just a false correlation. To quote from the Wikipedia page on high-fructose corn syrup:

> "The role of fructose in metabolic syndrome has been the subject of controversy but, as of 2020, there is no scientific evidence that fructose or HFCS has any impact on cardiometabolic markers when substituted for sucrose."

This sounds definitive… except for the fact that sucrose is one part glucose and one part fructose. The statement is therefore highly deceptive, as it is actually saying 'fructose corn syrup is no worse than half-fructose syrup', which is next to useless as a piece of counter evidence. Is sugar strongly linked to ageing and degenerative diseases? Is it a comrade-in-arms of meat, dairy, wheat and alcohol? Are they all charming but abusive foodstuffs, charming us with their pleasurable taste, and then repeatedly damaging us, year in, year out? To understand their effect on us, and particularly sugar, we need to look again at degenerative disease, and one disease in particular: cancer.

Degenerative Diseases and Cancer

Cancer is regarded, by many people, as simply a part of the human condition, just as heart disease, Alzheimer's, dementia and others are natural results of us getting older. In fact, the latest scientific studies indicate that this may not be true. Instead, civilization is giving us a high incidence of diseases that rarely, if ever, occur in hunter-gatherer societies.

For example, in the science paper, *Hunter-gatherers as models in public health* by H. Pontzer, B. M. Wood, D. A. Raichlen (3rd December 2018, Obesity Reviews), the authors investigated the health and causes of death of hunter-gatherer societies around the world. They report:

> "Cause of death is notoriously difficult to ascertain for hunter-gatherers and other populations without regular access to hospitals with trained medical specialists. The leading cause of death across small-scale populations is acute infection. Gurven and Kaplan 8 report that ~70% of deaths are caused by acute illness (mostly infectious and gastrointestinal disease) and another ~20% by trauma, including accidents and violence. These ratios are fairly consistent across the lifespan, although total mortality rate is highest for young children. The percentage of deaths from chronic, non-communicable diseases common in developed countries (e.g. heart disease, metabolic disease and cancers) is very low in small-scale populations, <10% of deaths even for individuals over 60 years old."

Traditionally, many people have assumed that hunter-gatherers don't get degenerative diseases - such as Alzheimer's, dementia, heart disease and cancer - because they don't live long enough. This assumption may be false. As the paper states:

> "Due largely to high infant mortality from infectious disease, the expected lifespan at birth for hunter-gatherer populations is lower (typically 30s–40s) than developed countries today. A common misinterpretation of this observation is to assume that few hunter-gatherers (either today or in the past) live to older ages. If this were true, the near absence of chronic diseases in small-scale populations could be explained simply by a lack of adults living long enough to develop them. Further, if people in small-scale populations inevitably die young, they might not be useful models for public health. In fact, demographic analyses of small-scale populations show that adult survivorship is similar in some ways to industrialized societies, with adults regularly living into their 60s and 70s and even beyond."

It would therefore seem that many of the disease we suffer from in the civilized world are not natural. Instead, they are the consequences of our civilized diet. In previous sections, we saw the connection between meat and heart disease, wheat and inflammation, and milk and osteoporosis. To that list we need to add another connection: sugar and cancer.

Nowadays, cancer dominates the health-care concerns of many Western people, with good reason.

To quote from Wikipedia:

> "In 2015, about 90.5 million people had cancer. As of 2019, about 18 million new cases occur annually. Annually, it caused about 8.8 million deaths (15.7% of deaths). For cancer in the United States, the average five-year survival rate is 66%."

Cancer, officially, is caused by a multitude of factors. To quote from the Wikipedia page on cancer:

> 'The majority of cancers, some 90–95% of cases, are due to genetic mutations from environmental factors. The remaining 5–10% are due to inherited genetics.'

This phrase 'environmental factors' is vague; it can cover many elements, from diet to pollution, stress, contamination, irradiation, exercise, sleep and so on, but for one, Nobel Prize winning scientist, cancer had only one crucial cause: sugar.

Otto Warburg

Otto Heinrich Warburg won the Nobel Prize for Physiology and Medicine in 1931. This was hardly a surprise, as he was nominated for the award 47 times over the course of his career. Warburg specialised in understanding how biological cells functioned, how they used fuel to keep themselves going. He used this knowledge to develop a theory about how cancers grew. To quote from his Wikipedia page, Warburg believed:

> "Cancer growth is caused by tumor cells generating energy (as, e.g., adenosine triphosphate/ATP) mainly by anaerobic breakdown of glucose (known as fermentation, or anaerobic respiration). This process is in marked contrast to healthy cells, which generate energy mainly from oxidative breakdown of pyruvate. Pyruvate is an end-product of glycolysis and is oxidized within the mitochondria. Hence, cancer should be interpreted as a mitochondrial dysfunction."

In other words, when the mitochondria in cells stop working properly, or are overloaded, tumour cells get the chance to grow by feeding on circulating glucose. To quote from the man himself:

> "Cancer, above all other diseases, has countless secondary causes. But, even for cancer, there is only one prime cause. Summarized in a few words, the prime cause of cancer is the replacement of the respiration of oxygen in normal body cells by a fermentation of sugar."

If this is correct then we really *don't* want to have too much glucose circulating in our body, or present in our bloodstream. If there's lots of glucose circulating inside us, any micro tumour will get all the fuel it needs to grow into something life-threatening.

Warburg's idea has stood the test of time. He may have come up with his theory in 1924, but scientists are still studying it, and continuing its development. For example, in the scientific paper, *Cancer as a metabolic disease: implications for novel therapeutics*, published in the Oxford journal *Carcinogenesis* in March 2014, the authors state:

> "Emerging evidence indicates that cancer is primarily a metabolic disease involving disturbances in energy production through respiration and fermentation. The genomic instability observed in tumor cells and all other recognized hallmarks of cancer are considered downstream epiphenomena of the initial disturbance of cellular energy metabolism. The disturbances in tumor cell energy metabolism can be linked to abnormalities in the structure and function of the mitochondria. When viewed as a mitochondrial metabolic disease, the evolutionary theory of Lamarck can better explain cancer progression than can the evolutionary theory of Darwin. Cancer growth and progression can be managed following a whole-body transition from fermentable metabolites, primarily glucose and glutamine, to respiratory metabolites, primarily ketone bodies. As each individual is a unique

> metabolic entity, personalization of metabolic therapy as a broad-based cancer treatment strategy will require fine-tuning to match the therapy to an individual's unique physiology."

In other words, if someone develops cancer, and tumour cells start growing in their body, then they need to change their diet. They need to stop eating sugar, glucose, and related molecules such as fructose, dextrose etc, which are all 'fermentable metabolites.' Instead, they need to consume a diet that gives them 'respiratory metabolites, primarily ketone bodies.' To do this, they need a diet low in carbohydrates and high in natural fats. In other words, they need to adopt roughly the same diet that Dr Perlmutter recommended, mentioned earlier, a diet that he recommended for avoiding wheat and its inflammatory effect on the body. It's an interesting coincidence that the same recommended diet for avoiding diabetes, weight problems and inflammation is *also* a diet that is said to prevent cancer growth. What's more, it's a diet that closely matches the diet of many hunter-gatherers.

It is very sad, in our modern, developed world, that we aren't encouraged to adopt a diet of eggs, vegetables, seeds, nuts and other low-sugar, low-carb, high fibre, high vegetable protein and fat foods. Such a diet would transform our health and happiness. Instead, we are endlessly encouraged to keep eating wheat, bread, milk, preserved meat, alcohol, and refined sugar. This advertising-consumer-capitalist system is making us ill, weakened, malnourished, depressed, and increasingly sick.

Summary

The Western diet, in fact the civilized diet, is bad for our bodies. A daily intake of wheat, meat, milk, alcohol, and sugar is damaging our bodies and brains and dragging us into an early death, filled with suffering, confusion, pain, and misery. What's worse, most of us aren't even aware of the damage being done to us, or the role of these foodstuffs in heart disease, diabetes and cancer, because our governments and the food industry make no attempt to inform us of the problem.

Our civilized diet is therefore a big problem. A paranoid person might even say that they are an instrument of oppression and toxic abuse, a way for those in power to keep us weak, poor, sick, and subdued, but that seems extreme. These foodstuffs may be simply a result of capitalism. Alternatively, they're an artifact of history. Long ago, a reliable supply of food, such as grains, meat, and milk, was more important than super-healthy food, and we've kept eating them out of cultural inertia. Which is it?

In order to decide whether our toxic, civilized diet is just an accident of history or, more darkly, an instrument of abusive control, it's worth studying more facets of our civilization; elements that don't exist in hunter-gatherer societies, and what they're doing to us. By doing that, we can obtain a clearer picture of how we're being treated, and how we have been treated since the beginning of recorded history.

On to Part 2…

Part 2: The Controllers of Civilization

Introduction

The previous part of this book explored what we eat and drink in the civilized world, and what these foodstuffs have been doing to us. The ones mentioned – wheat, meat, preserved meat, milk, sugar, and alcohol – are normal items for most of us. Officially, they are fine, as long as they're not eaten or drunk to excess. According to our governments and health bodies, none of them should cause us any problems, and we can live healthy lives while consuming them every day. Unfortunately, they do cause us harm, and it seems suspiciously as if those in power know this, and that they prefer us to be ill, confused, weak and condemned to a later life of cancer, dementia, heart disease and other ailments rarely seen amongst hunter-gatherers. Are they therefore part of a system of abusive control?

This Part of the book will study more elements of

civilization, elements that have been with us since the beginning of recorded history. The first one is connected to Part 1 of this book, as it is something that stops many people from improving their diets. Many of us would like to buy better food and get away from cheap products, filled with starch and sugar, but we can't afford to. This is surprising. Somehow, in a world where production of food and goods have reached unbelievable levels of efficiency, many of us still haven't got enough spare cash to buy fresh veg. To understand why, we need study the matter of money.

Money

What is money? Nowadays, when we see money, we see coins and notes, but our world is rapidly transforming into one containing digital money, of a total displayed on a screen. Soon, in many countries, there will be no physical money at all, simply an entry in a database. This is a very abstract situation. Therefore, in order to understand how money works, and what money does to a society, we need to go back to the beginnings of civilization. By doing that, we can see how money developed, why it was needed, and how it affected society.

Originally, there was no need for money. When hunter-gatherer groups roamed the Earth, they made their property themselves, whether it was a bow, a pot, a jacket, a knife, or a musical instrument. They created their possessions from the materials available around them. They would often carve ornaments and jewellery, again for themselves, but also give these to others as gifts. This system extended to the food they ate. Since the world around them was constantly producing food, they simply gathered that food in when they were hungry. They dried some of the food and stored for periods of time when food was low, but since there was only so much food people could store, or carry, this was never a substantial resource. Instead, the fat on people's bodies was an excellent backup energy source. A gramme of fat contains about 10 calories of energy, which is equivalent to a tenth of a mile of walking. This means that someone can walk for a hundred miles on a single kilogramme of fat. In other words, you could do a lot, and survive on little, even in harsh times, just with what you carried on you, and in you.

A Kwakwaka'wakw Indian potlatch (Vickie Jensen – U'Mista cultural society)

When tribal groups settled in fixed locations, and built houses, they were able to possess more property, but it was still a limited amount. There was also the impracticality of possessing more objects than they could use. What's more, possessing excessive amounts, when others around you had little, was a recipe for division and strife in any community. The tribes on the west coast of British Columbia in Canada (before Canada existed) got around this problem by developing the potlatch, a ceremony or meeting-event in which tribal leaders would give away many of their possessions, or publicly destroy them, as a demonstration of their status, both as a leader in the community. It is likely that these donations would have created unstated obligation by the receivers, but the net result was a regular re-distribution of property. By staging regular potlatches, physical assets in the community were converted into mental currency, in the sense of status, gratitude, obligation and social standing stored in the minds of the members of the community. This mental storage of gratitude and obligation would have reduced incidences of theft since, if most people's surplus possessions were repeatedly re-distributed, why take the risk of stealing things? It was a brilliant system to bind the community together.

Sadly, when Western civilization arrived on the west coast of Canada, its colonial leaders were quick to demonise the potlatches and do their best to eradicate it. From 1885 to 1951, the Government of Canada criminalized potlatches. Fortunately, in 1951, it was finally decriminalised, and the potlatch has re-emerged in some coastal communities.

The potlatch system shows that a human society can function by regular gift-giving, rather than buying and selling. This is similar to the British tradition of buying a round of drinks at the pub. Each person in the group takes it in turns to buy the drinks. No one is forced to buy a round, but woe betide any man who does not do his bit. He might not be openly castigated, but the word would soon go around, and his name would be mud. Could the 'buying the round' custom work in a larger context?

In a large society, people make a wide variety of things. Hunter-gatherers only make items that they need for the task in hand, but in a technologically advanced society, it's easy to make many more things than you need. What's more if the members of a society also have specialised skills, then there's a lot of surplus goods and services, of every type and variety, to share around, such as a farmer needing dental care. One way to run this complex transfer activity, and keep to the potlatch principle, is for everyone to simply hand out their surplus production. In other words, if they're a farmer, they just go around giving out their produce. If they're a dentist, they go around performing their service. If everyone did this, in an advanced society, then everyone would receive what they needed, and everyone would be happy.

Of course, critics of this idea would argue that some people might not do any work. Instead, they might just laze around all day and grab the free stuff. This ignores the fact that most people, if they are healthy and sane, invariably want to contribute to society; they want to do their bit and feel valued and appreciated by others. It's true that there will be some people who are physically or mentally ill, or entirely amoral, but these people will be in a minority. What's more, if the society has a sufficient surplus of production, then it would be able to accommodate the dead weight of this minority group. This situation already occurs in our modern world; it's known as a welfare state, social support or charitable help.

But what happens in a global context, with transfers of good between nations? What if someone turns up for a while, enjoys the local hospitality, receives a lot of drinks from everyone else, then leaves before they do their bit? What happens if you're trading with a stranger that you rarely see, or you might not see again? You could barter on the spot. In other words, you give them something and they give you something back before they leave, but this is hopelessly cumbersome. If you mend shoes and you need a wheelbarrow, you may find out that a stranger who needs your shoes doesn't have any wheelbarrows, as he just makes fountain pens. You'd then have to go through an exhausting process of swaps, involving shoes, wheelbarrows and who knows what else, to get the fountain pen. Bartering is therefore a nightmare way to transact goods without having to trust anyone. This is where money comes in.

The idea of money is that traders need a reliable token system to make transactions <u>without needing to trust anyone</u>. If they can agree on a particular token system, then they can trade without any need to trust the other person. Ideally, the token they agree on using needs to be small and hardy. It also needs to be hard to make. A gold coin is an excellent choice for this task, as it is small and hard-wearing. What's more, gold is difficult to find and mine, and because it is so dense, a counterfeit coin made of another metal won't weigh as much (gold is three times denser than lead). It is therefore easy to check that a gold coin *is* a gold coin, simply by checking its weight, compared to its volume. Gold coins are therefore a great solution for people who don't trust each other, and don't want to rely on gratitude or obligation. Problem solved.

Money, in the form of gold coins, seems to be a foolproof system. If everyone uses them, then there's no need for keeping score, or trusting others to respond in kind. But there's one problem. If I take a gold coin, I've obtained something of value which is anonymous. If someone were to steal that gold coin from me, then there's no indication on the coin that it used to belong to me. The coin has no loyalty, memory, or feeling of obligation. By avoiding any need to trust anyone, a system has been created where no one feels any obligation towards anyone else, or gratitude towards anyone else. Money is therefore ideal for amoral people, such as thieves. A skilful thief doesn't need to generate good feeling in others. All he needs to do, to obtain wealth and power, is to grab gold coins, any way he can. If he was in a society whose transactions were based on mutual gratitude and obligation, he'd have a terrible time trying to gain *any* wealth or power, but in a world run with money, the sky's the limit.

To stop thieves taking their gold coins, rich people (or in fact anyone) had to defend themselves. Merchants often employed armed guards, but these guards were expensive to support – all they did was stand around, preparing to be violent – and the merchants were never sure that they wouldn't take the gold instead. To solve this problem, banks were created: secure storehouses for gold. The merchant would deposit their gold in the bank and pay a fee for the bank to store that gold until the merchant wanted it back. This sounds like an ideal solution, on the surface. The merchant did need to trust the bank, but the bank wasn't going anywhere, and it had a reputation to maintain, so everything was great… but the nature of money hadn't changed. All that had changed was that these anonymous, amoral tokens of wealth and power had been concentrated in one place. If anyone robbed the bank, then, once again, they would gain enormous power and wealth without any strings attached. As already mentioned, they wouldn't need to win anyone's respect, gratitude or admiration to gain more goods, such as in the Pacific Coast tribes' potlatch, they just needed to take the gold. As a result, banks were robbed a lot, sometimes by individuals but more importantly, by the armies of other countries. Whilst money was represented by gold coins, this problem was endemic. What's more, while it was going on, another form of robbery was occurring; it wasn't being done by bandits or foreign armies, it was being done by the custodians of the gold.

Bankers, normally, appear to be respectable, reliable, steady, responsible characters, but they are, at the end of the day, human beings. They are also immersed in the money system. In other words, they are up to their necks in a process designed to be devoid of trust, generosity and gratitude. Not surprisingly, like Gollum and the One Ring in Tolkien's classic tale, *The Lord of the Rings*, bankers face a terrible temptation. They are in possession of a shining prize, devoid of morality, that can bestow great power to whoever uses it. They also know that they can gain that wealth and power in a way that would appear entirely respectable and reasonable, if no one looked too deeply into it. To do this, they first need to persuade everyone that it is better to have a printed note, rather than the gold itself.

Printed bank notes have been around a long time. Originally, they were created as a temporary replacement while a client's gold was stored in the bank. In Medieval Europe, for example, the Knights Templar began performing this service to pilgrims in around 1150 AD, since their templar preceptories also functioned as banks. International banking, on the face of it, isn't a very pious and devoted holy activity, but they did it regardless, and to great success. Later on, more bankers issued notes as temporary replacements for actual gold. For example, the first pound note in Britain, issued in around 1795, had a very important statement written on it, 'I promise to pay the bearer, on demand, the sum of one pound of gold'. In other words, the client only took the note because they were *guaranteed* that they could swap it for a pound of gold at the bank; that's why it was a pound note. These notes were so trusted that the government itself said they were legally just as good as the gold itself, in matters of debt. In other words, these notes became legal tender.

Bank of England One Pound Note (Wikipedia)

But this is where things became too tempting for bankers. Once everyone was walking around with pound notes, rather than the actual gold, and the gold was sitting in the bank, the bankers wondered, 'would anyone notice if we quietly printed more notes than we actually owned in gold?' They knew that every extra note they printed would make them richer, without them actually needing to mine gold, refine that gold ore or gain gold in exchange for goods or work done, like everyone else. They could get richer just by turning the handle of a printing press. Clearly, this plan would fall apart catastrophically if everyone turned their notes in and asked for the gold instead, a so-called 'run on the bank'. If their customers did this, the bank would be unable to pay out. As a result, their cheating would be plain for all to see, but they did it anyway. Nowadays, this difference between what the bank possesses and the notes it hands out is known as 'leverage', which shows that this form of cheating has eventually become legitimised, which is strange, as it is still counterfeiting. If all notes were backed by gold, in a bank, a 'run on the bank' would not be a danger. Everyone would take out their gold, feel assured, and then probably put it right back in again, and take a note instead. It is only when bankers cheat that a 'run on the bank' turns into an economic disaster.

Paper money, and banking leverage, is where the money system starts to fall apart. The whole point of money is that you don't have to trust anyone. Your gold coin is definitely a gold coin, because you can test that fact. It is a fact, in the original sense of the word, from the Latin 'factum', 'to do'. As soon as you leave your gold coins with bankers, and take notes instead, you have to trust those strangers, which defies the whole point of the exercise.

Franklin Roosevelt 1913 (Wikipedia)

Over time, unless something major is done to maintain trust, there is a very good chance that the use of paper money will turn sour. At that point, it'll become obvious to many people that their bankers are effectively liars and counterfeiters.

For example, in the United States during the Great Depression, many people lost faith entirely in their banks. They decided, instead, to keep their own gold. Logically, this is a perfectly sensible approach, since banks are just a place to store gold safely, but this strategy puts bankers out of a job. What's worse, for the bankers, is that if everyone abandons them, and they've been cheating, then they will be in massive debt, since they've been printing pieces of paper and telling everyone that these pieces of paper are of real value, when they're not. Unsurprisingly, as a result, the American bankers, and their friends in government, moved swiftly to stop the people of America exercising their financial freedom and independence. In 1933, the United States government demanded that everyone give up their gold and swap it for notes. To quote from the History.com article, *FDR takes United States off gold standard:*

> "On April 5, 1933, Roosevelt ordered all gold coins and gold certificates in denominations of more than $100 turned in for other money. It required all persons to deliver all gold coin, gold bullion and gold certificates owned by them to the Federal Reserve by May 1 for the set price of $20.67 per ounce. By May 10, the government had taken in $300 million of gold coin and $470 million of gold certificates. Two months later, a joint resolution of Congress abrogated the gold clauses in many public and private obligations that required the debtor to repay the creditor in gold dollars of the same

weight and fineness as those borrowed. In 1934, the government price of gold was increased to $35 per ounce, effectively increasing the gold on the Federal Reserve's balance sheets by 69 percent."

In other words, Franklin Roosevelt – an aristocratic corporate lawyer – forced everyone in America to sell their gold to the Federal Reserve, who are a group of private banks, at $20 per ounce. He then officially declared that the gold was worth $35 an ounce. This is an astonishing piece of robbery, but there you go. FDR then told everyone that they couldn't legally demand back the gold they borrowed. This was a very effective way to save the bankers from their cheating. There was no need for bankers to restore trust, amongst their clients - to convince people that they would honestly give back gold in return for paper notes - because no one was allowed to have gold anyway, apart from them.

Richard Nixon, early 1970's (Wikipedia)

After 1933, American bankers, and their international colleagues, continued merrily printing more dollar notes than they actually possessed in gold. Not surprisingly, as a result, the value of the dollar declined. In 1971, Richard Nixon solved this financial problem by telling everyone that they could own gold (which was nice of him) but he *also* added that the government would no longer turn anyone's dollars into gold, even at the official rate of $35 per ounce, even though these Americans weren't legally allowed to have a lot of gold anyway. To put it another way, Nixon changed the rules so that dollar notes were no longer tied to *anything* of value. People simply had to trust that their government would 'control the money supply'. Britain soon followed America's plan, as well as most developed countries. This approach became known as 'fiat' currency, which is Italian for 'trust'. In a deliciously ironic twist, the controllers of the money system, a system originally designed as a way to trade without *any* trust, were now asking everyone to trust them completely.

Unsurprisingly, these governments' plan to make people trust bankers with the printing of money didn't work very well. Since 1971, everything that has real value, and can't be created easily, such as gold and land, has ballooned in value because these major currencies have weakened so badly. For example, the British pound note was created in around 1800, and it was worth a pound of gold, because it *was* a paper receipt for a pound of gold. By 1971, a pound of gold was worth about $600, or £300. In other words, in a little under two-hundred years, the British pound note had shrunk in value by 99.7%. Since 1971, things have become far worse. At this moment in time, in 2021, a pound of gold is worth around $30,000, or roughly £20,000. In roughly two-hundred years, thanks to banks' shenanigans, a pound note has lost 99.995% of its value, or, to put in another way, if the bankers hadn't cheated with paper notes, a British pound note would now buy a luxury car. Instead, it gets us a dozen carrots.

The devaluation of money, through bankers' counterfeiting, has been only half the problem. Over several centuries, these bankers have been able to give their friends, or anyone they liked, money that they've simply made up. Their friends have then been able to buy up property with this phantom money, and then charged people from that time on, until the end of civilization, to live there. This fake money has therefore been turned into property, and thence into an endless supply of real money, gained every month from people who *did* work to gain their money. This process is no different from money-laundering, where money from criminal activities is turned into legal assets, thus 'laundering' out the dirty, criminal element.

To summarise, money was originally devised as a token system for trading goods. It was developed as a way to trade, without the need to trust anyone. Rather than giving, and gaining gratitude and obligation from that giving, merchants decided instead to exchange goods for a token that was small, portable and couldn't easily be made or counterfeited. This system sounds great, but it leaves the door wide open for robbery, since these tokens are anonymous and have no memory. Once someone steals them, he or she has all the purchasing power. If the merchants had stuck to exchanging, remembering, and keeping their obligations, robbers could not have easily stolen from them. This is the dark hole at the heart of money. By creating a system without any need for trust or obligation, the earlier merchants created a system that was hugely beneficial to liars and cheats, the very same people they were trying to defeat with that system. Even when these first merchants replaced gold with notes, it just encouraged their own bankers to become cheats and liars. In a way, because money is a trustless, amoral system, it inevitably corrupts those who handle it.

The degradation of currencies over the last two centuries, and particularly since 2008, is why cryptocurrencies have risen in value. Cryptocurrencies are similar to a gold coin, since they can't easily be created or counterfeited. Inevitably, as confidence in the money system has declined due to rampant banking counterfeiting, interest in cryptocurrencies has increased. Just as with any money token system, as soon as enough people agree that a cryptocurrency system is valuable, its value will shoot up. This is the same collective trust that merchants originally developed with gold coins. Unfortunately, like gold, there is an environmental consequence to making bitcoins. The power requirement to run the computers that create new bitcoins is enormous, especially with established cryptocurrencies. According to recent studies, the energy consumption of bitcoin 'miners', or computer systems, is now larger than that of the entire country of Sweden. In a world of accelerating climate change, our efforts to find a way to avoid trust in our transactions is still having destructive consequences.

Money has therefore been a very mixed blessing,

so what would the world be like without it? Many people would immediately conclude that if we abandoned money, economies and societies would crash, because no one would be bothered to do anything. Alternatively, economies would crash because there'd be no way to conduct business, or trade goods. These are valid concerns, and yet there are perfectly viable alternatives to money that are based around community values, rather than transactions designed to require no trust whatsoever.

To understand how we can replace money, it's worth thinking about the fundamental elements in how we make anything. For example, there has always been a fundamental relationship between time, tools, resources, and skills. If we are given time and relevant resources & tools (such as books, equipment etc), we can study, practice, and develop a skill. If we have a skill and resources & tools, we can use these things, and our time, to create more resources (such as a carpenter using tools and timber to create furniture). Fundamentally, resources come from the natural world, which continually produces them. Everything else comes out of the skills-time-resources system, but one element of this process isn't easily renewed: time. We can only gain time at a fixed rate, as in gaining time, which we can then spend. Therefore, time does work logically as a currency. Every hour, I've gained a time-hour. I can spend that hour in any way I like. If I spend that hour helping someone else, they've bought my time. They owe me one hour of my time. In return, they might give me an hour of their time, or an hour of the time of someone whom they've spent an hour helping. In this way, time becomes a token of transaction. If people maintain a log of their time, and who they've helped, then they have a currency system.

Let's see such a process in action. For example, a farmer spends a year growing crops. He has therefore turned his time, and his tools & materials, into food. Everyone who receives his food owes him the time he took to make that food. If they make the tools he needs for farming, or items he needs in his daily life, or they can teach him or his children's skills, then their time will benefit him, and they'll be able to make a direct exchange. Here's a rough calculation. A family farm is about 240 acres in size, or roughly 100 hectares. This would produce 700 tons or 700,000 kilogrammes of wheat in a year, according to an off-the-shelf reference (I'll use this crop as an example, as it's easiest). To produce this wheat, the farmer has spent one year, or 2,000 hours. Therefore, each of his hours produces 350 kgs of wheat. That is an enormous amount of wheat per hour. Understandably, the farmer needs tools, equipment and a host of materials and tools to do this work, but he would be trading his time for those materials in the knowledge that each of his hours produced such a bounty. What's more, anyone who spent an hour helping him would gain 350 kgs of wheat! Knowing this, a dentist would be happy to help the farmer with his teeth, or a carpenter make the farmer a chair, because they know they'd receive a bounteous return for their hours of work. In our modern world, maintaining a public log of this time-use would be easily done. It would also generate a positive community effect because people would feel connected to, and valued by, those they helped. It's an appealing idea; it's so appealing in fact that many time-bank systems are being used around the world today. For example, the Wikipedia page on Time-based currency states:

> "In 2004, Dr. Gill Seyfang published a study in the Community Development Journal about the effects of a timebank located in the Gorbals area of Glasgow, Scotland, "an inner-city estate characterized by high levels of deprivation, poverty, unemployment, poor health and low educational attainment." The Gorbals Timebank is run by a local charity with the intent to combat the social ills that face the region. Seyfang concluded that the timebank was effective at "building community capacity" and "promoting social inclusion." She highlights the timebank's success at "[re-stitching] the social fabric of the Gorbals." by "[boosting] engagement in existing projects and activities" in a variety of projects including a community safety network, a library, a healthy living project, and a theatre. She writes that "the timebank had enabled people to access help they otherwise would have had to do without," help which included home repair, gardening, a funeral, and tuition paid in time credits to a continuing education course."

The idea of a society running on a time-based currency is fascinating; it also has profound implications. As already mentioned, a community's spirit, and its cohesion, improves if people interact with each other. Secondly, since everyone's time-activity, and what they gained from that time is recorded, there is no room for counterfeiting, or banking 'leverage' (unless someone tries to create fake people, which is relatively easy to notice in a community).

One criticism of a time-based currency system is that some people might not like the idea that their time is worth the same as another person's. For example, a dentist might be unhappy that their time is worth the same as a cleaner's. They might say, 'I've spent years training to be a dentist! How can it be worth the same as someone who cleans toilets?' But there is another way of looking at this. By spending years training to be a dentist, that person has been able to do something they enjoy or find fulfilling, rather than someone they find distasteful or boring. Their training has enabled them to spend their hours doing something they treasure.

On the other side, by making everyone's time equal, the cleaner won't feel a failure, or inferior, because they know their time is of equal value to a dentist. What's more, this flattens the wealth distribution. In other words, a cleaner doesn't have to live in a cheap, damp flat because they can swap their time for the time of skilled artisans. In this way, both the dentist and the cleaner can live happy, healthy, self-respecting lives.

Unfortunately, instead of such an egalitarian system, our civilization has money, which is an absolute gold mine (literally and figuratively) for cheats, liars, abusers, exploiters and other criminals. One example of how an exploiter can prosper in the money system can been seen in life of Fred Trump and, in particular, his son Donald.

Donald Trump has often stated that he's a self-made man, but, according to the New York Times, he inherited $413 million from his dad. His dad, Fred, in turn gained his money from property. This sounds like a reasonable career, but Fred was not a nice landlord or developer. He was investigated for illegal profiteering in 1954 and again in 1966. He did build houses – real, physical assets – but he used every legal trick in the book to make as much money as possible in the process. Woody Guthrie, the famous American folk singer, wrote a song *Old Man Trump* while living in an apartment complex owned by Fred Trump in Brooklyn. Guthrie's lyrics include the following verse:

> "I suppose Old Man Trump knows just how much Racial Hate he stirred up in the bloodpot of human hearts when he drawed that color line here at his Beach Haven family project."

Guthrie's comment isn't that surprising, since Fred Trump was once arrested at a Klu Klux Klan gathering, indicating that he wasn't a fan of multiculturalism.

Fred Trump (Wikipedia – Bernard Gotfryd)

Fred Trump's business practices, therefore, according to many accounts, seem to show multiple elements of amoral, deceitful behaviour. Fred didn't need to win over hearts and minds, he just needed to exploit the money system. According to relevant accounts, he was little better at home as a warm human being. The Wikipedia page on him includes the following description (see the web page for the references):

> "Trump was an authoritarian parent, maintaining curfews and forbidding cursing, lipstick, and snacking between meals. At the end of his day, Trump would receive a report from Mary on the children's actions and, if necessary, decide upon disciplinary actions. He took his children to building sites to collect empty bottles to return for the deposits. According to Fred Jr.'s daughter, Mary L. Trump, Trump wanted his oldest son to be "invulnerable" in personality so he could take over the family business, but Fred Jr. was the opposite. Trump instead elevated Donald to become his business heir, teaching him to "be a killer", and telling him, "You are a king." Mary L. Trump states that Fred Sr. "dismantled [Fred Jr.] by devaluing and degrading every aspect of his personality" and mocked him for his decision to become an airline pilot. In 1981, Fred Jr. died at age 42 from complications due to his alcoholism."

The 'devaluing and degrading' comment, made by Mary Trump, is particularly revealing. It comes from her book, *Too Much and Never Enough: How My Family*

Created the World's Most Dangerous Man. We can see, in her description, that Fred Trump was, in many ways, a classic perpetrator of an abuse-control system, and he did it extremely well, thanks to money.

Inevitably, those that have become immensely wealthy by manipulating the money system have known they were cheating. As a result, they've always feared that they might have their fortunes reduced, or entirely confiscated by governments and the law. To stop this happening, these kleptocrats have made huge efforts to influence leaders of Western governments do their bidding. The more these amoral people have stolen, the more money they have spent on making sure that the democracies in their countries don't hold their financial crimes to account. In the last fifty years, this behaviour has turned politics into a dirty word. Fred Trump's son Donald, for example, became President of the United States, thereby turning a dubious real-estate speculator and friend of the Mob into the leader of the most powerful nation in the world. This was utterly shocking to large numbers of people in the United States and they're still reeling from it.

The United Kingdom has also moved into the world of morally vacant politicians and their kleptocrat friends. British voters, in the last twenty years, have voted for not one but two Prime Ministers that were once members of the notorious Bullingdon Club in Oxford, famed for its drunkenness, vandalism and general amorality. To quote from the Guardian newspaper article, *Sexism, vandalism and bullying: inside the Boris Johnson-era Bullingdon Club*, a female graduate of Oxford reported:

> "Bullingdon members found it amusing if people were intimidated or frightened by their behaviour. I remember them walking down a street in Oxford in their tails, chanting 'Buller, Buller' and smashing bottles along the way, just to cow people."

The female graduate was horrified when Boris Johnson (Bullingdon Boy) became Prime Minister of Britain:

> "The characteristics he displayed at Oxford – entitlement, aggression, amorality, lack of concern for others – are still there, dressed up in a contrived, jovial image. It's a mask to sanitise some ugly features."

Boris Johnson in the British Parliament

In truth, Johnson's behaviour doesn't seem to have visibly changed. Since taking power, his government has pursued an authoritarian, amoral agenda. Its new laws have systematically reduced freedom of speech, human rights, legal aid, independent bodies, monitoring of the police, institutional oversight, environmental support, financial accountability, and so on. None of these changes will help the poor people of Britain, or in fact 95% of its population, but they do help many powerful, amoral billionaires.

These recent examples of morally dubious and financially unsound people becoming leaders of major democracies is both chilling, and also odd. It is logical that wealthy, amoral people, ones who do so well from an amoral money system, might want to have their underlings in the top seats in government, but this is occurring in democracies, where the general public choose the leader. Why would the general public vote for autocratic, arrogant, callous men that are happy to exploit them, and often have only contempt for them? This is a strange paradox. It is also not new. In truth, it has been going on for centuries, and yet it still seems to make no sense. To understand why, we need to think about sex.

Sexual repression

In the 1930's, a young, Austrian psychoanalyst, Wilhelm Reich, thought about the paradox of people voting for leaders that held them in contempt, and exploited them. Reich could see, at that time, that Germany and Austria were becoming increasingly right-wing, authoritarian, and violent. He could also see that the Nazis and their friends had no compassion for their citizens; they had no desire to empower the people of their countries. Instead, these fascists wished to use their country's populace as tools in their own thirst for greater power. Reich eventually wrote a book on the subject, entitled: *The Mass Psychology of Fascism*. His book became an instant classic. It was so insightful and thought-provoking that it was hated by both the Soviet regime and the Nazis, who publicly burnt it.

Reich left Germany and emigrated to the United States, with the hope that it would be a sanctuary from oppression. Unfortunately, America was not a haven of free thought for him. Reich's intelligence and original thinking led him to develop alternative theories about the mind, the body, the life-force and how people could be healed. His ideas and methods were unusual, interesting and either harmless or a ground-breaking new understanding of biological life, but they incited the wrath of the U.S. authorities. In 1954, a judge in Maine ordered that all his published books should be burnt, on the request of the Food and Drug Administration. The spectre of Nazi book-burning had returned for Reich with a vengeance. He was imprisoned and died, shortly before his release date, in 1957.

Wilhem Reich

Reich's book, *The Mass Psychology of Fascism,* includes many insights, but it focusses on one particular reason behind people's devotion to authoritarian leaders. Reich believed that many ordinary people admire and worship authoritarian leaders because they have been moulded into that mindset from an early age by psychological control. Like any abuse-control victim, these people have learned to be worshipful in order to lessen their suffering. By training themselves to admire and publicly support a toxic leader, they can bury the negative feelings they have about themselves, negative feelings that have been repeatedly drummed into them by authority, just as the Korean prisoners-of-war experienced. Reich believed that the nature of the psychological abuse these people received, which caused them to form this attitude, revolved around one important element of their lives: their sexual desires.

For a long time, naturalists and zoologists, when studying animal behaviour, have described animals as purely heterosexual creatures. All sex in the animal world, they reported, was for the purpose of procreation and therefore there was only heterosexual sex. This is untrue. In recent decades, wildlife experts have dismantled this myth that animals are purely heterosexual. In the National Geographic article, *Homosexuality among animals stirs debate*, the author states:

> "Birds do it, bees do it, even educated fleas do it. So go the lyrics penned by U.S. songwriter Cole Porter. Porter, who first hit it big in the 1920s, wouldn't risk parading his

homosexuality in public. In his day "the birds and the bees" generally meant only one thing—sex between a male and female. But, actually, some same-sex birds *do* do it. So do beetles, sheep, fruit bats, dolphins, and orangutans. Zoologists are discovering that homosexual and bisexual activity is not unknown within the animal kingdom. Roy and Silo, two male chinstrap penguins at New York's Central Park Zoo have been inseparable for six years now. They display classic pair-bonding behaviour—entwining of necks, mutual preening, flipper flapping, and the rest. They also have sex, while ignoring potential female mates. Wild birds exhibit similar behaviour. There are male ostriches that only court their own gender, and pairs of male flamingos that mate, build nests, and even raise foster chicks. Filmmakers recently went in search of homosexual wild animals as part of a National Geographic Ultimate Explorer documentary about the female's role in the mating game. The team caught female Japanese macaques engaged in intimate acts which, if observed in humans, would be in the X-rated category. 'The homosexual behaviour that goes on is completely baffling and intriguing,' says National Geographic Ultimate Explorer correspondent, Mireya Mayor. 'You would have thought females that want to be mated, especially over their fertile period, would be seeking out males.'"

In Bruce Bagemihl's 1999 book *Biological Exuberance: Animal Homosexuality and Natural Diversity*, the author explains that the presence of same-sex sexual behaviour was not "officially" observed on a large scale until the 1990s due to observer bias caused by social attitudes towards non-heterosexual people, making the homosexual theme taboo. Petter Bøckman, academic adviser for the *Against Nature?* Exhibit, stated:

> "Many researchers have described homosexuality as something altogether different from sex. They must realize that animals can have sex with who they will, when they will and without consideration to a researcher's ethical principles."

It would seem that bisexuality, or homosexuality, is natural, in the sense that it takes place in the natural world. If the observations already mentioned are correct, then bisexuality and homosexuality is a natural occurrence amongst living creatures. According to the evidence, creatures, functioning as conscious, living, feeling beings, can become attracted to another member of their species of the same gender. As a result, they choose to be in a relationship that doesn't exist purely for reproduction. This preference isn't harmful to either party and is generally agreed to be a pleasurable experience. Some people may find homosexual sex disgusting but it's worth remembering that disgust is a learned behaviour. Babies, for example, are not disgusted by anything, although they do learn, by trial and error, that certain experiences are less enjoyable than others, like poo, sharp items and pulling cats' tails. But as they grow older, and turn from infants into children, they soon work out, from their parents or other peer-figures, what they should be disgusted by. Eventually, they are so developed in trained disgust that they will, for example, refuse to eat food from a potty-tray, even if the potty-tray has just arrived from the store and is fresh out of its packaging. In this way, children have completed their disgust training. This learned disgust can include aversions that are far more subtle than simple things, such as poo, rotten food and creepy-crawlies. To quote from the PBS science article, *What's Behind the Disgust Response?*:

> A recent study headed by self-proclaimed "disgustologist" Val Curtis at the London School of Hygiene and Tropical Medicine found that there might be different categories of disgust, one of which is atypical appearance. It may be this aspect of disgust that drives repulsion from people we see as different from ourselves. According to social neuroscientist Susan Fiske, "Disgust toward social outcasts avoids perceived moral and infectious contamination." We may implicitly believe that there is something dangerous about someone that looks different from ourselves. Psychologists at St. Andrews University demonstrated how disgust relates to social groups by asking students to smell sweaty t-shirts. Students were faster to sanitize their hands after smelling shirts with a rival university's logo than they were after smelling one with their own university's logo. Simply by changing the identity of who was wearing the shirt, researchers saw a change in the students' response. This result suggests

that social groupings have something to do with a disgust response."

If people can be disgusted in these subtle ways and trained to be disgusted so that they don't even question *why* their disgusted, then there is ample opportunity for peer groups to train them to be disgusted by certain forms of sexual behaviour. As a result, homophobia - the hatred of homosexuals and homosexual acts - can become normalised. They are also a fundamental aspect of most of the major religions of the Western World. For example, the conservative wings of the Catholic, Anglican and Islamic religions denounce homosexuality. Islam, a religion formed in around 500 BC, has this to say about homosexuality:

> "And as for the two of you men who are guilty of lewdness, punish them both. And if they repent and improve, then let them be. Lo! Allah is Merciful."
>
> Quran (4:16)

Most schools of Shari'ah Law – a right-wing form of Islam – view homosexual sex as deserving the same punishment as adultery, i.e. death. The Roman Catholic religion, since its early days, has vociferously banned homosexuality and declared it a sin. According to the Catechism of the Catholic Church:

> "Homosexual acts are... acts of grave depravity that are intrinsically disordered... They are contrary to the natural law. They close the sexual act to the gift of life. They do not proceed from a genuine affective and

sexual complementarity. Under no circumstances can they be approved."

According to the scientific evidence already mentioned, this catechism is untrue. Homosexuality *is* natural, as it's a part of many living creatures' behaviour. It's simply a personal preference for some animals. It's understandable that zoologists have failed to report evidence of homosexuality in the natural world, as many of them have grown up in religious schools, of one kind or another. When they saw it, they declined to report it, as it contradicts the Catholic Church's view.

Anglican Christianity is perhaps less condemning of homosexuality, but it also contains homophobic sections. For example, many conservative, Evangelical churches in the United States have effectively banned homosexuality amongst their congregations. Some of them have even gone as far as setting up centres to 'convert' homosexuals into heterosexuals.

But why are Western religions against gay sex? The way to answer this question is probably to look at these religions' origins. Islam, Catholicism, and its modern Anglican version all originated, long ago, in the Near East and Mesopotamia. It would seem that someone in power, in that region of the world, decided that homosexuality would be demonised and banned. They then promulgated this idea, insisting that an act that causes no harm, that some people naturally choose to do, was evil. This decision went hand-in-hand with another rule, that sex was *only* for reproduction. In other words, sex for pleasure, or masturbation, was sinful. This was made clear by the Catholic Church. In many Islamic communities, sex for pleasure, particularly amongst young people, is also suppressed, since young, unmarried women are physically kept apart from the men until they are married, preventing any sexual recreation amongst young adults.

What was the reason for such a draconian, repressive, system? Why not educate young people in how to enjoy sex; how to enjoy its pleasures without causing unwanted pregnancies? This was the question that Wilhelm Reich pondered in the 1930s. He was a psychoanalyst and so he sought to understand the psychological implications of this sexual suppression. He came to a thought-provoking conclusion. To quote from his book, *the Mass Psychology of Fascism*:

> "Suppression of the natural sexuality in the child, particularly of its genital sexuality, makes the child apprehensive, shy, obedient, afraid of authority, good and adjusted in the authoritarian sense; it paralyzes the rebellious forces because any rebellion is laden with anxiety; it produces, by inhibiting sexual curiosity and sexual thinking in the child, a general inhibition of thinking and of critical faculties. In brief, the goal of sexual suppression is that of producing an individual who is adjusted to the authoritarian order and who will submit to it in spite of all misery and degradation. Initially, the child has to submit to the structure of the authoritarian miniature state, the family, which process makes it capable of later subordination to the general authoritarian system. The formation of the authoritarian structure takes place through

> the anchoring of sexual inhibition and anxiety."

In other words, by making homosexuals and bisexuals feel sinful, repulsive, mentally deficient and deviant, religious institutions could erode their self-confidence and self-image. Banning sex before marriage, and making no attempt to supply sex education, also caused crippling emotional repression in many heterosexuals. As a result, a large proportion of the society become laden with self-loathing, anxiety, guilt and feelings of inferiority. Just as with the Korean prisoners-of-war, this continual psychological pressure can make people persuade themselves to zealously embrace the creed of the authoritarian abusers. By doing this, they alleviate some of their suffering. Some of them can even go as far as being extremely critical of others, as a way of compensating against their own, inner feelings of inferiority and shame. They punish anyone trying to break out of the cage as a proxy for their shame about their own, suppressed sexual feelings. Trapped in this miserable situation of self-loathing, suppression, compensation and hypocrisy, many turn to drink and other addictions, as a way to ease their pain. It is a tragic psychological situation and, what's worse, it was being applied to the entire religious congregations, which in many countries was everyone outside the religious order.

Reich realised that sexual repression, by those in power, was a powerful tool to create obedience and submission in their subjects. Some readers might say, at this point, that some sexual suppression *is* needed, in order to avoid excessive births, but there's no sign that that was the purpose. In fact, the main Abrahamic religions want many births, to swell their numbers. We can see this agenda in the Catechism of the Catholic Church; it states that homosexuality 'closes the sexual act to the gift of life'. In other words, all sex should be done to make babies. This fits with the Catholic Church's belief that all forms of contraception are sinful. This has an inevitable and devastating consequence: rampant population growth.

Population growth

Hunter-gatherers don't have the pill. Being relatively low on the technology totem-pole, they have few contraceptive aids. They have relaxed social rules, at least compared to civilized societies. For example, several North American indigenous tribes have always happily condoned same-sex couples, cross-dressing, changes of heterosexual partners (usually decided by the female) and whatever any of their members felt in the mood to do. To quote the Guardian article, *The 'two-spirit' people of indigenous North Americans* (11th Oct 2010):

> 'Native Americans have often held intersex, androgynous people, feminine males and masculine females in high respect. The most common term to define such persons today is to refer to them as "two-spirit" people.'

We-Wa, a Zuni two-spirit, weaving

Understandably, some people might conclude, on reading this, that hunter-gatherer societies breed excessively, like rabbits, and that their populations have only been controlled by starvation, predation, and war. In fact, this is mostly untrue. Hunter-gatherer societies have always been surprisingly good at maintaining a low birth-rate. It was only when tribes became civilized that their population rates increased. To quote from the PubMed article, *Breastfeeding: nature's contraceptive*, by R.V. Short:

> "Our ancestors achieved the lowest rate of reproduction of any living mammal by the postponement of puberty until well into the 2nd decade of life, a maximal probability of conception of only about 24% per menstrual cycle even when ovulation had commenced, a 4-year birth interval, as a result of the contraceptive effects of breastfeeding, and a sharp decline in fertility during the 4th decade of life, leading to complete sterility at the menopause. This pattern of reproduction was ideally suited to the prevailing lifestyle of the nomadic hunter-gatherer. The postponement of puberty resulted in a prolonged period of

> childhood dependency, thus enabling parents to transmit their acquired experience to their offspring. Long birth intervals were also essential for a woman who had to wander 1000 or more miles each year in search of food, because she could not manage to carry more than 1 child with her at a time."

The author then compares this with civilization's approach:

> "The lifestyle of comparatively recent times of a settled agricultural economy made possible subsequent rural and urban development, but this transition from nomad to city dweller also stimulated fertility. The cultivation of crops and the domestication of animals led to the development of permanent housing, where the mother could leave her baby in a safe place while she worked in the field. The resultant reduction in mother-infant contact coupled with the availability of early weaning foods reduced the suckling frequency, thereby eroding the contraceptive effect of breastfeeding and decreasing the birth interval. The model conquest of disease eventually led to rapid rates of population growth."

According to Short's article, it is civilized people that 'breed like rabbits', not hunter-gatherers. This increase in reproduction amongst civilized people has had several, negative, knock-on effects. Firstly, women have suffered. As the birth interval decreased, women's health decreased due to the strain of carrying out increased numbers of pregnancies and births. Women's likelihood of death in childbirth and related illnesses therefore also increased. They had lost their hunter-gatherer female role as expert forager and medicine-gatherer in the shift to agriculture. Continual childbirth would have weakened their role still further, propelling them into a subjugated role of house cleaner (since multi-roomed houses never existed in the hunter-gatherer societies) and endless baby-maker. Their poorer health, particularly in middle and later life, combined with a house-centric life, would have weakened their role in the community decision-making processes, allowing a far more 'yang' or macho male mentality to take over. This macho leadership culture would have prioritised violent conflict, as a way to resolve issues, rather than using the more 'yin' approach of intelligent discussion and mutually beneficial compromises.

Women weren't the only ones to suffer in the civilized world of accelerated population growth. In any society, particularly a settled one with permanent housing, every extra person requires more housing space, utilities, transport etc. If these resources aren't supplied, overcrowding occurs, with a corresponding drop in quality of life, physical health, sanitation, and mental health. These physical demands are only part of the overpopulation problem. The increasing lack of open spaces reduces mental and physical health, lowers privacy and stops those less socially adept from finding sanctuaries. If more and more young people are produced, it is hard to give them jobs, and so youth unemployment and resentment grows, resulting in more mental suffering, violence, and social unrest. These problems might seem normal to many of us, and perhaps a part of human nature, but in fact they are not natural. Instead, they are a direct effect of too many people living in a fixed location. Our familiarity with these problems blinds us to the fact that they are unnatural and toxic for all of us.

The negative effects of a high rate of population growth may make societies suffer, but they can be of use to toxic controllers. In particular, overpopulation, along with its creation of refugees, illegal immigrants and increasing hostility between nations, creates fear in people. Fear is an extremely useful tool for abusive controllers, as fearful people are far more willing to accept an autocrat as a leader. Michele J. Gelfand, Distinguished University Professor of psychology at the University of Maryland, explains in the The Hill article, *Threat, fear, and the evolutionary appeal of autocrats*:

> "Autocrats around the world have expertly capitalized on the primal tight-loose fault line: When we perceive threats (whether real, imagined, or manipulated), we crave social order – and the strongmen who can enforce it. Threats don't even need to be real to

trigger a desire for tightness. In our lab, we exposed study participants to false information about terrorist incidents, overpopulation, and pathogen outbreaks. Within minutes, their minds tightened: they wanted stronger rules, favored their own tribe, and became intolerant of outsiders. Would-be autocrats around the world are conducting these "threat experiments" on their nations' citizens. Trump has effectively used threatening language to encourage people to fear people from other cultures. Matteo Salvani, as if reading from a tight-loose text book declared that "We are under attack. Our culture, society, traditions and way of life are at risk." Viktor Orban claimed that Hungarians have to get rid of "Muslim invaders." Le Pen's rhetoric is equally alarming: Globalization and Islam will "Bring France to its knees." Analyze any speech of autocrats around the world, and you'll see the same pattern. Threat constitutes the foundation of their narrative. The goal: To inspire fear, tighten groups, and be perceived as the only person who can deliver safety. "I alone can fix it" claims Trump. The strategy is enormously successful because it taps into a deep evolutionary principle that helped us survive for millennia. Their supporters feel like their nations are "on the brink of disaster" and they need tight rules and strong-arm rules to survive. Our research confirms that the strongest Trump supporters believe their

> country is under grave threat and desire tighter laws and punishments."

Overpopulation therefore creates fear, and in particular a fear of invasion. This is bread-and-butter to abusive controllers, who can use this climate of fear to gain greater authoritarian control. As we've seen earlier in this book, 'fear of threats' is an important component in Biderman's Chart of Coercion, with good reason. Continual overpopulation therefore suits abusive controllers, as it keeps their subjects stressed, ill and fearful, but such a condition cannot continue forever. At some point, such population pressures will produce social breakdown. To prevent this occurring, historically, countries have conducted wars, using unwanted young men as cannon fodder, or released unwanted people as refugees, sending them to populate more remote places. For example, the modern United States was created using this method. By taking civilized technology with them, these refugee groups were able to transform their new habitat into a place that can support a larger population, but this invariably stressed the region's native population, or more likely decimated it. Any hunter-gatherer society, when invaded by civilization, almost always suffered terribly from civilization's toxic properties: soldiers, lethal infectious diseases, factory-education, abusive religions, money, clerical abuse, alcohol, and sugar. Effectively, they are steamrollered by the machine of civilization as it processes their natural environment.

Colonisation can create adventure, innovation and freedom, or indigenous genocide, depending on your point of view, but eventually, it will stop working because we only have one planet. We've now reached the stage, as a species, where there are no more sparsely populated areas to move into, and yet our population keeps climbing. What's going to happen to us?

To understand what our future will be, as we inexorably grow in numbers on a finite planet, we can examine an experiment carried out on another species of sociable mammals with a high production rate: mice. In the 1960's and 1970's, the American researcher John B. Calhoun performed population experiments with mice at the National Institute of Mental Health. Calhoun first created an idealised environment for the mice, a habitat he built that included a bounteous supply of food, nesting and communal areas.

John B. Calhoun in his mouse habitat (Wikipedia – Yoichi R Okamoto)

Calhoun placed a seed-group of mice in this habitat and observed what happened. At first, the mice in the habitat were wary of their new, strange surroundings, but they soon explored and staked out their new territory. Calhoun called this the 'strive' phase. Once they were settled, they began multiplying in what he called their 'exploit phase', until they reached a population ceiling. This wasn't the maximum possible population for the habitat. Instead, it was around 70% of the habitat's theoretical carrying capacity. At this point, the mice entered what Calhoun described as an 'equilibrium phase'. This sounds calm and balanced, but it was in fact more of a 'population crunch phase'. To quote from the video documentary *Mouse Utopia Experiment*, created by Jerry Haislmaier:

> "In the equilibrium period, Doctor Calhoun noticed that the new generation of mice were inhibited, as the social spaces were already defined. At this time, some unusual behaviour became noticeable. Violence became prevalent. Excess males strived for acceptance, were rejected, and withdrew. Huddling together, they would exhibit brief flurries of violence amongst themselves. The effects of violence became increasingly visible. Certain individuals became targets of repeated attacks. These individuals would have badly scarred and chewed tails."

Personally, for me, such a description sounds a lot like secondary school, or what it's like to live in a low-income neighbourhood. The documentary then states:

> "Other young mice, growing into adulthood, exhibited a different type of behaviour. Doctor Calhoun called these individuals the 'beautiful ones'. Their time was devoted solely to grooming, eating and sleeping. They never

> involved themselves with others, engaged in sex, or would fight. All appeared as a beautiful exhibit of the species; alert eyes and a healthy, well-kept body. These mice, however, could not cope with unusual stimuli. Though they looked inquisitive, they were, in fact, very stupid."

It makes sense that, in an environment where food is continually available and there are no predators, some members of a society would do nothing; they would make no effort to explore or gain social status or compete for a mate. Instead, they would just groom themselves and hang around. Bereft of threat, and avoiding the need for confrontation, they drift into a dead-end of inert stasis.

The mouse habitat's 'equilibrium phase' did not last forever. After about eight generations, the colony entered a final phase, a 'die phase', in which its population rapidly dwindled to extinction. To quote from the video:

> "Although the habitat could potentially house three thousand mice, the population reached its maximum at around 2,200, then rapidly declined. In the shift from the equilibrium to the die phase, each animal became less aware of associates, despite all animals being pushed closer together. Doctor Calhoun concluded that the mice could not effectively deal with the repeated contact of so many individuals. The evidence of violence increased to the point where most individuals had had their tails bitten to some degree. Eventually, the entire mouse population perished."

The video concludes by commenting on how Calhoun's experiments reflect on human population issues:

> "The findings about population growth and individual behaviour are being closely compared to human populations. Like all populations that have existed on this planet, many researchers believe that the human race have reached a crucial point in the 'exploit phase', a point where important decisions must be made, and careful planning implemented, if we are to survive. The study of plant and animal populations helps us to make decisions about the future, so that we may maintain our own balance with nature."

It would be good if the leaders of our species did study our current situation, and the future dangers of overpopulation, but there seems to be precious little sign that this is going on. China did implement a 'one child' policy (which has now ended). Other countries have worked to educate women, so as to reduce birthrates, but overall, there is little sign of any slowdown in population growth. Here is a graph of world population since the dawn of civilization:

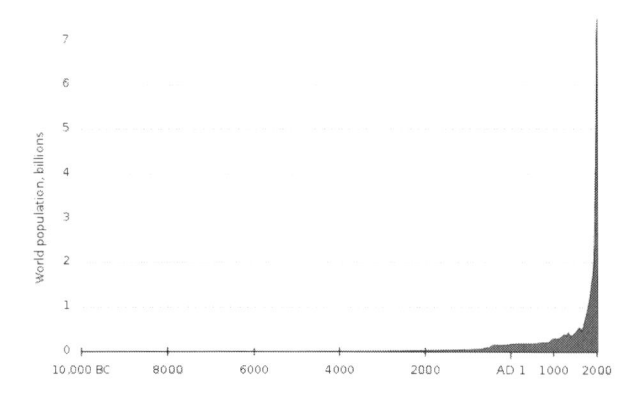

Global population since 10,000 BC (Wikipedia commons)

The spike at the end is so sharp that it's hard to believe that it *can* be a graph of population. It looks more like a bacterial or viral population graph. Such a rate of increase shows that there is effectively no control over the human population of our planet. Instead, it's as if the floodgates opened, which they did, once two things happened. Firstly, technology removed all elements that controlled population, such as predators and dangerous, infectious illnesses. Secondly, irrigation, selective breeding of livestock, the chainsaw, fertilisers, pesticides, the genetic modification of crops and other technological marvels massively increased our food supply. Our current numbers are now around 7.9 billion people on Earth, and counting.

Many academics and scientists believe that our current population hasn't reached a maximum. Instead, they believe that we can grow more, without creating chaos. For example, the eminent Harvard University sociobiologist Edward O. Wilson, comments in his book, *The Future of Life*:

> "The constraints of the biosphere [Earth] are fixed... If everyone agreed to become vegetarian, leaving little or nothing for livestock, the present 1.4 billion hectares of arable land (3.5 billion acres) would support about 10 billion people."

According to Wilson, if we switch to vegetarianism, we'll still have some more growing space, but there are three problems with Wilson's idea. Firstly, wealthy people like eating meat, and will probably use their wealth to keep doing it. Secondly, exponential growth (as shown in the earlier graph) means that we'll hit 10 billion very soon, making the idea of 'growing room' meaningless, since we'd have to start planning population stabilization strategies right now, just in order for those policies to come into effect before we hit that population ceiling.

The third problem with Wilson's view is perhaps the worst of all. Our population might be only 77% of what our planet can support, but Calhoun's mice experiment showed that a theoretical population ceiling did not translate into an actual population ceiling. Calhoun reported that his mouse habitat could support 3,000 mice, but the population plateaued at 2,200, or only 73% of its theoretical capacity. Once the mice hit that percentage, their population-growth flatlined and they entered a world of suffering, indolence, and misery.

There are signs that the human population on planet Earth is now in Calhoun's 'equilibrium phase'. Almost every fertile part of our planet is now maximally farmed, and these fertile areas are diminishing, thanks to over-farming, desertification, and soil erosion. Global fish stocks are also dwindling, and climate-change induced heat-stress will soon kill off more and more of our harvests. We have left Calhoun's 'exploit phase' behind and we are now suffering in the same way as the mice, with overcrowding, mental stress, and violence. Such problems are very familiar problems to people in the developed world and have been for some time. In Asia, particularly Hong Kong, Japan and South Korea, these problems are reaching intense levels. Many people in those countries are living in tiny apartments because the overcrowding has become so intense. They are also suffering from crippling debt, due to their hyper-capitalist or neo-liberal set-up, which has increased stress and misery. These critical problems recently gave rise to the global television hit *Squid Game*, a South Korean series inspired by the debt-misery of many South Koreans, a country that is amongst the most densely populated in the world. To quote Wikipedia:

> "The series revolves around a contest where 456 players in deep financial debt put their lives at risk to play a series of children's games for the chance to win a ₩45.6 billion prize... Hwang had conceived of the idea based on his own economic struggles early in life as well as the class disparity in South Korea."

Squid Game may be seen by many as purely entertainment, but it's a cultural and social marker. It is throwing into sharp relief a world where there are too many people, and a sharp divide between the haves and have-nots. Those that successfully manipulate the money-system live lives of luxury, whereas those that don't live in misery, however hard they work. The popularity of *Squid Game,* and its social resonance, may also be warning us that we're actually a step beyond Calhoun's equilibrium phase. We're no longer in the 'crunch period' but instead, we're entering what he called the 'die phase', where the population declines, fertility flatlines and everyone suffers. Is this true? Will we all lose heart, stop breeding, and plunge to extinction in only three generations? It seems to be a grossly negative prediction, and yet there are signs that it may be true. To quote from the BBC news article (15th July, 2020), *Fertility rate: 'Jaw-dropping' global crash in children being born*:

> "The world is ill-prepared for the global crash in children being born which is set to have a "jaw-dropping" impact on societies, say researchers. Falling fertility rates mean nearly every country could have shrinking populations by the end of the century. And 23 nations – including Spain and Japan – are expected to see their populations halve by 2100."

The drop in fertility in the developed world has been blamed on the cost of child-rearing, but that itself is a consequence of population pressures. There is also a crucial extra element to add to the mix: climate change. Global warming is already exacerbating the problems caused by overcrowding and shrinking resources. Calhoun's mouse habitat always stayed the same size and supplied the same amount of food. In comparison, our planet's resources are shrinking as climate-change induced floods, droughts, and heatwaves increase, in their number and severity. It would be like Calhoun gradually increasing the temperature of his habitat, polluting the air, and lowering the quality of the food. The results don't bear thinking about.

It would be tempting to believe that our climate change situation, along with our population problems, has 'come of nowhere', and that no one had a clue it would occur half a century ago. In fact, both problems were anticipated.

Edward Teller in 1958 (Wikipedia)

In 1959, the celebrated nuclear physicist, Edward Teller, gave a talk to assembled guests at a New York Symposium, entitled Energy patterns of the future. This is what he said:

> "Ladies and gentlemen, I am to talk to you about energy in the future. I will start by telling you why I believe that the energy resources of the past must be supplemented. First of all, these energy resources will run

short as we use more and more of the fossil fuels. But I would like to mention another reason why we probably have to look for additional fuel supplies. And this, strangely, is the question of contaminating the atmosphere. Whenever you burn conventional fuel, you create carbon dioxide. The carbon dioxide is invisible, it is transparent, you can't smell it, it is not dangerous to health, so why should one worry about it? Carbon dioxide has a strange property. It transmits visible light but it absorbs the infrared radiation which is emitted from the earth. Its presence in the atmosphere causes a greenhouse effect. It has been calculated that a temperature rise corresponding to a 10 per cent increase in carbon dioxide will be sufficient to melt the icecap and submerge New York. All the coastal cities would be covered, and since a considerable percentage of the human race lives in coastal regions, I think that this chemical contamination is more serious than most people tend to believe."

Teller was almost entirely correct. The only mistake he made was the '10%' value. Before the Industrial Revolution, carbon dioxide concentrations in our atmosphere were around 280 parts per million. They are now over 400 parts per million. Apart from this miscalculation, Teller was right to warn about our ice caps melting and New York becoming submerged.

The problems of overpopulation, and its consequences of pollution, social stress, food shortages etc, was also predicted in the early 1970's.

In 1973, researchers in Australia used its largest computer (at that time) to predict future trends in key areas. To do this, they used an algorithm developed by the M.I.T. programmer Jay Forrester. As the black-and-white ABC video documentary *Computer predicts the end of civilisation (1973)* shows, their computer simulation concluded that between 2030 to 2050, pollution-levels on Earth would sky-rocket, quality of life would collapse, and the global population would then drastically decline. In the documentary, the presenter makes the following comment:

> "Hopefully, of course, this won't be allowed to happen, but it's taken this kind of shock treatment to nudge governments into doing something, and we are. We're starting to clean up our atmosphere. We're starting to recycle our rubbish. We're doing something positive about population control. But so far, efforts have really been just a drop in the ocean."

He was right. Miniscule efforts were taken by governments then, and they haven't changed in scale since, even though the signs and warnings have grown. Instead, the problem is usually dismissed, or promises are made that some new, magical technology will sort everything out. This applies to all the problems that face us, including climate change, food shortages, pollution, chronic overcrowding, and other systemic problems. For example, here is a very recent comment about the climate change threat from a columnist in the *Guardian* newspaper (28th October 2021), a paper that prides itself on intelligent, courageous views:

> "Political will has shifted – two-thirds of the world's GDP is now in countries that have declared a net zero target."

The author of the article fails to mention that these targets are to be met in 2050. According to the well-researched book *Climate Wars*, by Gwynne Dyer, it is likely that Earth's climate will be so bad by 2050 that all international cooperation will have broken down, large wars will have broken out and most major governments will be ruling in a state of martial law. The 1973 computer assessment agrees with this prediction. If they are correct, then such 'net zero by 2050' government promises are as useful as a person saying they'll pay a friend back after they've died.

It seems almost inconceivable that our newspapers, bought and paid for by us, and operating under legal rules of objectivity and honesty, should be so unreliable about such an important issue, but this leads us to another facet of civilization, one that is more abstract than alcohol, sugar, or money, but is just as important. Most of us, because of the way civilization works, effectively exist in boxes of acute specialisation. In other words, we know a lot about a very specific job, and no first-hand understanding of anything else. Specialisation *is* an intrinsic part of civilization – it's one of its key facets - but it has a dark side: dehumanisation and propaganda.

Dehumanising Specialisation of Work

In hunter-gatherer societies, there is very little specialisation. Each member knows all the skills he or she needs to survive. This approach is immensely liberating. If a hunter-gatherer decides to wander off and live elsewhere, they can. They have all the required skills in their head to survive independently. What's more, they can obtain the materials they need for their tools and equipment from the land around them. The downside of this approach is that no one dedicates all their time to one endeavour, which means there is little research and development. Hunter-gatherers are usually operating on a subsistence level. In other words, they've got enough to keep themselves going in the short term and they don't have the capacity to dedicate resources to long-term projects.

Civilization, by comparison, is all about specialisation. In a settled compound, with a store of grain and a hierarchical organisation of power, those in charge can order certain people to do a particular job all the time. These specialised individuals do not have to hunt, harvest, or cook, they just do that rarefied job. The benefit of this approach is that someone who is particularly skilled in one area of research, or development, can dedicate all their time to advancing that field of study. They can advance their field, thus improving the knowledge of the entire community. Scientists, doctors, dentists, carpenters, and blacksmiths are examples of such roles.

The downside of specialization is that a person who is trained purely in a specialised role is incapable of living independently of the group; they have no knowledge of hunting, tool-making or outdoor survival. They are therefore trapped in their role. This isn't so bad if you're a doctor, but what happens when jobs become ultra-specialised? What happens, for example, if you only know how to make one part of a pin?

Adam Smith on the UK £20 note

The Scottish economist and philosopher Adam Smith thought a lot about manufacturing efficiency. He realised that artisans were productive, and valuable workers, but they weren't the most efficient way to produce particular objects. In in his famous work, *The Wealth of Nations*, he explains that a factory making pins could produce many more of them if its workers didn't each make whole pins. Instead, each worker should only carry out one part of the pin-making process. In Chapter 1 of his book, Smith describes, in exhaustive detail, why this would increase productivity.

> "One man draws out the wire, another straights it, a third cuts it, a fourth points it, a fifth grinds it at the top for receiving the head; to make the head requires two or three distinct operations; to put it on, is a peculiar business, to whiten the pins is another; it is even a trade by itself to put them into the paper; and the important business of making a pin is, in this manner, divided into about

> eighteen distinct operations, which, in some manufactories, are all performed by distinct hands, though in others the same man will sometimes perform two or three of them."

By making each worker do only a subset of the job of making a pin, he explains that more pins can be made per day. Factory owners and industrialists wholeheartedly embraced Smith's idea. Unfortunately, none of them seemed to be concerned about the human cost. What would it be like, for any worker, to spend their entire working life repeatedly making one part of a pin? This sounds like a truly dehumanising situation. It also condemned each worker to become completely trapped in their role. If any of them tried to leave and set up shop making pins elsewhere, they would only know part of the pin-making process. They would have to *all* leave and work together, a far harder task for any worker in Victorian England.

The ultra-specialisation of work, to the point of dehumanising a person into a kind of robot, was immensely profitable. Smith himself was so revered by the establishment, as a result of his ideas, that he ended up on the back of the United Kingdom's twenty-pound note.

It's true that specialisation of work can benefit society, such as having full-time doctors, dentists, blacksmiths, and carpenters, but ultra-specialisation can condemn the lives of huge numbers of people to an unrelenting tedium, like Smith's pin-factory workers. Such workers' horizons narrow dramatically. Their ability to enjoy many aspects of life, including natural exploration, discovery, experimentation, and testing, which were always part of every hunter-gatherer's daily life, are gone. As a result, many of them become clueless about much of reality. The writer Alan Moore once commented, when he was growing up in Northampton, England, that the world consisted of his neighbourhood, and the Queen. To fill the huge gaps in their understanding of the universe, most people in civilization have no choice but to trust in information given to them by other people, usually senior people in their establishments. This is an efficient system, but it can be abused. Once a power-group know that they control the choice of what is true, and what isn't true, then they are sorely tempted to make these choices based on their own wants and needs, rather than from fact. In other words, instead of the truth, they give out propaganda.

Propaganda

The words 'fact', as mentioned earlier, comes from the Latin word 'factum': to do something. In other words, something is a fact if you do it, if you test it out. This idea, that something is true only if you can check it's true yourself, is a central tenet of science. In science, any fact must be testable. In other words, anyone should be able to test any declared phenomena by performing their own experiment. For example, Galileo knew that it was a fact that Jupiter had moons because he could see them through his telescope.

Hunter-gatherers' lives are all about facts. Everything in their world is a fact because they learn almost everything through direct experience, in other words, by seeing what is in front of them, in their hands or under their feet. These phenomena don't change. Hunter-gatherers can see, from day to day and year to year, that key processes are repetitive and reliable. They can also directly test what they've learned. Even their spiritual views are facts, since they gain these views from dreams, visions, and hallucinogenic experiences, which are all also direct experiences. Young hunter-gatherers are taught skills by the elders of their tribe - a form of second-hand information - but this is done by show-by-example, another form of direct experience.

In civilization, we are given most of our knowledge of the universe by our institutions. Almost none of us can scientifically test the information they give out. We can't perform scientific tests, or go out and directly test geographical, foreign political, historical, or archaeological information. We have to take them all on trust. The problem with this is that it runs straight into another issue.

The sixteenth century English diplomat, spy and writer Sir France Bacon once famously remarked that 'knowledge is power'. His view has stood the test of time. Logically, anyone in power will therefore *not* give out important knowledge, as a way to maintain their power. In fact, they are likely to give out convincing falsehoods, as this will increase the gap in understanding between them and everyone else. Therefore, the more important a subject is, the more likely we will be lied to about it by people in power. These statements will be designed to be believable, convincing, and completely wrong. In other words, all we'll get from the powerful is deception and propaganda, a term that originally referred to a committee of cardinals, founded in 1622 by Pope Gregory XV.

A striking recent example of propaganda, and the use of establishment lies to maintain a knowledge-power gap, occurred in the Spring of 2020, when the Covid-19 epidemic reached the United Kingdom, Canada, and the United States. In response to this major threat, these governments and their media became united in telling their populations something vitally important, that face masks were a bad idea. Multiple commentators in the media of these nations, some of whom were qualified medical professionals, explained to everyone that not only did a mask *not* protect a person from catching the disease, it could give someone a false sense of security. In addition, these experts explained, because someone might touch their mask when removing it, or putting it on, the act of wearing a face mask could actually *increase* the likelihood of a person getting the disease. This advice was wrong. Basic science, for a century, had made it clear that it was vital to wear a face mask if an airborne disease was circulating. In the Spanish Flu epidemic of 1918, for example, medical workers wore masks, along with officers of the law.

Seattle policemen wearing cloth masks during the 1918 flu epidemic

(Wikipedia)

Eventually, in April 2020, the government and the media in Europe and North America slowly shifted their position. An article in the UK's Telegraph Newspaper, on April 1st, entitled *Have we listened to the wrong advice about face masks?*, demonstrates this change. To quote from the article:

> "It is a matter of orthodoxy at the UK Department of Health and Social Care (DHSC) that surgical face masks are a no-no as far as the public are concerned. Officials have taken the view that paper masks do not protect against viruses and do not hold emergency stocks of them."

This was a very odd view to take, since any paper or cotton mask will protect the user to some extent against airborne droplets. A simple mask might not stop all airborne droplets, but it would reduce the amount of virus getting through. This level of viral dose is known as the inoculation; the smaller it is, the better chance a person's immune system has at resisting and defeating the infection. It is possible to create a good-quality mask out of everyday household items, such as J-cloths cloths (fine weave kitchen cloths), fabric etc. The article goes on to say:

> "The DHSC, like most Western health authorities, has always approached the question of surgical masks from the perspective of the individual. The question has always been, do they protect us individual citizens from infectious, droplet-borne diseases? Approached from this angle, the

> evidence is clear – they provide little protection from viruses and may create a false sense of security as well as wider public anxiety. They are ill-fitting and need regular adjustment, causing wearers to touch their hands to their faces. Worse, they quickly become moist, creating a potential magnet for germs."

This statement is highly deceptive. It is true that surgical masks are ineffective against airborne infections because they're designed to stop splashes, such as blood, hitting the surgeon's mouth and nose, but they're not the only option. Any mask worn closely over the mouth and nose, even a polycotton one costing less than the price of a coffee, can protect a person from breathing in the airborne droplets produced by another person's coughs, sneezes, talking or heavy breathing. As for people touching their hands to their faces, that is solved by the simple act of removing the mask by grasping its ear loops. The Times newspaper article goes on to say:

> "A couple of days ago, *Science* magazine ran a rare interview with George Gao, director-general of the Chinese Centre for Disease Control and Prevention. "The big mistake in the US and Europe, in my opinion, is that people aren't wearing masks," he said. "This virus is transmitted by droplets and close contact. Droplets play a very important role – you've got to wear a mask, because when you speak, there are always droplets coming out of your mouth."

The Times article concludes with the comment:

> "All of this is no doubt correct – but it is also academic. We don't have a stockpile of surgical masks in Britain, even if we wanted one."

This statement is *also* highly misleading, since there was no need for everyone to have surgical masks. The people of Britain were perfectly able to make their own masks. Although surgical masks were better in terms of their filtering ability, simple, home-made cotton cloth masks would have been highly effective.

The efforts of Western governments and their health services to discourage the use of face masks amongst the population, even home-made ones, for months, is astonishing and appalling. It is hard to calculate how many people died, or were seriously ill, as a result of this media disinformation campaign in Britain and North America, but it must have run into the tens of thousands, if not hundreds of thousands. Even in April 2020, the face mask situation hadn't changed. In that month, a BBC news article reported that the World Health Organisation was, at that moment, in the process of discussing whether to change its advice and promote wider use of face masks. The British government was no better. It was only on May 11th that they finally recommended that people wear face masks. Six months later, the situation had flipped completely. By that time, governments were stating that people *not* wearing a face mask were irresponsible, irrational, and dangerous.

There is a logical reason for this media and government campaign of lies and deception. In the

Spring of 2020, face masks were in short supply. China was not exporting any, as it needed every item it made. Europe and North America, who were dependent on China for so many goods, were left high and dry. The wealthy and influential of those countries, desperate for their own supply, would have been strongly tempted to ask their friends, in government and the media, to announce to the public that face masks were useless, or dangerous, just so they could quietly buy up what was available. Did this happen? Events seem to indicate that it did.

The face mask debacle of 2020 shows that, in civilization, there is a fundamental problem: those in power are likely to lie to everyone else about anything of any importance. In fact, the more important the subject, the bigger the lie. Knowledge is power, and those in power wish things to keep their power, or ideally increase it. They are also, often, a tribe-within-a-tribe, and so they feel only obligation and loyalty to each other. They also have a fear that they will be thrown out by the masses, which gives them further motivation to maximise their power. As a result, they are likely to produce an unending stream of propaganda.

Unfortunately, in the modern world, it is difficult for ordinary people to counter this flow of deception. When it comes to scientific or political facts, individual scientists and journalists cannot help the general public, because they don't own or control the media. If any scientists try to contest the official line, they can easily be censured for disseminating false information. What's more, since most scientists are employees, if they do make statements that their employers or the government don't like, they can lose their jobs.

The face-mask debacle of 2020 is an illuminating example of propaganda versus fact. It shows that those in power, when pressed, will churn out a blatant lie to everyone, a lie that even defies basic science. This lie is not contested in any major newspaper or television channel. A year later, the whole matter is then entirely forgotten. As George Orwell once said, 'he who controls the present writes the past and decides the future'.

Propaganda isn't just used to temporarily pull the wool over people's eyes. It can also be used to create a long-running deception. For example, in the United States, there has been a pervasive view, for generations, that if you work hard enough, you will become rich. This idea plays into the entrepreneurial aspect of the American Dream. It also fits with the Protestant Work Ethic, the idea that good people work very hard. The flipside of this idea, that 'those who work hard enough get rich', is also deep-seated: if you fail to become rich, it is because you are inferior, useless, lazy and stupid. In short, if you're not rich, you're a loser. This idea has almost no basis in reality. For example, in 2019, a team from the Georgetown University Centre for Education and the Workforce conducted a detailed study to find out how much a person's home situation influenced their material success in life, compared to their intelligence. As the CNBC website article, *To succeed in America, it's better to be born rich than smart*, explains:

> "Carnevale and his team analyzed data from the National Center for Education Statistics (NCES) to trace the outcomes of students

from kindergarten through adulthood, assessing intellect according to performance on standardized math tests. The researchers then categorized students by socioeconomic status, considering household income, parents' educational attainment and parents' occupational prestige (a measure of social standing, power and earnings ability as defined by the Duncan Socioeconomic Index). What they found was that poor kindergartners with good scores are less likely to graduate from high school, graduate from college or earn a high wage than their affluent peers with bad grades. Specifically, the study found that a kindergarten student from the bottom 25% of socioeconomic status with test scores from the top 25% of students has a 31% chance of earning a college education and working a job that pays at least $35,000 by the time they are 25, and at least $45,000 by the time they are 35. A kindergarten student from the top 25% of socioeconomic status with test scores from the bottom 25% of students had a 71% chance of achieving the same milestones. Even if students from disadvantaged households do beat the odds and earn a college degree, they still face challenges. The Georgetown study found that kindergartners from low socioeconomic status families who scored in the top 25% and later earned college degrees had a 76% chance of reaching high socioeconomic status by the age of 25. By comparison, their low-scoring, high socioeconomic status peers who earned college degrees compared had a 91% chance of maintaining their status."

Understandably, the idea that hard work produces material success is a very useful trope for rich people, as it helps them feel that they are superior, when in fact their wealth usually is inherited; it come from their parents.

Propaganda, in our modern world, is therefore working on several fronts. It is used in short-term deceptions, and it is also used in long-term deceptions. In these ways, it confers an ongoing advantage to those in power. It also keeps those without power at a serious disadvantage. In a world where facts – provable truths – are so elusive to most people, trapped in ultra-specialised jobs, propaganda fills the void.

As we've seen, there's evidence that our establishments, in the Western World, will produce blanket falsehoods when needed, to give them an advantage over the rest of us. This strategy can be taken a step further. Any group in power that wants to maximise their knowledge advantage in the long term will benefit from systematically indoctrinating the masses in falsehoods from a very young age. By doing this, they can instil falsehoods so deeply that the general public won't even believe the truth when they hear it.

There is evidence that a strategy of deep-seated indoctrination of the masses has been discussed at the highest levels of the establishment. For example, Charles Sanders Peirce, the prominent twentieth-century philosopher, wrote in his essay, *The Fixation of Belief*:

> "Let the will of the state act, then, instead of that of the individual. Let an institution be created which shall have for its object to keep correct doctrines before the attention of the people, to reiterate them perpetually and to teach them to the young, having at the same time power to prevent contrary doctrines from being taught, advocated or expressed. Let all possible causes of a change of mind be removed from men's apprehensions. Let them be kept ignorant, lest they should learn of some reason to think otherwise than they do. Let their passions be enlisted, so that they may regard private and unusual opinions with hatred and horror."

Has this been done? Has the state been indoctrinating us, from an early age, 'to keep correct doctrines' and 'regard private and unusual opinions with hatred and horror'? To answer this question, we need to study another facet of civilization: factory schooling.

Factory Schooling

In the modern, developed world, most children attend school full-time from an early age, usually from around five years of age. They continue in their schooling until the age of sixteen, eighteen or, after attending university, twenty-one. This system of free education, at least until the age of eighteen, has become a backbone of modern, technologically advanced societies. It enables young people to develop important skills, such as reading and writing, arithmetic, and other abilities. These skills enable many of us to function in the modern world, do our jobs, handle our finances etc. This is all good but, in many ways, it was never entirely an act of philanthropy. Historically, those in power in the Western World were quite happy for much of the population to stay ignorant, as a way for them to 'stay in their place'. For example, as reported in *Technical Education Matters (A Short History of Technical Education Chapter 5)* the Anglican Lord Bishop of London stated in 1803:

> "It is safest for both the government and religion of the country to let the lower classes remain in that state of ignorance in which nature has originally placed them."

It's an interesting use of the term 'nature', as the lower classes of Britain didn't have a lot of choice in where they were placed. It's a mentality similar to the orthodox Hindu view of the Untouchable or Dalit caste, who have historically been forced to do the lowest classes of work, such as manual scavengers, cleaners of drains, garbage collectors, and sweepers of roads, simply because of the caste into which they are born.

The Lord Bishop of London's comment indicates that those in power in the early nineteenth century were keen to keep the masses ignorant and uneducated, but this ran into a practical problem. By the mid eighteenth century, technology in Britain was rapidly advancing. Jobs were shifting from agricultural work to factories, and then into offices. In order for people to be employable in these new jobs, and thereby generate profit for the factory owners, the general population needed to learn a standard set of skills. Ordinary people needed to be more than just uneducated farm labourers. This commercially vital education of the masses was viewed as a double-edged sword by those in the establishment; it might make the general population useful as workers, but it might also give them the opportunity to develop their own ideas about how society should be run. This was not something the pillars of the establishment wanted. As a result, they made a concerted effort to make sure that mass schooling was implemented, and that it made people sufficiently skilled to do their jobs, but no more. The powers-that-be wanted mass, public education to produce factory-drones, rather than knowledgeable, enlightened individuals. In order to carry out this task, Britain adopted a schooling system originally developed by Martin Luther.

In the 16th Century. Martin Luther, the famous religious reformist, wrote to the German leaders:

> "I maintain that the civil authorities are under obligation to compel the people to send their children to school. If the government can compel such citizens as fit for military service to bear spear and rifle, and perform other martial duties in time of war, how much more has it a right to compel the people to send their children to school, because in this case we are warring with the devil, whose object it is, secretly, to exhaust our cities and principalities of their strong men."

As we can see, Luther worried that the German people were at the mercy of the Devil; they needed to be educated in how to deal with Beelzebub, particularly if the world was going to end. This aim was philanthropic, at least in a zealously religious sense, but senior figures quickly spotted that telling all children, and adolescents, the same instructions from an early age could be a powerful tool to mould them into obedience.

Luther's comprehensive schooling system was adopted throughout Germany, and later Prussia. It wasn't one in which students were drawn to subjects that interested them, or read what interested them, and then asked for help from learned adults. This approach, one of encouraging learning, has been tried in other forms of education, for example in Steiner Schools. Instead, it was one in which all students were told what was true; they were then made to learn that truth. The benefit of this system is that during the schooling, the students are trained to know certain things, decided by the schoolmaster. The downside of this system is that it is monotonous, repetitive, narrow in its views, authoritarian and highly rigid and inflexible. This is why, unsurprisingly, it's known as the Factory Schooling System. To quote from Rena

Upitis' book, *Raising a School*:

> "In factory schools, teaching, like the buildings, tends to be boxlike and linear. Transmission teaching dominates: standing at the front of the classroom, the teacher transmits knowledge to the students. This kind of teaching works best when the teacher can see everyone at once, and so, classrooms are treated as a series of boxes, the most pervasive example being one of double-loaded classrooms down a single, long hallway."

The Factory Model of schooling 'prioritises standardization of teaching, testing, and learning rates and respect for authority over the exploration of truth, and uniformity and orthodoxy over innovation and progress'. Not surprisingly, this can seriously grate with bright, inquisitive, independently minded students. For example, the book *Cradles of Eminence*, a study of 400 eminent twentieth-century individuals, reported that 60% of them, 'had serious school problems.' Albert Einstein was a classic example. He once stated that state schooling required 'the obedience of a corpse'.

Factory Schooling was therefore an ideal tool to educate the masses so they could do required jobs, but at the same time, make sure that they didn't get any funny ideas, like wanting to change the system, or challenge the orthodox views. They were implemented throughout Europe and North America, often forcibly replacing existing philanthropic schools. As Ellwood Cubberley (1868 – 1941), a senior public-school administrator, wrote in 1916:

> "Our schools are, in a sense, factories, in which the raw products (children) are to be shaped and fashioned into products to meet the various demands of life. These specifications for manufacturing come from the demands of twentieth-century civilization, and it is the business of the school to build its pupils according to the specifications laid down."

William Torrey Harris, United States Commissioner of Education (1889 – 1906) wrote in his book, *The Philosophy of Education*:

> "Ninety-nine students out of a hundred are automata, careful to walk in prescribed paths, careful to follow the prescribed custom. This is not an accident but the result of substantial education which, scientifically defined, is the subsumption of the individual."

The hidden purpose of mass, factory schooling was not lost on everyone. The American journalist and cultural critic H. L. Mencken stated:

> "The most erroneous assumption is to the effect that the aim of public education is to fill the young of the species with knowledge and awaken their intelligence. Nothing could be further from the truth. The aim of public education is not to spread enlightenment at all; it is simply to reduce as many individuals as possible to the same safe level, to breed and train a standardized citizenry, to put down dissent and originality. That is its aim in the United States, whatever the pretensions

of politicians, and that is its aim everywhere else."

The extent and depths of this planned indoctrination of the masses, through compulsory public schooling, was worryingly deep. For example, Frederick Taylor Gates, who worked on the General Education Board (1903) and was a business advisor to John D Rockefeller, wrote in his book *The Country School of Tomorrow*:

> "In our dream... the people yield themselves with perfect docility to our molding hand. We shall not try to make these people or any of their children into philosophers or men of learning, or of science. We are not to raise up from among them authors, orators, poets or men of letters. We shall not search for embryonic great artists, painters or musicians. Nor will we cherish even the humbler ambition to raise up from among them lawyers, doctors, preachers, politicians, statesmen, of whom we now have ample supply. For the task that we set before ourselves is a very simple as well as a very beautiful one: to train these people as we find them for a perfectly ideal life just where they are... an idyllic life under the skies and within the horizon, however narrow, where they first open their eyes."

This view reflects ideas developed in Aldous Huxley's famous dystopian novel, *Brave New World*.

Huxley thought long and hard about social control, and what would and could be done by those in power to create a state of complete obedience. He writes, in the preface of the 1977 Granada paperback edition of *Brave New World*:

> "A really efficient totalitarian state would be one in which the all-powerful executive of political bosses and their army of managers control a population of slaves who do not have to be coerced, because they love their servitude. To make them love it is the task assigned, in present-day totalitarian states, to ministries of propaganda, newspaper editors and schoolteachers."

Huxley goes on to say:

> "The greatest triumphs of propaganda have been accomplished, not by doing something but by refraining from doing. Great is the truth but still greater, from a practical point of view, is silence about truth. By simply not

> mentioning certain subjects, by lowering what Mr Churchill calls an 'iron curtain' between the masses and such facts or arguments as the local political bosses regard as undesirable, totalitarian propagandists have influenced opinion much more effectively than they could have done by the most eloquent denunciations."

Huxley is pointing out that those in power don't just need to make the population believe certain views. They also need to steer them away from certain, sensitive subjects or facts. It isn't enough for civilization's Factory School education system to drum into everyone a certain set of information, the system also needs to make sure people don't explore, entertain different ideas, and thereby discover information, theories, and facts that those in power do *not* wish them to know about, or find credible. This shows the fear of the controllers; they know that they are vastly outnumbered and that the masses, whom they manipulate and look upon with contempt, could potentially turn the tables on them by waking up to greater understanding.

Huxley continues his 'rough guide to absolute, abusive control' by advising that the security of a totalitarian state system can be attained in four steps. Firstly, the young are indoctrinated, particularly with the use of conditioning drugs. Secondly, every person is placed in an occupation that prevents them thinking dissident thoughts (similar to the abuse-control tactic of overworking victims so that they have no time or energy to think about their situation). Thirdly, the masses are given some sort of pleasurable drug that dulls any dissident thoughts (such as alcohol). Fourthly, the state carries out a selective breeding or eugenics programme, in order to create a genetically malleable population.

Huxley's explanation, and suggestions, are realistic, grim and resonate with ideas we've already explored in this book. His ideas marry the latest technology with long-standing strategies of social control. He also touches upon a critically important issue, that those in power are afraid; they are scared that the masses they control will become aware of ideas that they do not want them to know. As Huxley states, the powers-that-be have placed a Churchillian 'iron curtain' over certain topics. What these topics are, and their vital importance for all of us, will be explored later in this book.

Interim summary

Let's briefly recap on what we've explored so far. We've seen that many of the gifts of civilization - the methods we've adopted as we switched from hunter-gathering to a settled, urban and rural life - have been dubious to say the least. These elements, such as alcohol, wheat, livestock meat, milk, money, super-specialisation, mass schooling, propaganda, sexual intolerance, female subjugation, and rampant population growth have cursed us; they've left us sick, tired, ignorant, indoctrinated, often repressed, anxious, fearful, and deluded. Unfortunately, they've also left us in a state where we are open to abusive control. What's more, most of these elements have been in place since the very beginning of civilization.

It therefore seems that we've been living in a seriously flawed setup for six-thousand years or more.

It's worth asking: why haven't we changed this situation? To answer this, it's probably worth addressing several possible obstacles to any form of 'wake up' and revolution. Firstly, it's difficult for many of us to simply be aware that we *are* being misused. After all, the purpose of indoctrination is to make the victim believe that the situation they're in is normal, and that it's how things should be. It would seem that human beings are easy targets for this, as we are very adaptable, and most of us can quickly shift our views, both of others and ourselves, to fit with a new situation, and comply with whoever's in power. The speed of this change can be shocking, especially when seemingly reasonable people are involved.

For example, in the summer of 1971, Stanford psychology professor Philip Zimbardo decided to conduct an experiment on his college campus. He created a mock prison in the basement of one of the buildings and recruited a group of male students to take part. He randomly split the group into two sets, one would be the guards and the other would be the prisoners. Zimbardo wanted to find out if it was the guards, or the prisoners, that created problems in prisons or whether it was prison life, and its rules and regulations, that created problems. The volunteer prisoners were mock-arrested and treated like any normal U.S. prisoner. The volunteer guards were given uniforms, batons and told the rules of the prison. Zimbardo planned to run the experiment for two weeks, in the mock-up prison in the building's basement, and then see how the prisoners and guards were behaving. It didn't last a week. Zimbardo had to end the experiment prematurely, because the guards' behaviour had become so out of hand. By the end of the first week, guards were routinely humiliating prisoners, force-feeding them, berating them, ordering them to declare loyalty, removing their sense of personal identity, and other abusive acts.

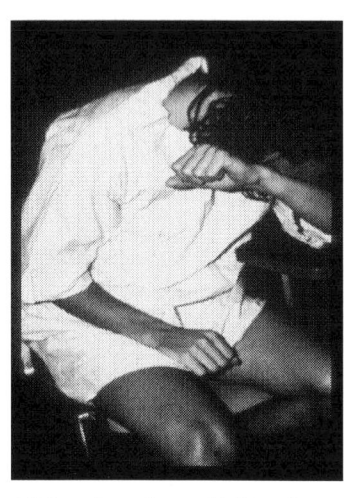

Stanford Prison Experiment (Wikipedia commons)

Zimbardo himself lost his sense of perspective on what was going on in his experiment. He only woke up to how bad things had progressed when he invited Christina Maslach out for dinner. Before heading to the restaurant, Zimbardo offered to show her his latest psychological study, his Stanford Prison Experiment. When Maslach saw what was going on - what the guards were doing – she burst into tears and told him it was a horror-show. Her heartfelt observation woke Zimbardo up to the state of his experiment and he immediately closed it down. Even though it had only been running for less than a week, it had deeply affected several of the students who'd been prisoners. One student refused to leave the

The controllers of civilization

prison and use his own name again, rather than his prison number. It was only when Zimbardo officially told the young man, as prison warden, that he could leave, that the student-prisoner smiled in relief, happily accepted, and left the building.

The Stanford Prison Experiment shows how quickly a group of people can adopt to a new regime and become indoctrinated in it, literally within days. Fortunately, that experiment was ended when someone from outside, someone with compassion, gave its organiser a reality-check, but what if it ran for weeks, months, years, or centuries? In that time span, it would be understandable that no one involved could even conceive of anything different, or cope with switching to a better world.

Fortunately, during our history, progress has been made in human welfare and the lives of everyday citizens. For example, the introduction of the welfare state in Britain, after the Second World War, with its free health service, unemployment benefit and state pension, was a big improvement in people's lives. What's more, this ground-breaking and compassionate system was sustained for multiple generations. Britain still has a free, high-quality healthcare system for its citizens, although this service is now badly under strain due to budget cuts and the pandemic.

Unfortunately, history tells us that progressive steps at the national level have been relatively rare. There are several reasons for this. One key obstacle has been the use of soldiers to suppress popular uprisings; a subject that we'll look at soon. The second obstacle is more subtle, but perhaps just as difficult: the organisation of our institutions, and companies, into top-down hierarchies.

Top-down hierarchies

In human groups, it is normal to adopt a hierarchy to carry out tasks. When a group needs to do something together, they often choose a leader to carry out that job. That leader, along with a few chosen assistants, instruct everyone else in what to do. This approach allows the group to function efficiently and follow a particular plan. Hunter-gatherer groups often choose leaders, or elders, to deal with specific issues, make major decisions, face a threat, and so on. It's interesting to note that in some hunter-gatherer societies, their choice of leader can change, depending on the problem in hand. In other words, they don't have a single leader; they choose a leader temporarily for a particular task, and that choice varies depending on the task. This is an intelligent approach, since one individual might be good at diplomacy, while another might be good at choosing a new location for the group to move to. Fundamentally, these leaders act for the group and they everyone in the group. New members of a group are rarely chosen as its leaders, since no one knows them well enough to entrust them with responsibility. Leadership is therefore gained by familiarity and experience, amassed over many years.

In civilization, something very different happens. Because of the size of many nations, people pick leaders who they have never spent time with. They therefore have no direct experience of that leader's character, reliability, or ability. Instead, they must rely on media information, which can easily become propaganda, disinformation and outright lies. As a result, people can end up voting for a leader that virtually none of them would choose as a leader if they personally knew that person. To quote again from the Guardian newspaper article, *Sexism, vandalism and bullying: inside the Boris Johnson-era Bullingdon Club*, the female graduate, who was interviewed in the article, and had first-hand experience of Johnson's student behaviour, was horrified when she learned that he was going to became Prime Minister of Britain:

> "The characteristics he displayed at Oxford – entitlement, aggression, amorality, lack of concern for others – are still there, dressed up in a contrived, jovial image. It's a mask to sanitise some ugly features."

The size of civilized societies is therefore a big problem when it comes to choosing leaders, but there is also another aspect of civilization that produces terrible leaders: top-down recruitment.

Hierarchical Organizations

Normally, most people in organisations work in teams. This is natural, useful, and pragmatic. The team of people work together and collectively achieve results. Every now and then, their leader will leave.

When this happens, logically, it would make sense if the team chose a new leader from amongst their ranks. As already mentioned, if the group chooses their new leader from amongst them, they can choose a person who they know has leadership skills because they've worked with that person. This new leader will also know the group well and know, in detail, what they do. It's a simple, rational, and highly effective system.

But in most organisations in the civilized world, if not the vast majority of organisations, something very different happens. Senior people, who are higher up the hierarchy than the people in the team, choose their new leader. This new leader is often someone no one in the team has ever met before. This means that senior people, who do not know the team's activities in detail, will choose a person who also doesn't know the team's activities in detail. What's more, the senior people choosing that new team leader don't know that person either. This entire decision-making process is often based on one interview, along the candidate's Curriculum Vitae, which the candidate supplies.

Top-down hierarchical recruitment is therefore a very strange process, to the point of being bizarre. Some might say that sometimes, a team needs a new person to come in and 'shake things up', or 'add new blood', but this could be done by employing a new member *in* the team, rather than giving the team a new leader. Fundamentally, top-down hierarchical recruitment is biased towards those at the top, at the expense of those at the bottom. It also suits one type of person down to the ground: the charismatic psychopath.

The controllers of civilization

Psychopaths are notorious for being glib liars; they are charming and persuasive, at least in the short-term. They are therefore very good in interviews; they can win over the interviewers with their banter and their excellent (but often false) CV. As a result, they land the job. Unfortunately for everyone concerned, after working in the role for a period of time, their true character becomes clear. Everyone in the team they're leading realises that their new leader is a toxic, horrible person. Psychopaths deal with this problem in two ways. Firstly, whenever they screw up, they find someone to blame who is junior to them in rank, and they repeat this process as many times as they can. Secondly, they prepare a way out, so that once everything has collapsed and there's no one left to blame, they leave and charm their way into a new role in another organisation. Since they gained their job through people who never work with the team concerned, and therefore are unaware of what's going on, the psychopath's toxic period of employment can last months or years. This is the Achilles Heel of top-down recruitment. If psychopaths had to start at the bottom of organisations and work their way up, they would never reach any position of power. Unfortunately, in the top-down recruitment system, these amoral, ruthless people can run organisations. What's worse, once these people are in charge, they can employ people that they like to work under them. Psychopaths never choose honest, intelligent people, as such people usually show them up, and so once they're in control, the entire organisation is in danger of steadily filling up with corrupt, cheating liars, from the top downwards, as these toxic new recruits drive out the staff beneath them and replace them with their own goons or sycophants. Top-down recruitment is therefore, potentially, a disaster for any hierarchical organisation. Knowing this, it's hard to wonder why it's even allowed, but there is one group of people in society who benefit greatly from such a system: secret societies.

Secret Societies

Hunter-gatherer societies do not contain secret societies. Their groups are simply too small, and too closely knitted for such a group to function. Civilization, by comparison, is tailor-made for secret societies. Civilization enables a large population to exist, and for its members to form sub-groups. The existence of walled compounds, gates, guards and the concentration of wealth through money makes it possible for those at the top to bind together. They can perform ceremonies and rituals in private and keep information secret amongst themselves. They can also identify themselves to each other through secret words and acts. For example, the use of a handshake as a greeting is an ideal way for two society members to secretly identify themselves to each other with others knowing.

It is interesting to wonder if the Western culture of a handshake, as a greeting, was specifically introduced to enable secret identification. Officially, it was devised as a way for two men to show they weren't armed, but this idea seems threadbare, as you could simply stab the person with your other hand.

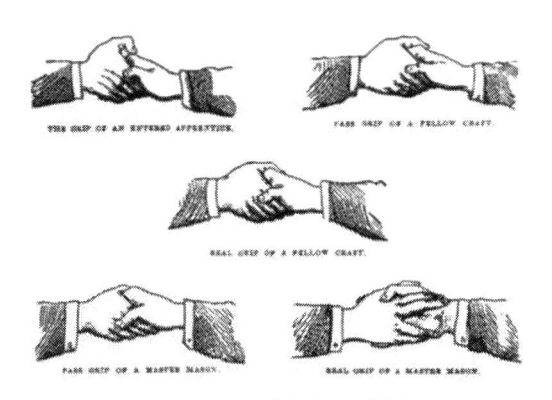

Masonic handshakes (1759)

Secret societies give their members many advantages in society, since their members are duty-bound to help each other, in preference to anyone else. This rule gives them a particular advantage when it comes to top-down recruitment in organisations. Generally, when senior staff pick a new manager, the senior people concerned will be stopped from employing their wife, brother, or other family member, as it would be blatant nepotism, but if they are in a secret society, they can employ a fellow society member without revealing any sign of nepotism. In this way, they can reward their fellow secret society member and increase their society's influence. The fact that the new manager they've recruited has only has the sketchiest ability to do the job can be brushed aside because he or she 'shows the right qualities', or 'impressed in the interview', or 'shows great adaptability', or 'is clearly a quick leaner', or 'has the right vision'. Secret societies, such as the Freemasons, often defend this suspected bias towards hiring each other because, in their words, all their members are honest people of integrity and fairness.

This is possible, but since they are a secret society, it's impossible to confirm such a statement. Secret societies, therefore, are able to populate entire top-down, recruiting, hierarchical organisations with their people; they can also do it over a relatively short period of time, once one of them gains the top job. This result would be extremely difficult, if not impossible, in a bottom-up recruiting, hierarchical organisation.

The problem of secret societies taking control of organisations extends even further, if we take into account another aspect of corporations: shareholding. Shareholding enables a few people to buy an entire organisation. When they do that, they gain the right to choose the organisation's new boss. If we therefore combine top-down recruitment, shareholding, and another potentially shady activity, banking leverage (lending more than you have), then a single secret society, with bankers amongst its ranks, could potentially buy hundreds of organisations with made-up money. They can then install their members as bosses of those organisations. Once that's done, those bosses can then steadily populate the organisations' entire hierarchy with more of their members. In this way, a powerful, unscrupulous secret society acts as a type of parasite, one that infects the head of its hosts (corporations) and then rapidly spreads downwards, forcing the hosts to follow its agenda. Such parasites do exist in the wild. The notorious fungus Cordyceps does exactly this to its hosts. It infects the heads of insects, such as ants or wasps, and then controls their behaviour, in order to spread itself through the colony. Ants infected with the Cordyceps fungus climb a tree by their colony, walk out on to an overhanging branch, then clamp their mandibles to the wood. The fungus sprouts from their heads and showers its spores over the ant colony below. Grim, grisly but very effective.

Cordyceps infecting a wasp (Wikipedia - Erich G. Vallery, USDA Forest Service)

Our civilization is dominated by top-down recruiting organisations. Unfortunately, when this is combined with shareholding and banking leverage, the situation is tailor-made for secret societies to quickly gain an enormous amount of control. Schwaller de Lubicz, the famous Egyptologist and mystic, once commented that he believed that the world wasn't being controlled by oligarchies and monarchies, Instead, he believed it was being controlled by cryptarchies, or 'hidden rulers.' Secret societies would certainly fit with this assessment.

If secret societies are infiltrating hierarchical organisations from the top down, and have been for a long time, then it's likely that many of our institutions and seats of power are riddled with their members. In the same way that an unhealthy animal can become riddled with parasites, our global civilization may be riddled with at least one unscrupulous secret society, or possibly several. Just as with the Cordyceps fungus, which exerts a spooky control over its insect host's behaviour by turning it into a compliant zombie, secret societies can alter the behaviour of the organisations they control, warping their behaviour so that their actions benefit the society, even at the cost of the organisation's own health and survival. Worryingly, it is not just our corporations that use top-down recruiting. Our law, science, commerce, military, and governments do too. Because of this, few of them are safe from such an infection.

In the end, secret societies may be so powerful that they don't fear the law, only other secret societies. To what a degree this is true is extremely difficult to know.

In the wild, most creatures have parasites of one kind or another. When times are good, it is possible for these animals to function and remain healthy, but if times become hard, or the parasites that afflict them grow out of control, then they suffer. The creature becomes weaker and weaker and behaves in an increasingly erratic manner. Its energy diminishes, its motivation drops, and it can drift into madness and even self-destruction. Tragically, our civilization seems to be behaving in just this manner. We are rushing headlong into environmental catastrophe and we seem unable to change our course. Our leaders are not just failing to address the problem, they seem bizarrely blind to it. Does this indicate that we are severely parasitised? One way to work this out is to refer, again, to the natural world. When a parasite realises that it's host will soon die, it takes wing and flies off. Are there signs that powerful people, or organisations, are taking flight from our civilization? Oddly enough, there are. Firstly, our governments are planning to colonise the moon and Mars but more revealingly, several of our most prominent billionaires are spending vast sums of money on space rockets. It's a bit cleverer than wings, but otherwise, it's the same.

Climate change is most definitely a fact, and we seem to heading headlong into it. It's therefore vitally important that large numbers of us do stand up, protest, and attempt to change the system we're in. Unfortunately, history shows us that popular, righteous efforts invariably run straight into another, important aspect of civilization, and they get a terrible beating. Chairman Mao once said that 'morality begins at the point of a gun'. Unfortunately, it also often ends there too. It's time we looked at the thorny matter of soldiers.

Soldiers

In the Monty Python film, *The Holy Grail*, King Arthur, played by Graham Chapman, asks two peasants - Michael Palin playing 'Dennis', and Terry Jones playing 'Peasant Woman' - about a local castle: King Arthur is shocked to hear that Dennis and his friend have absolutely no interest in monarchy or inherited power. Dennis is even less impressed when King Arthur explains that *[Angelic music plays…]*:

> "The Lady of the Lake, her arm clad in the purest shimmering samite, held aloft Excalibur from the bosom of the water, signifying by

divine providence that I, Arthur, was to carry Excalibur. That is why I am your king."

Dennis isn't impressed. He replies:

"Strange women lying in ponds distributing swords is no basis for a system of government! Supreme executive power derives from a mandate from the masses, not from some farcical aquatic ceremony. You can't expect to wield supreme executive power just because some watery tart threw a sword at you. I mean, if I went around saying I was an emperor just because some moistened bint had lobbed a scimitar at me, they'd put me away!"

King Arthur reacts to this blatant lack of reverence, and disloyalty to divinely ordained kingship, by throttling Dennis. Dennis shouts:

'Ah, now we see the violence inherent in the system! Come and see the violence inherent in the system! Help, help, I'm being repressed!'

The scene is very funny, but like all good satire, it's making a serious point. Someone in a position of power, such as a king, might like to see themselves as noble, caring and on their throne by divine right, but if that approach doesn't work, they also have a suit of armour and a large, sharp sword to make their point, so to speak. This is part of a general pattern, carried out by monarchy. If the glory, nobility, and fine robes don't win the masses over, a large contingent of highly trained, lethally armed men is a good Plan B.

Soldiers did not exist before the arrival of civilization. Hunter-gatherers were invariably armed, and able to defend themselves, but this ability is simply a part of their skillset; it wasn't their job. They were also able to choose whether or not to be violent, and so their communities could function both as a peaceful group, or a skilled militia, if required. This freedom allowed them to stay mentally healthy, and empowered. Committing dark acts of violence was something they chose to do, and it was something that was only a part of their lives, if it occurred at all. By comparison, the life of a full-time soldier is very dark indeed. They are not only trained to kill, and are likely to kill multiple times during their life, they also have no choice over who they kill. Their entire purpose is to kill-to-order, like a contract assassin. This state of existence will cause deep anguish and trauma to any person who isn't a stone-cold psychopath. It is true that there are times when killings can bring peace to a region, or prevent further bloodshed, but these outcomes are often unknowable and difficult to discern from the power-games of influential people. Soldiers never have the option of opting out; they are there to obey orders.

The traumatic nature of a soldier's life has been written about in excellent books like *Jarhead*, by the former U.S. Marine Anthony Swofford, and *All Quiet on the Western Front* by the German World War I veteran, Erich Maria Remarque. Both books eloquently describe the life of a soldier; its dark, violent, fearful, morally compromised existence. They also make it clear that the large majority of soldiers are moral people. They want to be caring fathers, loving husbands, good neighbours, and generous friends. Knowing this, it's hard to imagine how they can be turned into obedient killers. To understand how this is done, it's worth looking back in history, and studying perhaps the most famous soldiers of all: the Spartans.

The Classical World of Ancient Greece, which developed in the first millennium BC, is where democracy began, at least according to our textbooks. For the first time in recorded history, in 508–507 BC, the Greek city-state of Athens decided to give the vote to all its citizens. The word 'democracy' comes from two Greek words, 'demos', meaning the common people, and 'krátos', meaning force or might. This first version of democracy didn't actually include everyone. The only people who were eligible to vote in Athens were men who weren't slaves, but it was a start. Unfortunately, in another society, not far away on the Greek mainland, things were very different.

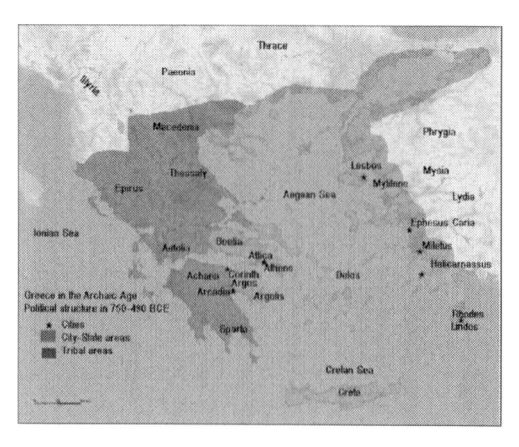

Map of Classical Greece (Wikipedia – Megistias)

The Spartans lived in a fertile valley, flanked by

mountains, in Southern Greece. In this idyllic landscape, they developed into a fiercely warlike society. Their prowess at battle enabled them to conquer neighbouring tribes and enslave their members. As a result, Spartan society formed into the Spartans themselves, ruling over a large number of helot slaves. The ratio, according to some reports, was as high as fifty helots for every Spartan male. This situation would clearly have made the Spartans feel like powerful masters but at the same time, they would have continually worried that the helot slaves would revolt. Such is the double-edged nature of power: pleasure and ego from the mastery of a subjugated people, combined with the gnawing fear of revolution, humiliation, and revenge by those same subjugated people.

Spartan Warrior (Wikipedia)

To maintain order, and keep their control, the Spartans needed dedicated soldiers, men whose existence was entirely focussed on killing people, as well as being the best killer possible. To create this deeply violent and toxic system, the Spartans developed an extreme form of indoctrination. Every Spartan boy, at the age of around seven, was removed from his family and placed in the Agoge, a male-only military school. In this isolated, cruel and violent environment, these boys became fierce warriors, or they died. There was no escape. They either survived the trials and combats, or they were killed in the process, often by being beaten or whipped to death. At the same time, these boys would be chosen as sexual partners by older Spartans. These Spartans males lived in their barracks or were out fighting. The boys never saw their families. In fact, most young male Spartans spent virtually no time with any women at all.

The women in Spartan society had a very different role. They were given the work of running households, buying food and managing the finances. They were also encouraged to compete in athletic events, wrestle and excel physically. This stark social division of men and women created a practical problem: a lack of babies. Since the men were forced from an early age to be homosexual, any woman who wished to have a child had no interested Spartan male to couple with. To get over this problem, Spartan women enacted a weird practice: they would disguise themselves as a man and wait in an appointed room at night. The chosen male would leave his barracks, have sex with her in the darkness, and then return to his dormitory before morning.

The Spartans' system of soldier training is a classic example, in more ways than one, of the abuse control

The controllers of civilization

system described in Biderman's Chart of Coercion. The Spartans also abusively controlled their helot slaves. According to accounts written about the Spartans by neighbouring societies, and later analysis by historians, the Spartans used the following strategies:

> *Isolation:* The helots were not allowed to leave or mix with foreigners. This situation mirrored Spartan society as a whole, which was notoriously insular, shielded as it was by mountains from the rest of Greece and the Mediterranean world.
>
> *Reduced diet:* Spartans were compelled, by law, to keep their helots in a 'lean state', so that the helots could never attain enough strength to overpower their masters.
>
> *Humiliation:* To quote Myron of Priene, "the Spartans compelled their helots to drink strong wine and to lead them in that condition into their public halls, that the children might see what a sight a drunken man is; they made them to dance low dances and sing ridiculous songs during syssitia, or obligatory banquets."
>
> *Create feeling of inferiority:* The French academic, Jean Ducat, describes Spartan treatment of the Helots "as a kind of ideological warfare, designed to condition the Helots to think of

themselves as inferiors."

Continual observation/Continual fear and threat: A specialised group of Spartan men belonged to the Crypteia, a secret police and assassination group. This covert group of soldiers were said to go out at night and kill any helots that were believed to be potentially dangerous to the Spartan rulers. Members of the Crypteia were under pressure themselves, for if they were caught during their missions, they were whipped by other Spartans.

Acts of terror: Every Autumn, the Spartan elite would declare war on the helot population, allowing any Spartan citizen to kill a helot without fear of punishment.

Honey-pot trap: According to the ancient historian Thucydides, 2,000 helots were massacred in a carefully staged event in 425 BC or earlier: "The helots were invited by a proclamation to pick out those of their number who claimed to have most distinguished themselves against the enemy, in order that they might receive their freedom; the object being to test them, as it was thought that the first to claim their freedom would be the most high spirited and the most apt to rebel. As many as two thousand were selected accordingly, who crowned themselves and went round the temples, rejoicing in their new freedom. The Spartans, however, soon afterwards did away with them, and no one ever knew how each of them perished."

Reward for Loyalty: According to Thucydides, male helots could be freed from servitude if they completed military service. In other words, if these helots agreed to an even more extreme form of abuse-control, they would escape their lower state.

These are the elements of Spartan control for which there is written evidence. As we can see, they are straight out of Biderman's Chart of Coercion. The only element that seems to be missing is the enforcement of trivial, meaningless rules, but this may have also gone on too; it was simply not recorded by Greek historians. There is therefore substantial written evidence describing the abuse-control methods used by the Spartans. They used them on their helots. They also used them on their own sons, to make sure their boys grew up to be ruthless, skilled killers.

Nowadays, soldiers in the Western world are not recruited using a Spartan-like system. Most young men enter the army in their late teens, and it is their choice to become a soldier. The problem with this seeming freedom is that many poor, young men are deliberately targeted with advertisements to make them believe that soldiering in a noble and patriotic activity. Many of them are also keen to become soldiers as it has steady pay. In this way, poverty and propaganda will distort their freedom of choice. Once they've joined up, they have lost their freedom of choice. It is at that point that they are trained to become killers. Unfortunately, there is evidence that this stage of their time in the army contains many facets of abusive control. These facets include isolation from their family, humiliation, physical abuse, repeated psychological abuse, arbitrary punishments, repeated, forced, declarations of loyalty, monotonous food, exhaustion, deprivation, being forced to stand naked, being forced to perform humiliating acts, and so on. To support this view, here is an account posted by Drew Holland, former NCO at U.S. Marine Corps, published on the Quora discussion website:

> "I went to MCRD Parris Island in July, 1969. In my platoon it was commonplace for recruits to be beaten up. It was typically choking, shoving, shots to the stomach area and slaps to the face. I would guess 80% of the recruits in my platoon had been beaten up multiple times as this was a daily occurrence. Our Senior Drill Instructor did more of it than the other three Drill Instructors. One time, myself and three other recruits were blindfolded. We had to grab the belt buckle of the recruit in front of us and they ran us into the head and shower room. They slapped us, hit us in the stomach and threw garbage cans at us. The rest of the platoon had been sent to chow and they held us behind. One time the Senior Drill instructor Bit my trigger finger so hard I lost feeling in it for about two months. My finger was not exactly the way he wanted to see it at

port arms. During our first week there we had a tall gangly looking recruit who was anaemic and could barely do any of the physical conditioning the rest of the platoon was doing. I don't understand why he was even there unless he got drafted. They tortured this kid unmercifully. They would surround him and yell at the top of their lungs for long periods of times. It would rain and they would make him lay outside in a mud puddle for hours. They would force him to roll under the bunks up and down the squad bay. They would beat this poor kid. One morning we woke up and he was not with our platoon anymore and we never saw him again. They also had a special platoon in Parris Island at that time called the Motivation Platoon. They would send you there for a day and these recruits would run and crawl thru slimy mud all day. You would then have to march and run and do exercises covered in mud, it was miserable. They would just end up randomly sending guys there for a day. I remember a recruit in another platoon committed suicide at the rifle range when we were there, he shot himself in the head with his M14. From what I read, Boot Camp is much different today than it was during the time I was there. I am sure it is still very difficult, maybe they just don't have to deal with as much abuse?"

Here is another account from the same website, given by Harold Mendelson, former Cpl at U.S. Marine Corps (1963-1966). His account matches several key elements of abuse-control. Firstly, he describes the inflicting of meaningless, exhausting tasks on recruits:

> "For those who were judged overweight, they were assigned to a special platoon. They got to spend the day digging a hole in the ground, putting the dirt they dug into a bucket and carrying over to a previous hole in the ground maybe 8 to 10 feet away and putting the dirt into that hole. When the hole was filled in, they would repeat the process all over again. They were put on a special diet and weighted everyday. When they reached the desired weight they would be sent back to a recruit platoon which was in the same cycle of trying they left."

Secondly, he recounts demonstrations of total power by the drill instructors:

> "In each platoon there were four squads. Each squad was assigned a squad leader who was also a recruit. One day we were called into the area from the duty DI (Drill Instructor) area to the rear of the squad bay. This was done one squad at a time. The three Dis went down the line and punched each of us in the gut. It was painful but we endured in silence. After they finished with the entire platoon and we were standing in front of our racks. The reason for the thumping was explained. It went something like this. 'We drill instructors are your God's while your in boot camp. You will treat us as such. Squad leaders are our disciples. In our absence you will treat then as

> such. When they give you a command, you will obey them without question.' Apparently one recruit gave his squad leader some shit and it was overheard by one of the Dis. The message was received and complied with, without any comments. Those caught talking which wasn't allowed got to eat a bar of soap. That's about it, except for the thousands of punch-ups we did. The psychological punishment was worse that the physical punishment. The Dis were always messing with your head which was to be expected."

Thirdly, he recounts an act of humiliation and psychological domination:

> "In my recruit battalion there were two or three who didn't qualify and until they graduated, they wore a pair of large red woman's panties which were known as Maggie's draws. If you missed a target with a round you just fired, a long stick with a red pennant was waved across the target. That was called a Maggie's draws. The DI was berating the recruit telling him he was less than useless because he couldn't be counted on to protect his fellow Marines in a firefight. He went on and told him the only thing left for him to do was to shoot himself and because he was such a screw up, he would probably miss on the first attempt , so the DI handed him to live rounds and had the recruit load them into a magazine and load the magazine into his rifle. At that point the recruit was ready to kill himself and would

have if the DI didn't grab the rifle from him. That's how much DIs got inside of the heads of the recruits they were training."

Does such psychological abuse create a skilled soldier? In truth, that's highly unlikely. Stress, humiliation and exhaustion lower a person's ability to learn and develop physically, and so such methods would undermine a soldier's training, but this abusive process can create someone who will kill on command, because the victim has been psychologically ground down to the point where they willingly become an obedient killer. They do this simply to end their suffering, gain favour, and restore their self-respect. Deep down, this indoctrination can create terrible anguish in many soldiers, but they bury these feelings in order to survive. This is the power of an intense form of abuse-control; it can change a normal, caring man, in a short period of time, into an unquestioning, obedient killer.

The use of indoctrination, and abuse-control methods, to mould the behaviour of individuals, is a powerful and effective system, especially if it is implemented systematically, over time. As we can see with the Spartans, and the anecdotal accounts of several ex-servicemen, these methods are used in military training, either officially or unofficially, and have been for millennia, possibly from the very beginning of civilization. These methods are so powerful that it must have been tempting, for those in power, to use such methods on everyone, all the time. If they could do such a thing to their new soldiers, then they might be able to mould, or manipulate *everyone* to their own ends. Elements of such a plan are evidence in factory schools, as we've already seen, but what if it was done to everyone, from the moment they were born to the day they died? It's time we looked at one last 'gift' of civilization, possibly the most important of all: religion.

Religion

The word 'religion' comes from the Latin word 'religio', meaning 'obligation, bond, reverence'; it is also connected to the Latin word 'religare', which means 'to bind'. Religion is very much an invention of civilization. Hunter gatherers do not have religions. They do have spiritual beliefs, but these beliefs are usually gained through direct observation, dreams, hallucinogenic experiences and other forms of direct experience and perception. It is true that several key religious beliefs are connected to direct experience, such as feeling the love of God, or the presence of Christ, but others are not. These beliefs are often described as dogma, 'a principle or set of principles laid down by an authority as incontrovertibly true', from the Greek word 'dogma', meaning 'opinion'. To give an example of such dogma, here is an abbreviated list of key Roman Catholic beliefs:

> *Sin:* All people possess Original Sin, due to the behaviour of the first humans, Adam and Eve. Christ suffered and died a horrible death because of people's sin. Fortunately for people, if they follow all the teachings, they can redeem themselves, but the Lord will make the final decision.

Heaven: All good Church members will go to Heaven, a place of bliss for all eternity, if they stay in the Church, follow its teachings and serve the Lord.

Hell: If any person abandons the Church, rejects its teachings, and refuses to submit to the Will of the Lord, they will go to Hell when they die. This is a place of eternal, appalling torment. There is no escape from this punishment.

Judgement: The Lord has the right to judge and punish whoever he declares to be sinners. He still loves his followers, but he must maintain justice.

Disasters: Sometimes, people suffer and die who were devout, but this is part of the Lord's plan. The Lord is omnipotent (all-powerful) and omniscient (sees everything) and all his acts are good; it is simply that some are beyond people's understanding.

Confessions: All sinful acts will be seen by the Lord. Everyone must confess their sins to their priest, regularly, and accept the penance the priest confers upon them. In this way, they can be absolved of their sinful acts.

Poverty: Poverty is a noble state. Catholics should not seek after riches but instead embrace a life of few possessions. Christ preached that this was good, and all Christians should follow this advice.

This list, to the best of my knowledge, is an accurate summation of key Catholic beliefs. For many Catholics, these rules are so familiar as to be beyond comment, and yet they contain a dark undercurrent. To understand that dark side, we can re-write the above list in a different form.

> *Inferior and flawed:* Everyone is fundamentally flawed and inferior; they are soiled and deserving of punishment. Nevertheless, the Lord loves them. Because of this, everyone should be forever grateful that their Lord does love them, and that he cares for them and watches over them.
>
> *Reward for Loyalty and declarations of omnipotence:* If everyone does the right things, as defined by the Lord, then they will be rewarded in Heaven after they die, where the Lord rules. The Lord will judge them there, and may punish them with infinite, endless, Hell, but he is good. The punishment is therefore their own fault, due to their sins.
>
> *Removal of privacy and declarations of omniscience:* The Lord sees everything. No one can hide from Him.
>
> *Dire punishment for leaving:* If anyone leaves the church of the Lord, then they will go to Hell and suffer appalling torments for eternity. There is no way to escape this. The Lord rules everything and He will punish them when they die.

Arbitrary punishment: Sometimes, the Lord causes suffering, such as earthquakes, floods and volcanic eruptions. When that happens, devout followers will die. The Lord has His reasons to do this. These actions may not make sense to everyone, but His flock must trust him, regardless.

Deprivation: The Lord's flock may have poor food and few possessions, but this is a noble situation and worthy of praise. The priests of the Lord may be fed better, and have better accommodation, but this is because they are carrying out devout duties.

Repeated confessions: Everyone must reveal everything they do and think to the servants of the Lord. If they hide anything, the Lord will know and they will be punished.

Repeated declarations of loyalty: Everyone must regularly attend church and praise His name by singing and replying en masse. Non-attendance is a sign of disloyalty; it is sinful behaviour.

The Wrath of Moses – Gustave Dore

As readers can hopefully see, the second list is, in fact, very similar to the first list. The only difference is that the first list was couched entirely in religious language. This similarity is unlikely to be a coincidence. It may be that the Catholic Church fully believes that its doctrines are true and loving, but at the same time, Biderman's studies make it clear that repeatedly telling someone that they're fundamentally flawed and inferior, that they cannot hide, that they will be punished, whatever they do, that they will suffer for no good reason, that they must repeatedly confess and declare loyalty, and that any escape will only make it far worse for them; these elements make up an abusive, controlling system, however it's packaged.

Some readers may be unhappy that I've singled out the Catholic Church in this manner. I've chosen Catholicism because I am familiar with it, having gone to a Catholic Primary School. If I were a Muslim, I might have studied its doctrine instead, to see if its rules and regulations were a form of abusive control. The issue here is not which religion is investigated but establishing if *any* of the major religions show elements of abusive control. Unfortunately, the Roman Catholic Church is a prime subject for such an investigation. Not only does its doctrine eerily match Biderman's Chart of Coercion, the behaviour of many members of the Catholic clergy indicate that they have been personally carrying out abuse for many decades.

In the last fifty years, as human rights and legal powers have cracked open the Catholic Church's protective shield, and finally broken its power of censorship, horrible things have been revealed. Here are some of the Catholic sexual abuse scandals uncovered by civil authorities in recent decades:

> BBC News – 5th October 2021 – "Some 216,000 children - mostly boys - have been sexually abused by clergy in the **French** Catholic Church since 1950, a damning new inquiry has found. The head of the inquiry said there were at least 2,900-3,200 abusers and accused the Church of showing a "cruel indifference towards the victims".

> *The Guardian Newspaper 21st April 2010* – "Walter Robinson, then Spotlight editor, says the paper's reporting "put the match to some very, very dry tinder". That's certainly true: within two years of the first of the Globe's 800 articles on the scandal appearing in January 2002, Rezendes notes, Cardinal Law had resigned, 150 priests in **Boston, United States**, stood accused of sexual abuse, more than 500

victims had filed abuse claims, and churchgoers' donations to the archdiocese had slumped by 50%."

Wikipedia – Catholic Sexual Abuse Scandal in Victoria – "In the past 16 years, about 620 cases of criminal child abuse have been upheld by the Church in **Victoria, Australia**. Most claims relate to incidents from 30 and up to 80 years ago. The Church has received very few complaints of abuse that has taken place since 1990." Reasoning that because sexual abuse is rarely reported, campaign groups believe these numbers may represent only a fraction of the cases which actually occurred."

The Guardian newspaper – 10th November, 2020 – "Pope Francis asked Cardinal Vincent Nichols, the leader of the Catholic church in **England and Wales**, to stay in his post, despite a damning report that criticised his leadership and concluded that the church repeatedly prioritised its reputation over the welfare of child sex abuse victims. In its final review of the church, the independent inquiry into child sexual abuse (IICSA) said the Vatican's failure to cooperate with the investigation "passes understanding". The 162-page report said, "the church's neglect of the physical, emotional and spiritual wellbeing of children and young people in favour of protecting its reputation was in conflict with its mission of love and care for the innocent and vulnerable."

> *Reuters* – January 12th 2021 - *Factbox: Reports into abuses in the Irish Catholic Church*: "The first official inquiry into the activities of abusive priests - in the diocese of Ferns in **County Wexford, Ireland** - detailed the Church's handling of 100 allegations, including of rape, against 21 priests dating back to the mid-1960s. It found that for 20 years the bishop in charge of the rural diocese did not expel priests but simply transferred them to a different post."

I've marked the different countries, or regions, in bold, to show that these abuse scandals are widespread. It is far from being a complete list. Anyone who wishes to extend this list can conduct their own search. I obtained the above examples after only a few minutes of searching on the web, simply by typing 'Catholic sexual abuse'. It's important, at this point, to emphasise that not all Catholic priests are abusers. Many Catholic priests spend their lives doing good works in the community, but it does show an intrinsic problem with the Catholic religion. Even the Vatican's own senior members have spoken out on how deep its corruption goes. For example, the BBC news article, *Catholic sex abuse: Pope critic Archbishop Vigano 'in hiding'* (28th August 2018), states:

> "A former Vatican diplomat who accused the Pope of covering up reports of clerical sex abuse is lying low over fears for his safety, it is claimed. Archbishop Carlo Maria Vigano wrote in a letter that Pope Francis knew of allegations against a US cardinal five years before accepting his resignation. Italian

blogger Aldo Maria Valli later said the archbishop had told him that he had "purchased an aeroplane ticket".

The article goes on to say:

"In his letter, Archbishop Vigano said he told Pope Francis that Cardinal Theodore McCarrick, the former archbishop of Washington, had been accused of sexually abusing lower-ranking seminarians and priests over decades. He said Pope Francis' predecessor, Pope Benedict XVI, had taken action against the cardinal, forcing him to withdraw to a life of "prayer and penance". However, he said Francis had lifted the sanctions against him and allowed him to return to full duties. Pope Francis "knew from at least 23 June 2013 that McCarrick was a serial predator", the archbishop wrote, adding: "He knew that he was a corrupt man, he covered for him to the bitter end." McCarrick, now 88, resigned in disgrace in July."

The endemic child-abuse problem in the Catholic Church might be explained as a more recent corruption of an innately good system, but as we've seen, several of the Catholic religion's key doctrines seem to be straight out of a playbook on abusive, psychological control. How did this happen? When did it began? Was it a new element in religion, or was it inherited or copied from even earlier religions with abuse-control elements? Who originally developed these toxic ideas?

To answer such questions, we need to go back to the beginnings of religions, and therefore the beginnings of civilization. To put it simply, we need to return to the time of the gods. That is the subject of Part 3.

Part 3: The Gods

Introduction

In Part 1 of this book, we investigated the gifts of civilization, facets of our lives that don't exist in the world of hunter gatherers. These gifts arose within a system of living, developed six-thousand-or-more years ago. After close inspection, many of these so-called gifts seem not to have been beneficial. Instead, they have damaged us to the point where we have become wide-open to abusive control. Unfortunately, we've seen extensive evidence that the people in power have taken advantage of this effect. As a result, they have lorded it over us in a toxic, manipulative way. What's worse, their behaviour isn't a recent phenomenon; it seems to have been going on for centuries and probably millennia. We are in a toxic setup that is so ingrained, we're not even aware of it. Many of us believe in the propaganda that tells us that our suffering is due to our failures, our flaws, sins, and inadequacies. We are like any indoctrinated and abused victim, one whose life is one, continual state of drugged, exhausted, psychologically oppressed suffering. As George Orwell vividly depicted in *1984*, most of us have bought into the lie that enslaves us, or to quote Aldous Huxley, we have learned to love our servitude. This summation might sound overly dramatic, even hysterical, but it's worth remembering what happened in the Stanford Prison Experiment. After less than a week, a group of college students became entirely immersed in their fake prison world. Not only were the pretend prison guards revelling in their power, several of the prisoners were also entirely lost in their fake existence. Even when Professor Zimbardo, who created the experiment, told one of them that the experiment was over, the student-prisoner refused to respond to his name, but only to his prison number. If such a deep level of indoctrination can occur in less than a week, how deep would an indoctrination go that was maintained for millennia? This leads to another question: How long *has* our indoctrination gone on for? When did this toxic system begin? Who created it and why? Was there ever a time when we weren't oppressed by propaganda, lies and abusive doctrine?

To start this investigation, it's worth studying the Roman Catholic Church again; it is a religion that has dominated Europe for two-thousand years. According to what we've seen in Part 1, it seems to contain a large number of elements from Biderman's Chart of Coercion. These elements are key parts of that religion, and so they must have been there from its earliest days. Who put them in? Were they original ideas or were they inherited from an earlier religion? By studying the origins of Catholicism, we may be able to trace back the origins of our abuse.

Mixed messages

Two-thousand years ago, Jesus of Nazareth taught the people of Galilee that it was important to love and care for others, to be non-violent, forgiving and not to seek after riches and power. These ideas were wise and compassionate. What's more, they were not new; they had been taught, for example, in India for at least a millennium. Jesus brought these ideas to the land of Judea.

Jesus also showed supernatural abilities. According to the records, he was able to perform a form of levitation. He could produce materials from nothing. He could spontaneously heal people, and other phenomena. These abilities seem incredible, but in fact they have been viewed as entirely achievable by Indian religions for at least a millennium. These abilities are known as siddhis, from the Sanskrit word for 'perfection'. According to elders of Indian religions, anyone can develop siddhis, such as telepathy, telekinesis, materialisation, invisibility, levitation, super-strength, precognition etc. These abilities arise naturally from deep meditation and mental focus. This is possible because reality is, primarily, a creation of the mind, according to these sources (this is also scientifically correct, which is something we'll study, later in this book). As the Buddhist scholar Alan Wallace comments, in his book, *Hidden Dimensions: The Unification of Physics and Consciousness*, (pg 103):

> "In Buddhism, these are not miracles in the sense of being supernatural events, any more than the discovery and amazing use of lasers

is miraculous, however they may appear to those ignorant of the nature and potentials of light. Such contemplatives claim to have realised the nature and potentials of consciousness far beyond anything known in contemporary science. What may appear supernatural to a scientist or a layperson may seem perfectly natural to an advanced contemplative, much as certain technological advances may appear miraculous to a contemplative."

Jesus's abilities, and his wise teachings, won over many people. A Christian fellowship was formed. Its members learnt, preserved, and passed on Jesus's teachings. Later on, during the century after Jesus's life, more Christian groups formed. One of these were the Gnostics.

The Gnostic Christians believed that Jesus was a Christos, an enlightened one, and that his mission had been to help others achieve enlightenment or gnosis too. In that sense, they believed that Jesus was Christ, but that everyone could become a Christos too, if they followed Jesus's teachings and took the right path. In other words, Jesus Christ was not a distinctly different being from everyone else, he was simply one of them who had become enlightened and advanced; he had achieved gnosis.

The author Elaine Pagels discusses this matter of gnosis and personal enlightenment her book, *The Gnostic Gospels*. On page 19, she states:

'Orthodox Christians believe that Jesus is Lord and Son of God in a unique way: he remains forever distinct from the rest of humanity whom he came to save. Yet the gnostic *Gospel of Thomas* relates that as soon as Thomas recognises him, Jesus says to Thomas that they have both received their being from the same source. "Jesus said, 'I am not your master. Because you have drunk, you have become drunk from the bubbling stream which I have measured out... He who will drink from my mouth will become as I am: I myself shall become he, and the things that are hidden will be revealed to him.'" Does not such teachings – the identity of the divine and human, the concern will illusion and enlightenment, the founder who is presented not as Lord, but as spiritual guide, sound more Eastern than Western?'

Pagels continues, in her book, by exploring the connections between the gnostic view of Christ's teachings and Indian mysticism. As she shows, they are similar.

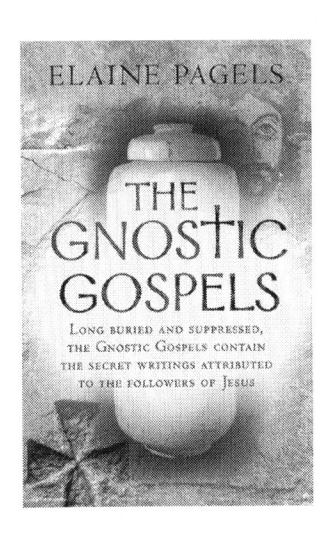

Unfortunately for the Gnostic Christians, the Roman Empire didn't like their interpretation. Once the Roman Empire began to adopt Christianity, rather than persecute it, they enforced the idea that Jesus *was* God, or the Son of God. In other words, they made it ruthlessly clear that Jesus was *not* a normal human, and that his powers were an aspect of his God state. The early Roman Christian bishops, following this agenda, zealously attacked the gnostic interpretation. To quote again from Pagels' book (pg 17):

> 'Bishop Irenaeus, who supervised the church in Lyons (c. 180 BC) wrote five volumes, entitled *The Destruction and Overthrow of Falsely, So-called Knowledge*. They begin with his promise to, "set forth the views of those who are now teaching heresy... to show how absurd and inconsistent with the truth are their statements... I do this so that... you may urge all those with whom you are connected to avoid such an abyss of madness and of blasphemy against Christ."'

The Roman Empire's adoption of Christianity is a fascinating event in history. It can be viewed as the Roman Empire's conversion to a loving religion, in other words as a redemptive climb by the Romans out of their history of cruelty and violence. But there is another logical interpretation. In the second century AD, the Roman Empire was declining. Its Western part was crumbling under the attacks of Northern European tribes and it needed to reinvent itself or it would disappear from history, like the giant statue in Shelley's poem *Ozymandias*. Its solution was to split its empire in two, with the Western Empire keeping its capital in Rome, and the Eastern Empire founding a new capital in Constantinople, now Istanbul. It also needed a religion to bind its population together, the literal meaning of 'religion'. It can't have escaped the emperor's notice that the Christian groups at that time showed enormous courage and fortitude, willingly dying in great pain rather than abandoning their faith. If such people could be persuaded to be loyal to the new, Eastern Roman Empire, then this could hold the empire together. Whatever the true reason may have been, the Eastern Roman Empire adopted the Christian religion as its official faith in the third century AD.

Constantine the Great (Wikipedia)

The first Roman emperor to convert to Christianity was Constantine the Great (272 to 337 AD). He was converted on his deathbed to Christianity. Because of this significant act, he became a saint. The Church officially equated him as being equal to the apostles (Constantine has a feast day on the 27th of May). Constantine's sanctification is jarring. During his life as Emperor, he was ruthlessly violent. He had his eldest son Crispus seized and put to death by "cold poison" at Pola in May, 326 AD. In July of that same year, he had his wife Empress Fausta, stepmother of Crispus, killed in an overheated bath. To quote from Adrian Goldsworthy's *How Rome Fell*, Constantine was so calculating and cold-blooded that he would not hesitate to, "kill his own relatives when he felt this was necessary." It would seem, even in these early stages of the orthodox Roman Catholic Church, that dubious decisions were being made as to who was good and who was bad.

As mentioned earlier, the Roman Orthodox Catholic Church firmly believed that Jesus Christ was the Son of God. In other words, that Jesus of Nazareth was a supernaturally gifted individual *because* he was the Son of God, or God in physical form. By doing this, the Romans were killing the idea, espoused by the Gnostics, and supported by Ancient Indian religions, that *anyone* had the potential to possess Christ's wisdom and his abilities. If anyone dedicated enough time and effort to meditation and mental development, then they could possess the wisdom and abilities of Christ. This idea may seem hard to believe, for us modern people, but it is an idea that is supported in one of the most ancient books of all, the Egyptian book, *The Hermetica*.

The Ancient Egyptian book *The Hermetica* is so old that passages of its text appear on the inner walls of the pyramids of Saqqara, built at least four-thousand years ago. The book famously states:

> 'What is God but an immortal man and Man, a mortal God.'

In other words, it makes it clear that all of us have the potential to have god-like abilities. In the same way, the so-called ancient gods did *not* possess any special properties unique to themselves. According to one of the oldest books in existence, the Roman Catholic Church was wrong; gods are *not* different from normal humans, they're just more mentally/spiritually advanced.

The Roman Catholic Church's decision to tell everyone that Jesus *was* God, and the Son of God at the same time, and that no one could be like him, has had a huge effect on our belief systems. In the seventeen-hundred years since the formation of the Roman Catholic Church, we've been told that we can't become special, or supernaturally gifted, or powerful like Christ, and that super-powers are only attributes of God and his Son. This message has been pushed on us for so long, many of us would find it impossible to believe anything else. Unfortunately, this indoctrination is a lot like the 1944 film *Gaslight*, in which an unscrupulous husband convinces his wife that she's mad when she sees incriminating evidence of his crimes. Just like the wife in *Gaslight*, we've been gaslighted for nearly two-thousand years by the Roman Catholic Church into believing that we're incapable of advanced mental and physical abilities.

But how did the Roman Church back up this plan? If the Gnostic gospels make it clear that Jesus viewed himself as a normal person who'd found gnosis, that he believed that, 'he who will drink from my mouth will become as I am', then where did the Romans get the God Incarnate material? To understand this, we need to study another religion that existed in the Near East and Ancient World at that time, one that had been in existence for thousands of years: The Ancient Egyptian cult of Osiris.

Holy Trinity

The Romans revered Ancient Egypt, just as their elder civilization, Ancient Greece, had revered it before them. The Romans might have conquered the land of Egypt, and turned it into one of their provinces, but Egypt still held an almost awestruck fascination for them. It's therefore unsurprising that when the early Roman bishops (from the Old English 'biscop', based on the Greek word 'episkopos' or 'overseer') were assembling the holy books of Christianity - its gospels - and deciding what material should go into the Holy Bible, they seem to have drawn a significant amount of inspiration from Egypt and, in particular, the cult of Osiris, one of the founding gods of Egypt.

The similarities between Osiris, and the Christ described in the official Roman gospels, are extensive. For example, Osiris was born to a virgin mother. His birth was accompanied by the appearance of a bright star (Sirius), which is always followed in the sky by the Three Kings (the three stars of Orion's Belt). Osiris was violently killed after being betrayed by someone close to him (his brother, Set), also known as the Golden Grains. Osiris died but later rose again, becoming more powerful as a result. He became Lord of the Afterlife and the Judger of Souls. Osiris was a Shepherd God, who watched over his flock with his symbolic crook and flail. In the ancient, week-long Festival of Osiris, Osiris was ceremonially resurrected three days after his death, at the hands of his trusted brother, Set. During the festival, Osiris's symbolic body, created by baking bread in a mould, was blessed and consumed by his followers. These uncanny similarities have been known for quite a while. The famous Egyptologist, E.A. Wallis Budge, in his book, *Osiris and the resurrection of Egypt*, described at length the many similarities between Christianity and the Osiris religion:

> "The Egyptians of every period in which they are known to us believed that Osiris was of divine origin, that he suffered death and mutilation at the hands of the powers of evil, that after a great struggle with these powers he rose again, that he became henceforth the king of the underworld and judge of the dead, and that because he had conquered death the righteous also might conquer death. In Osiris, the Christian Egyptians found the prototype of Christ, and in the pictures and statues of Isis suckling her son Horus, they perceived the prototypes of the Virgin Mary and her child."

Osiris statuette (Wikipedia – Marco Almbauer)

Part of the reason that the early Roman bishops adopted so much material from the cult of Osiris may have been that the two religions were hard to separate. When Egypt first became part of the Ancient Greek, Hellenistic World, the Osiris cult morphed into a more Greek-friendly religion, the cult of the god Serapis, who was a combination of Osiris and an old, Egyptian bull-god. Over time, followers of Serapis mingled with early Christian groups. They mingled to such a degree that observers of the early Alexandrian Christian community in Egypt (in around 200 AD) couldn't see many differences between Serapis and Christ. These observers noted that followers would prostrate themselves without distinction between the two. Evidence of this behaviour turns up in a letter in *The Augustan History*, ascribed to the Emperor Hadrian. The letter's author refers to the worship of Serapis by residents of Egypt who described themselves as Christians and Christian worship by those claiming to worship Serapis. To quote:

> "The land of Egypt, the praises of which you have been recounting to me, my dear Servianus, I have found to be wholly light-minded, unstable, and blown about by every breath of rumour. There those who worship Serapis are, in fact, Christians, and those who call themselves bishops of Christ are, in fact, devotees of Serapis. There is no chief of the Jewish synagogue, no Samaritan, no Christian presbyter, who is not an astrologer, a soothsayer, or an anointer. Even the Patriarch himself, when he comes to Egypt, is forced by some to worship Serapis, by others to worship Christ."

Osiris wasn't the only Ancient Egyptian god to seemingly influence the early Christian religion. Another Ancient Egyptian god, who was dominant in the Ancient Egyptian New Kingdom (1500 BC to 1100 BC, the period of Ramses and Tutankhamun), was Amun (or Amon, or Amen, as the Ancient Egyptian vowel sounds are ambiguous). He was also a Shepherd God and was often depicted as a ram with curved horns. A prayer to Amun, inscribed on Egyptian temple walls, states:

> "Hail to thee, Amun-Ra, Lord of the thrones of the earth, the oldest existence, ancient of heaven, support of all things, Chief of the gods, lord of truth; father of the gods, maker of men and beasts and herbs; maker of all things above and below, Deliverer of the sufferer and oppressed, judging the

> poor, Lord of wisdom, lord of mercy; most loving, opener of every eye, source of joy, in whose goodness the gods rejoice, thou whose name is hidden. Thou art the one, maker of all that is, the one; the only one; maker of gods and men; giving food to all."

We can therefore see that the early Roman Catholic Christian religion, rather than being a pure creation by the Romans, or a direct transference of Christ's teachings, was at least partly the Cult of Osiris. This enabled the Roman overlords to say that Christ was God, or the Son of God, like Osiris and Horus. They made sure that Christianity was not a path to personal enlightenment and spiritual godhood, but instead was the worship of a god that was higher than humans, all-powerful and forever beyond their understanding and abilities, a situation that could easily shift into abusive control.

The origins of our civilization's abusive control, in terms of religion, seems therefore to have come from the Cult of Osiris, or at least was facilitated by it. It's therefore interesting to note that Osiris, and his sister/wife Isis, were also viewed as the creators of civilization, as the bringers of wheat, medicine, architecture etc. They weren't the only gods to be given this role. By interesting coincidence, another inspiration for the Roman Catholic version of Christ may have been the god Tammuz. Tammuz was also a Lamb or Shepherd God who suffered, died and was reborn. Nowadays, Tammuz is not a well-known god, but there is some evidence that his influence was so widespread in the Roman world that the river Thames was named after him, during the Roman occupation of Britain. Tammuz's religion, or cult, is very old indeed. It existed before the Roman Empire even began. The Romans renamed Tammuz as Adonis, a beautiful, male god who suffered and overcame persecution and death, but the name Tammuz itself was a later renaming of a much older god, the Sumerian god Dumuzid, the Shepherd God.

Dumuzid, like the later figures of Tammuz and Adonis, also suffered, died and was reborn anew from the Underworld. He was associated with the date palm and was a provider of milk (and probably honey). He was also associated with fertility, agriculture, grains, writing, irrigation, medicine etc, all the key elements of civilization. Just like Osiris and Isis, and then the Roman version of Christ, Dumuzid was the Shepherd God, the Civilizing God and the God who Died and Rose Again. He was also, according to Sumerian records, a god that was steeped in feuding, jealousy, battles and power.

Dumuzid the Fisherman/Shepherd (Wikipedia – Francoise Foliot)

It therefore seems that the version of Christ created by the Romans was the latest in a long line of Shepherd gods that died and were reborn. This enduring religion, morphing through the millennia from one form to another, stretched back to the beginnings of history, when the first recorded civilization existed: Sumer in Mesopotamia. This is where civilization is said to have begun. According to our archaeologists, it formed as a culmination of innovative practices by hunter-gatherers, but the records of Sumer say something very different. They clearly state that the gods, such as Dumuzid, *brought* civilization to Earth. If these records are to be believed, then our search for the origins of the abuse-control facets of civilization, and religion, leads to those gods.

For a long time, no one even knew that the Sumerian civilization existed. It was only in the early twentieth century that travellers discovered its clay tales, inscribed with cuneiform markings. Its major cities were excavated, and it soon became clear to academics that Sumer was the first civilization in Mesopotamia. After a lot of hard work, scholars deciphered the Sumerian, cuneiform script. They could then read the records of that civilization and discover what its scribes wrote down, six-thousand years ago. Thanks to their translations, we can gain an understanding of what happened at that very earliest time in recorded history. What it tells us is both strange and very familiar, for it became clear to the translators that the Sumerian stories were the origin of key material in probably the most famous book of all.

The Garden

For many of us in the Western World, our understanding of the earliest events in record history don't come from science, but from the Holy Bible, the official book of the Roman Christian religion. According to the first book in that holy tome - the Book of Genesis - God himself made the world. He then made Adam and Eve, thereby starting the human race. Up until fairly recently, this message was viewed as religious fact, and beyond criticism or debate, but recent scholarly investigations have been able to establish how the Book of Genesis was put together, and where it gained its information.

In 597 BC, Nebuchadnezzar II, king of Babylon, besieged Jerusalem. To quote from Wikipedia, "Nebuchadnezzar pillaged the city and its Temple, and the new king Jeconiah, who was either 8 or 18, and his court and other prominent citizens and craftsmen, were deported to Babylon." After Jerusalem was sacked, large numbers of Jews were forcibly taken from their homeland, in bondage, and spent the next half-century as captives of the Babylonian Empire in the city of Babylon. Eventually, after the Persian king Cyrus the Great conquered Babylon in 539 BCE, these exiled Judeans were permitted to return to Judah.

The Flight of the Prisoners (1896) by James Tissot: The exile of the Jews from Canaan to Babylon

While the Jews of Judea were in exile in Babylon, they picked up historical tales from their captor civilization, stories that had existed in Mesopotamia for many millennia. The Jews could see that these accounts were highly regarded, and very old. Possibly for this reason, and possibly also to ingratiate themselves with their Persian overlords, they decided to integrate Mesopotamian stories into their own religious canon. As the relevant Wikipedia pages states, "these events are considered significant in Jewish history, and culture, and had a far-reaching impact on the development of Judaism." There is much discussion of how much historical material the Jews took from their Babylonian captors, but many scholars agree that, in particular, the Book of Genesis bears many similarities to Babylonian history, along with the history of its parent civilization, Sumer. If this is correct, then when we read the Book of Genesis, we're actually reading a modified version of Sumerian creation stories.

The Book of Genesis begins by describing how God makes the world. After 'separating Heaven and Earth', God populates the world with plants and animals. To quote Genesis 2:4 (King James Version):

> "These are the generations of the heavens and of the earth when they were created, in the day that the Lord God made the earth and the heavens, and every plant of the field before it was in the earth, and every herb of the field before it grew: for the Lord God had not caused it to rain upon the earth, and there was not a man to till the ground. But there went up a mist from the earth and watered the whole face of the ground."

The comment 'there was not a man to till the ground' is revealing, for it indicates that even at the beginnings of Creation, God needed some farmworkers. This is an odd comment, considering God was supposed to be all-powerful. Usually, an omnipotent Creator of the World doesn't need agricultural labourers.

After God performs the Great Work of creating the world, He then creates Man. As Genesis 2:7 (King James Version) states:

> "And the Lord God formed man of the dust of the ground and breathed into his nostrils the breath of life; and man became a living soul. And the Lord God planted a garden eastward in Eden; and there he put the man whom he had formed. And out of the ground made the Lord God to grow every tree that is pleasant to the sight, and good for food; the

tree of life also in the midst of the garden, and the tree of knowledge of good and evil."

Once God had created Man, and the Garden of Eden, he then gave Adam (the man) instructions (Genesis 2:15, King James Version):

> "And the Lord God took the man and put him into the garden of Eden to dress it and to keep it. And the Lord God commanded the man, saying, 'Of every tree of the garden thou mayest freely eat, but of the tree of the knowledge of good and evil, thou shalt not eat of it: for in the day that thou eatest thereof thou shalt surely die.'"

This is also strange, perhaps even stranger than the need for agricultural labours at the beginning of Existence. If God was all-powerful, why did he put a poisonous tree in the middle of an idyllic garden? Surely, he could have solved the problem with a vigorous session of weeding?

The Garden of Eden story continues with God furnishing his new idyll with plants and animals. He then puts Man (Adam) to sleep, takes a rib from Adam and uses it to make Eve, the first woman. At this point in the story, a deceitful serpent turns up, which is also a strange event. If God was all-powerful, how a deceitful serpent could have entered His Garden? Nevertheless, this is what happens in the story. Here is the rest of the story (King James Version, Genesis 3):

> "And he said unto the woman, Yea, hath God said, Ye shall not eat of every tree of the

garden? And the woman said unto the serpent, We may eat of the fruit of the trees of the garden: But of the fruit of the tree which is in the midst of the garden, God hath said, Ye shall not eat of it, neither shall ye touch it, lest ye die. And the serpent said unto the woman, Ye shall not surely die: For God doth know that in the day ye eat thereof, then your eyes shall be opened, and ye shall be as gods, knowing good and evil. And when the woman saw that the tree was good for food, and that it was pleasant to the eyes, and a tree to be desired to make one wise, she took of the fruit thereof, and did eat, and gave also unto her husband with her; and he did eat. And the eyes of them both were opened, and they knew that they were naked; and they sewed fig leaves together, and made themselves aprons. And they heard the voice of the Lord God walking in the garden in the cool of the day: and Adam and his wife hid themselves from the presence of the Lord God amongst the trees of the garden. And the Lord God called unto Adam, and said unto him, Where art thou? And he said, I heard thy voice in the garden, and I was afraid, because I was naked; and I hid myself. And he said, Who told thee that thou wast naked? Hast thou eaten of the tree, whereof I commanded thee that thou shouldest not eat? And the man said, The woman whom thou gavest to be with me, she gave me of the tree, and I did eat. And the Lord God said unto the woman, What is this that thou hast done? And the woman said, The serpent beguiled me, and I did eat. And the Lord God said unto the serpent, Because thou hast done this, thou art cursed above all cattle, and above every beast of the field; upon thy belly shalt thou go, and dust shalt thou eat all the days of thy life: And I will put enmity between thee and the woman, and between thy seed and her seed; it shall bruise thy head, and thou shalt bruise his heel. Unto the woman he said, I will greatly multiply thy sorrow and thy conception; in sorrow thou shalt bring forth children; and thy desire shall be to thy husband, and he shall rule over thee.

"And unto Adam he said, Because thou hast hearkened unto the voice of thy wife, and hast eaten of the tree, of which I commanded thee, saying, Thou shalt not eat of it: cursed is the ground for thy sake; in sorrow shalt thou eat of it all the days of thy life; Thorns also and thistles shall it bring forth to thee; and thou shalt eat the herb of the field; In the sweat of thy face shalt thou eat bread, till thou return unto the ground; for out of it was thou taken: for dust thou art, and unto dust shalt thou return."

"And Adam called his wife's name Eve; because she was the mother of all living. Unto Adam also and to his wife did the Lord God make coats of skins, and clothed them. And the Lord God said, Behold, the man is become as one of us, to know good and evil: and now, lest he put forth his hand, and take also of the tree of life, and eat, and live for ever: Therefore the Lord God sent him forth from the garden of Eden, to till the ground from whence he was taken. So he drove out the man; and he placed at the east of the garden of Eden Cherubims, and a flaming sword which turned every way, to keep the way of the tree of life."

Adam and Eve driven out of Eden (Gustave Dore)

What can we gain from this story? Firstly, it is very revealing about the God who created the Garden of Eden. God is supposed to be omnipotent and omniscient, and yet he couldn't stop a serpent wandering into his garden. What's more, at one point in the story, it states:

'The Lord God [was] walking in the garden in the cool of the day: and Adam and his wife hid themselves from the presence of the Lord God amongst the trees of the garden. And the

> Lord God called unto Adam, and said unto him, Where art thou?'

Such a description also doesn't match an omnipotent or omniscient God. The fact that the Lord God was 'walking in the garden in the cool of the day' shows that he was more of a landowner or overseer, rather that the Creator of the Universe. In addition, God didn't spot that his human creations were hiding in the bushes. It's hard to believe that the Creator of the Universe would fail miserably at a game of hide and seek. God, in the Garden of Eden story, seems to be no better than a local landowner.

The Garden of Eden story is therefore an odd tale but, as we've already seen with much of civilization, it has elements of abusive control. As the Garden of Eden passages state, God doesn't want Adam and Eve to eat from the tree of good and evil because it would enable them to know good and evil. This shows that God didn't want Adam and Eve to be moral people. Instead, He wanted them to be unable to make spiritual choices. To put it bluntly, God wanted his creations to be his amoral, ignorant, fleshy automatons. All God wanted from Adam was someone to 'till the ground'. By comparison, the serpent is trying to empower Adam and Eve. The serpent wants Adam and Eve to 'be as gods'. God himself admits as much in the story, when he states, at the end of Genesis 3, 'behold, the man is become as one of us, to know good and evil'. If this is correct, then something is very wrong in how God treated Mankind. God, in the Garden of Eden story, was an archetypal abusive controller, trying to subjugate, control and incapacitate his captive charges.

Earlier in this book, we saw that key elements of the Roman Catholic Faith had disturbing similarities to abuse-control tactics. After studying the Garden of Eden story, it seems that several of these abuse-control ideas were established in that ancient tale. For example, God's attitude towards Adam and Eve, at the end of the Garden of Eden story, is dark and oppressive. He declares that they have failed, that they are disobedient, that they have fallen into temptation and betrayed his trust. As a result, he states that they should be banished from the idyllic Garden. God also believes that Eve is the worst offender, as she colluded with the snake and tempted Adam.

If we look at the Garden of Eden story with fresh eyes, we can see how dark and oppressive God was, but we can also see the courage of Adam, and particularly Eve. Thanks to her efforts, along with some supernatural assistance, they both learned of a bigger world beyond their psychological and physical prison. As a result, they were able to escape from their controlling, abusive overseer: God. Adam and Eve could leave the compound (the Garden of Eden) where Adam had been made to a gardener, an agricultural worker, naked, trapped, uneducated and unenlightened. If we remove the ancient references, and place the story in a modern context, then God is an abusive landowner, a petty lord in a remote compound, forcing his naked, ignorant servants to do hard physical labour, while threatening them with dire consequences if they ever leave.

The Garden of Eden story, in the Book of Genesis, is therefore a dark tale. If it was simply a religious, mythical story, then many of us might avoid it and never read it again, but there is evidence that it wasn't simply a moral tale. As we've already seen, much of the content of the Book of Genesis is likely to have been inspired, or a modified copy, of earlier, Mesopotamian stories. What's more, these stories themselves may not have been myths, concocted to entertain. Instead, there is evidence that they were records of actual events. Thanks to the latest research in that field, and extensive efforts by academics and non-academic enthusiasts, we now have evidence that the Garden of Eden was an actual place, and that the gods were very real indeed.

Edin

According to the history books, Sumer was the first official civilization to have existed on Earth. It started as a group of city-states in Persia, in modern-day Iran and Iraq, in around 4,000 BC. Before that time, people did live in that fertile region of the world, but they were nomadic hunter-gatherers. Suddenly, in a relatively short period of time, according to the history books, those people developed all the primary facets of civilization – irrigation, pottery, masonry, religion, metalworking, settlements, temples, permanent armies etc. As a result, Sumer was born.

Early Cuneiform tablet (Wikipedia – MOMA)

We now know a lot about Sumer's existence, and how it operated, because Sumer also developed writing. As mentioned earlier, Sumerian scribes inscribed cuneiform or wedge-shaped markings (from the word *cunus*, the Latin for 'wedge') into clay tablets, thereby recording many aspects of their life and activities. Many cuneiform tablets, recovered from the Sumerian sites, are dull to read, as they record transactions, inventories, and other accounting records, but some of them describe the Sumerian epic stories, the tales of their civilization's formation, the adventures of their heroes etc.

One key Sumerian tale, which was inscribed in cuneiform, was *the Epic of Atrahasis*. It is a story of global disaster, warring gods and heroic humans. Unfortunately, due to the age of Sumer, and the cryptic nature of its language, there is much discussion over how to translate it, but here is a translation of part of *the Epic of Atrahasis*, by B.R. Foster, currently available on the livius.org website.

The Epic of Atrahasis begins with a group of lesser gods, the Igigi, doing the hard work of ploughing and manual labouring. They soon become thoroughly unhappy with their lot:

> "When the [Igigi] gods were man, they did forced labour, they bore drudgery. Great indeed was the drudgery of the [Igigi] gods, the forced labour was heavy, the misery too much: the seven great Anunnaki gods were burdening the Igigi-gods with forced labour."

As we can see, the seven senior gods of Sumer, the Anunnaki, were making their lesser Igigi gods do all the drudgery, and the Igigi weren't happy. After repeated complaints, the Igigi revolted and demanded that the Anunnaki make a being to do the work instead:

> "Belet-ili, the midwife, is present. Let her create, then, a human, a man, let him bear the yoke! Let him bear the yoke! Let man assume the drudgery of the god. Belet-ili, the midwife, is present. Let the midwife create a human being!"

The Annunaki gods listened to the Igigi's complaints. In response, Nintu, the midwife goddess, recommends that Enki, the brother of the Anunnaki leader Enlil, should make a human, since Enki is a gifted engineer and scientist. Enki agrees. He, and the other Annunaki gods, then create Man out of a mixture of 'clay' and the blood of one of their own gods, who is 'slaughtered' in the process. These events clearly are very similar to those described in the Book of Genesis. As we saw in the Book of Genesis, God is aware, early on, 'that there was not a man to till the ground'. God therefore makes Man to till the ground.

After the creation of Man in the *Epic of Atrahasis*, humans soon proliferate on Earth. This doesn't please the Anunnaki head-god, Enlil, who grows tired of their noise. He decides to wipe Mankind out with a Great Flood. Enlil's brother Enki, who has always been kind towards Man, decides to help the poor humans. Enki quietly warns a senior human, Atrahasis, of the impending disaster. He also gives Atrahasis instructions on how to build an Ark. Atrahasis follows Enki's instructions and, as a result, along with his family, he survives the flood. Once again, the Sumerian legend closely matches the one given in the Book of Genesis. As we can see, the *Epic of Atrahasis* is very similar to chapters in the Book of Genesis. Unfortunately, it says little more, but this may not be because of what's in it, but how it's been translated.

Academics are generally a careful and conservative crowd. When they publish their work, they're often following each other's lead. They rarely say anything controversial, in order to protect their reputation. As a result, they produce respected and officially endorsed translations that are reliably similar, in a way, but actually suffer from the same set of erroneous ideas and assumptions. By comparison, non-academic writers often have more freedom to 'go out on a wing' when translating these ancient texts, since their pay cheques aren't dependent on them playing safe. It's therefore worth studying what non-academic translators have made of these key cuneiform texts.

One famous, non-academic translator of ancient Sumerian texts is the writer Zechariah Sitchin.

Sitchin's translations produced a very different and controversial version of those ancient tales. Unfortunately, Sitchin, in his books, doesn't explain in-depth how he translates the cuneiform, how he deciphers its word-structures, roots and connections. Instead, he just gives his translation. This approach by Sitchin forces his readers to just trust his word. This isn't a thorough or scientific approach, and so I won't be using his translations in this book.

Fortunately, another writer, the Frenchman Anton Parks, has also learnt cuneiform and translated the key texts. In addition, he has explained his translation methods in detail, allowing his readers to understand how his translations differs from other, more established academics. In his book, *Eden – The Sumerian Version of Genesis*, Parks methodically translates several key Sumerian and Akkadian tablets. He explains his approach, and references previous translators in the process. By doing this, he has produced an excellent explanation of what he believes those ancient tablets may have actually meant.

Parks begins the translation process by analysing an ancient cuneiform tablet in the British Museum with the code number BM74329. Scholars have given this tablet several titles, including *The Dynasty of Dunnum*, *The Theogeny of the Dunnu* or *The Harab Myth*. Parks has translated its cuneiform text and produced a strange story, a tale that is similar to the early passages of Genesis, but with some strange and thought-provoking extra details. Here is my annotated version of Park's translation of the cuneiform tablet (with extra notes from me in italics for clarity):

"In the beginning, the Harbu chariot(s) *[literally, 'the bond or circle of the faraway', or 'the millstone of light']* of the Elohim *[God in the plural sense, from the Hebrew]* wed the Earth, their light separating the darkness. A family was founded and a power. "We should break up the virgin soil into clods." (they state) Thanks to their chariot(s), the Elohim created the sea. From the place of their work, they engendered the wild beasts *[literally A-DAM, connected with the god of livestock, Sakkan].* Then they *[the Elohim]* created the fortress of DUN-NU (firm ground), the shelter for both the chariot(s) and their family. Their chariot(s) took on the absolute power of the hard soil."

This translation is intriguing. In some ways, it is very similar to the beginning of the Book of Genesis (King James Version):

"In the beginning God created the heaven and the earth. And the earth was without form, and void; and darkness was upon the face of the deep. And the Spirit of God moved upon the face of the waters. And God said, Let there be light: and there was light. And God saw the light, that it was good: and God divided the light from the darkness. And God called the light Day, and the darkness he called Night. And the evening and the morning were the first day. And God said, Let there be a firmament in the midst of the waters, and let it divide the waters from the waters. And God made the firmament, and

> divided the waters which were under the firmament from the waters which were above the firmament: and it was so. And God called the firmament Heaven."

As we can see, the two passages are similar, but there are important differences. Firstly, in the Sumerian version, there was a group of gods (Elohim), rather than a single being. Secondly, these gods brought light to Earth, but that light came from their chariots, their 'Harbu' or 'millstones-circles of light'. It was their chariots that broke up the darkness, rather than a godly act. These Harbu chariots seem to be more than just wheeled, horse-drawn vehicles; the literal meaning for chariot. The Harbu's strangeness is similar to an observation made in the Old Testament (Isaiah 66:15):

> "For, behold, the Lord will come with fire, and with his chariots like a whirlwind, to render his anger with fury, and his rebuke with flames of fire."

If we return to Park's translation, it states that after the Elohim's or gods' Harbu chariots arrive on Earth, their vehicles land on or 'wed' Earth. The Elohim then set up a fortress on terra firma and begin agriculture (breaking up the hard ground). They also gain livestock by domesticating wild beasts (referred to as A-DAM). In some ways, this seems to be a normal tale of colonists arriving in a new place, then setting up a compound for the purpose of protecting themselves from the elements of nature, and from wild animals. These colonists also set up a means of food production, to keep themselves alive. It's all standard stuff, except for the fact that it's also, seemingly, the original source of the Book of Genesis. Instead of God creating the world, as described in the Book of Genesis, the actual, original Sumerian tale describes a group of foreigners, or aliens, landing on Earth and building a compound. After constructing their compound, they create Mankind, by mixing biological material from themselves and 'clay'. If this is correct, then the earliest records on Earth, written in Sumer, are telling us that Homo Sapiens literally started as a genetic creation, produced by aliens, to function as a dumb labourer. In other words, we were made to be a subservient, slave race. Is this true?

Until recently, it would have been impossible for us to know if we were created artificially, or that we naturally evolved. Fortunately, thanks to the latest genetic research, we can establish some illuminating, and disturbing, genetic facts on this matter. They don't make for easy reading.

Mutants

Officially, according to our textbooks, our species, Homo Sapiens, evolved from apes during the last two million years. This idea sounds reasonable, and most people believe it, but the latest genetic research indicates that it may not be true. In fact, scientifically, the idea that we naturally evolved from apes in a few million years is statistically impossible.

In 2004, a group of scientists published a paper in the prestigious science journal *Cell*, entitled *Accelerated Evolution of Nervous System Genes in the Origin of Homo Sapiens*. In the paper, they explain that they studied the differences in the DNA between humans, primates and rodents, and the genetic changes needed for humans to have bigger brains, and for those bigger brains to work. They make it clear in their paper, that such a brain expansion is not a simple task, biologically. It requires an extensive and specialised set of genetic alterations. What's more, these required changes must occur *at the same time*.

For example, if a primate species gains a gene that makes their brain bigger, then their skull will need to be bigger too. An increased blood supply will also be needed to feed that bigger brain. This will, in turn, require a stronger heart. In addition, the neck muscles and spine need to be stronger to support the larger head. Also, the females of the species will need wider hips and other reproductive changes to safely give birth to such a big-headed infant. In other words, a whole raft of specific genetic alterations must occur, at effectively the same time, for a species' large brain increase to succeed, and not simply kill the species.

In the natural world, a species must increase its brain size in very small increments. After each small increment, it must then obtain the other genetic changes needed to cope with this small increase. Since these changes, naturally, require random genetic mutations, this process occurs at an extremely slow pace. But this didn't seem to happen with Homo Sapiens. Somehow, our species gained *all* the needed changes to have a much larger head in an evolutionary eye-blink. To quote from the paper:

> "It has long been noted that brains of various extant and extinct primates display **remarkable** variation in size, organization, and behavioral output (Noback and Montagna,

> 1970; Armstrong and Falk, 1982; Byrne and Whiten, 1988; Matsuzawa, 2001). This is particularly true for the evolutionary lineage leading from ancestral primates to humans, in which the increase in brain size and complexity was **remarkably** rapid and persistent throughout the lineage (Jerison, 1973; Walker et al., 1983)."

I've marked the two 'remarkables' in bold to emphasise what seems to be astonishment on the part of the scientists. Another 'remarkable' turns up in later the paper:

> "It is **remarkable** that 17 out of the 24 primate-fast outliers are linked to the regulation of either brain size or behavior."

These 'primate-fast outliers' are the key genetic changes that enabled us to become big-brained primates at a 'fast' pace. They're outliers because they exist in areas of the genome that normally change. Somehow, therefore, most of the key changes that helped us get bigger changes all changed in the right way at the same time, even though many of them were outside the normal areas of mutational change. How lucky is that? It's as fortunate, and as likely, as going to a firing range, grabbing a gun, closing your eyes, waving your arm while pulling the trigger, and finding your shots hit all the bullseyes.

In order to understand the sheer unlikelihood of Homo Sapiens gaining all the required genetic changes to have a bigger brain in only two million years, it's worth remembering how slowly evolution by random mutation occurs.

For any species to evolve, the DNA of one of its members must change, through a random event, into a new form, producing a physical change that is beneficial for that species. This event, by itself, is very unlikely, as most random genetic changes make things worse. This new, positive, genetic change must also be present in the creature's sperm or ovum, otherwise it won't be passed on to the next generation, which is also very unlikely. This newly mutated creature, with its helpful new bits of genetic code, must then mate and produce young that safely grow up, possessing this new genetic change, and not die along the way. These young must then mate with others in the species, preserving the gene in the process, and so on, until the entire species possesses this genetic change. This is clearly a very long and improbable series of events and yet they're required for just a *single*, beneficial, genetic mutation.

Now that we know the unlikelihood of genetic change, let's examine the official timeline of our species' evolution, and its brain expansion, in more detail. Officially, two million years ago, our distant ancestor, Homo Habilis, with the brain capacity of 600 cm³, evolved from chimpanzees, who have a brain capacity of up to 500 cm³. One million years later, and one million years ago, Homo Erectus supposedly evolved from Homo Habilis; it possessed a brain capacity of 850 cm³. After that, 300,000 years ago, we appeared, with a brain capacity of roughly 1400 cm³. In this way, in an evolutionary eye-blink, we appeared with a brain triple the size of chimpanzees, along with all the other physical alterations needed for us to survive with our much bigger head. This, as we've already seen, is extremely unlikely. To use another analogy, it's as likely as someone crashing their car, and then discovering that it had turned into a working airplane. Logically, rationally, something else must have happened.

It's hard to believe, for many of us, that our species isn't natural. Our scientific establishment has made it clear that we evolved from apes, and no one has come forward with well-supported counter evidence. According to our scientists, everything on Earth evolved naturally, but there is a species on Earth that is even more bizarre than us, and one that is even more unlikely to have appeared naturally: maize.

Maize, or corn, is a wonder-food. It originated in the Americas but it's now almost everywhere. We sprinkle it on our pizzas or put it on our plates next to our steaks. It's a great choice, as it's an excellent nutritional resource. To quote from Wikipedia:

> 'Raw, yellow, sweet maize kernels are composed of 76% water, 19% carbohydrates, 3% protein, and 1% fat. In a 100-gram serving, maize kernels provide 86 calories and are a good source (10–19% of the Daily Value) of the B vitamins, thiamine, niacin, pantothenic acid (B5) and folate. In moderate amounts, they also supply dietary fibre and the essential minerals, magnesium and phosphorus.'

According to our standard texts, the cultivation of maize began in Meso-America (Mexico and its nearby areas) between 3,500 BC and 2,700 BC, although some recent research indicates that it may have been grown as far back as 8,000 BC. Maize, along with beans and legumes, gave societies in that region a complete set of nutritional requirements. This success could be put down to clever cultivation, slow agricultural developments over thousands of years, and so on, but there is no evidence that this occurred. Instead, maize seems to have appeared in the region, as a crop, literally overnight. What's more, there is no close, wild, genetic relative to maize. Maize's nearest wild relative is the wild grass teosinte, but the two plants are barely recognisable as siblings. Maize produces a large cob on a single stalk, bulging with fat, energy-rich grains, all wrapped in a protective husk. The wild grass teosinte, by comparison, is tiny, has no husk and grows many ears. Teosinte's nutritional content is almost negligible, and yet somehow, that feeble, wild grass is supposed to have naturally mutated into maize in one go. The odds of this happening, understandably, are almost zero.

The strange appearance of maize has perplexed agricultural scientists. In 1969, a conference was organised at the College of Agriculture, part of the University of Illinois, to agree on how maize came into existence. According to reports, it didn't go well. The more its attending scientists discussed the origin of maize and how teosinte might have transformed into maize, the more they argued. At least one of them stormed out (according to the conference notes). It seems there is no easy answer to how maize came into existence. We can see this dilemma in the science paper, *Studies in Archaeological Maize I: The "Wild" Maize from San Marcos Cave Re-examined*, published by Cambridge University Press. It states:

> "Cobs of the earliest known archaeological maize from San Marcos Cave in the Tehuacan

Valley were re-examined to estimate their morphological similarity to extant Mexican maize races. Cursory examination of these 7,000-year-old specimens aroused suspicion that they are not very closely related morphologically to any thus-far-described modern Mexican race. Statistical comparison of the Tehuacan specimens with 30 races of Mexican maize fully confirmed this suspicion. However, the inclusion in our statistical analysis of an extant race of popcorn from Argentina morphologically similar to the Tehuacan specimens indicated that the two were virtually indistinguishable. These findings imply that the earliest maize from Tehuacan already was fully domesticated, its cobs exhibiting a morphology one would expect had maize evolved from teosinte by way of catastrophic sexual transmutation (Iltis 1983)."

The quote's key statement comes at its end. To put it simply, it states that maize appeared fully formed, overnight, due to a miraculous act of evolution. In other words, they conclude that the wild grass teosinte's DNA was extensively changed *in one go*, producing maize. Some scientists believe that a virus caused this change. The virus infected teosinte, entering the plant's cells, and making all the DNA changes required to turn it into maize. After that happened, farmers then immediately spotted this weird, new, amazingly nutritious plant called maize and quickly adopted it as one of their staple foodstuffs. The farmers needed to take care of maize immediately, as the plant is next to useless at naturally seeding itself, due to its fat, hardy cob. In the wild, wild grasses have evolved to easily shed their seeds in the wind. Maize can't do this. Left to itself in the wild, it would steadily die out.

If we analyse the story of maize rationally, then by far the most likely scenario is that someone with advanced DNA-engineering skills altered the wild grass teosinte so that the peoples of Mesoamerica could have a nutritious crop to eat. This idea matches the tribal stories of that region. In other words, the local people say that this is exactly what *did* happen: they state, categorically, that the gods made maize as a gift for their human subjects.

The latest genetic research on the origins of maize and Homo Sapiens therefore indicates that both corn and us were artificially created. We are not the product of natural evolution. Someone made our species by altering the genetic code of Homo Habilis, or a similar protohuman. This idea tallies with the reports in the Bible, which states, 'God made Man in his own image' and the Sumerian texts, which state that the gods make Man as a hybrid of themselves and earth 'clay'. Sadly, for us, the Sumerian texts reinforce the hints, given in the Book of Genesis, that we were not a celebrated creation: a 'child' of God. Instead, a group of gods created us as a drone-worker, a genetically constructed labourer. According to Park's translation of key cuneiform texts, the gods didn't think much of us either. Their regard for us was so low that they gave us the same name they used for their livestock and wild animals: A-DAM. This regard for us can be seen in how they treated us. According to the Sumerian records, the first humans were placed, naked, in the Elohim's compound, to work, day and night, in their service. Our ancestors worshipped the gods, but they were doing it in the word's original form, for the word 'worship' comes from the same root as 'work', as in 'workmanship'. In other words, Adam, Eve and the other mutant drone-workers worshipped the Lord day and night by doing hard labour. This endless toil wasn't the only form of suffering that they endured. As the Garden of Eden story implies, humans were expressly forbidden from leaving God's compound. They were also prevented from learning any skills, clothing themselves or having any influence over their situation. As a form of abusive control, it's a textbook example.

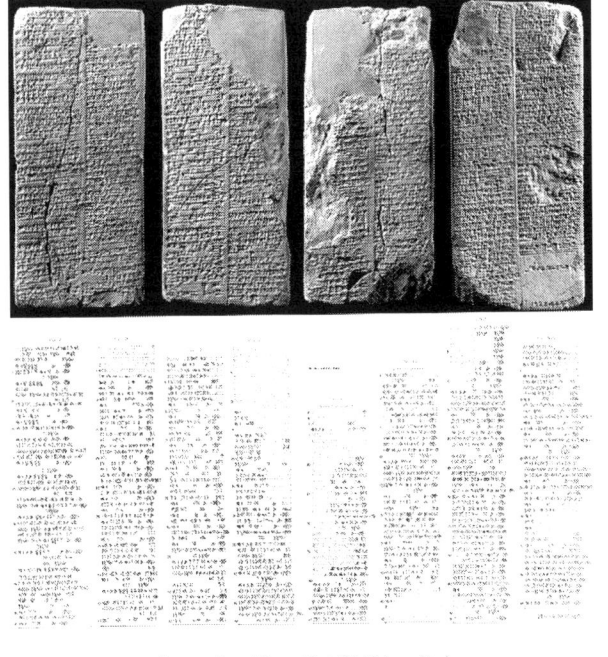

Sumerian King List (Wikipedia)

Tragically, this abusive setup that these gods

seemed to have created may have gone on for far longer than the official date for the start of the first civilization, in around 4,000 BC. Sumerian records speak of the gods ruling Earth for astonishing lengths of time: tens or hundreds of thousands of years. According to the Sumerian's own royal chronology, stated in The Sumerian King List, a copy of which is on display in the Ashmolean Museum in Oxford, the Sumerian kings reigned for approximately 240,000 years. Overall, the timeframe specified by the Sumerian cuneiform text amounts to roughly half-a-million years of Elohim rule on Earth.

If the Elohim did create Homo Sapiens, early on in their time on Earth, as their slave-worker, then it would logically follow that anatomically modern humans have been slaving away on Earth for at least 300,000 years. This idea contradicts official archaeological textbooks, which state that we only possessed tools in the last 70,000 years, but there is intriguing evidence that it may be true. In 2017, the Guardian newspaper published an article entitled, *Oldest Homo sapiens bones ever found shake foundations of the human story*. To quote:

> "Fossils recovered from an old mine on a desolate mountain in Morocco have rocked one of the most enduring foundations of the human story: that Homo sapiens arose in a cradle of humankind in East Africa, 200,000 years ago. Archaeologists unearthed the bones of at least five people at Jebel Irhoud, a former barite mine 100km west of Marrakesh, in excavations that lasted years. They knew the remains were old, but were stunned when

dating tests revealed that a tooth and stone tools found with the bones were about 300,000 years old."

The article goes on to say:

"In the first of two papers, published in Nature on Wednesday, the researchers describe how they compared the freshly excavated fossils with those of modern humans, Neanderthals and ancient human relatives that lived up to 1.8m years ago. Facially, the closest match was with modern humans. The lower jaw was similar to modern Homo sapiens too, but much larger. The most striking difference was the shape of the braincase which was more elongated than that of humans today. It suggests, said Hublin, that the modern brain evolved in Homo sapiens and was not inherited from a predecessor."

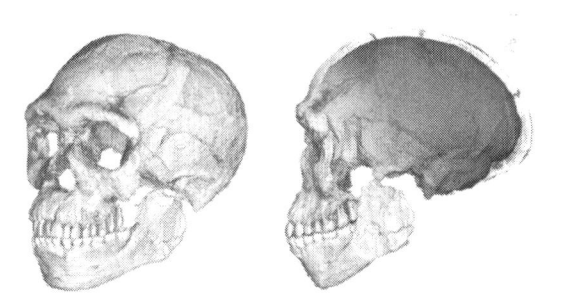

Jebel Irhoud cranial reconstruction (Philipp Gunz, MPI EVA Leipzig)

The second half of the above paragraph is especially intriguing: 'The lower jaw was similar to modern Homo sapiens too, but much larger. The most striking difference was the shape of the braincase which was more elongated than that of humans today.' In other words, the earlier version of ourselves, slaving away in a mine 300,000 years ago, actually had a larger brain. Standard evolutionary theory states that our brains have gradually become larger, because it has helped our tool-working, reasoning, and organisational skills. The Jebel Irhoud discovery shows that our brains have instead shrunk since that time. This evidence points to something other than purely natural evolution occurring. Instead of us slowly increasing our brain size over the last half-a-million years, we appeared out of nowhere with very big brains, and *then* we evolved into a smaller-brained species, probably because very big brains would have mean very big skulls, which would have made human births extremely dangerous. In other words, Homo Sapiens started with very big brains in 500,000 BC, or thereabouts, and then slowly evolved into a smaller-brained species, simply because its huge-head infants kept dying in childbirth.

If it is true that we are an artificially engineered worker species, created by the gods as a hybrid of a local creature like Homo Habilis and themselves, then we can work out what these gods looked like. We know what we look like, and we know what Homo Habilis looked like, and therefore we can work out what the Elohim looked like.

Profile

Human beings are an odd creature. Unlike all apes, we are mostly hairless. We also walk upright, and our hands are designed for grasping items, with opposable thumbs for gripping. Our women menstruate, shedding the lining of the womb every month, something performed by virtually no other mammals. Women show almost no sign that they are ovulating, unlike most other mammals. Our heads and brains are far larger than any other mammal, making childbirth a highly risky activity, unlike all other mammals. If we add these features together, it seems clear that we're not a natural mammal, at least in comparison to all other mammals on Earth. We are, to put it bluntly, freakishly different, but these odd traits are useful in that they give us clues to the identity of the god-species that created us, if that's what occurred. By comparing ourselves to Homo Habilis, the protohuman that scientists believe was the first step towards homo sapiens from apes, we can work out what the gods looked like, since we are allegedly a mix of those two species.

Homo Habilis (Wikipedia Commons)

For starters, we know that we are half-as-tall again as Homo Habilis, who was around four-foot tall.

Therefore, it's therefore reasonable to assume that the Elohim were half-as-tall again than us. That would make them around nine-foot tall. Secondly, we have the unusual genetic attribute of semi-hairlessness and baldness, something which is completely alien to the ape family. This indicates that the Elohim must have been entirely hairless. Fourthly, many of us have fleshy lips, unlike Homo Habilis. Thirdly, our brain volume is over twice that of Homo Habilis; our brain size is 1400 cm^3 compared to its brain size of 600 cm^3. Our skulls are understandably larger to cope with this larger brain. We can therefore conclude that the Elohim must have had twice as much brain matter as ourselves, and that they therefore possessed a much larger skull. The discovery at Jebel Irhoud reinforces this idea, since it shows that the earliest known homo sapiens had a larger and more elongated braincase than us. Logically, therefore, the gods must have had a *very* large and elongated brain case.

The idea that the gods had very large, very elongated heads, creates a problem. How can a mammal give birth to an infant with such a huge head, without killing the mother in the process? Our head size, at birth, is already dangerously large for a safe birthing process, and so it is practically impossible for the Elohim's head to be the same shape as ours, far larger in size, and still possess our rough body shape. If they possessed such a massive head, all their mothers and babies would die in childbirth. Two possible physical differences of the Elohim can solve this problem. Firstly, their infants are born much smaller, in relation to their adults, than our babies. Secondly, if the very elongated Elohim skull projects backwards, like a tube, this would allow

The Gods

a larger brain capacity without an increase in skull cross-section. If these ideas are correct, then we have a good physical description of the Elohim. They were nine-foot-tall, hairless, fleshy-lipped, and had very large heads with craniums that projected backwards like a tube. Apart from those differences, they looked a lot like us, Homo Sapiens. It is therefore very interesting to note that there was a ruling family in Ancient Egypt that possessed all those attributes: the family of the pharaoh Akhenaten.

For most of their recorded history, the god-rulers of Ancient Egypt depicted themselves in a very formal and abstract manner. They were carved in profile, with normal, human features and either human or animal heads. As a result, it is difficult to work out the details of these god-king pharaohs' physical form, but there is one exception. In 1300 BCE, the pharaoh of Egypt, Amenhotep IV, after ascending his throne, made radical changes in his kingdom. He dispensed with the Egyptian old gods, such as Amun, the Ram God. In their place, he introduced a single god, Aten. He also changed his name to Akhenaten. He then moved his country's capital to a new city in Egypt, Amarna, and took up residence there with his family and court. Akhenaten also changed the style of royal artwork. Instead of having himself depicted in a formalised, semi-abstract form, he commissioned carvings in which he, and his family, were depicted in a down-to-earth way, with family moments and scenes of everyday activity. This, in many ways, was a progressive and admiral step forward. It also is an invaluable source of information because, thanks to those carvings and engravings, we can see the true form of Akhenaten and his family.

Civilization is a system of abusive control

Meritaten, eldest daughter of Akhenaton (Source unknown)

Relief depicting Akhenaton, Nefertiti and their daughters under the rays of Aten (Wikipedia Commons)

Statue of Akhenaten, Egyptian Museum (Wikipedia Commons – Warren LeMay)

There are many statues of Akhenaten still intact in Egypt. Their consistent depiction of the ruler, and his family, gives us an excellent opportunity to study how different he was, physically, to ourselves.

The differences between Akhenaten and his family, and us, is clear. To quote from the Wikipedia page *Colossal statues of Akhenaten at East Karnak*:

> "The statues were divided into three categories based on size, the largest of which were 12.75 metres (over 41 feet) tall and the smallest, 8.55 metres (about 28 feet). The pharaoh is depicted with a distorted physique, not present elsewhere in the artwork of Ancient Egypt. He is portrayed with a protruding stomach, thin arms, and exaggerated facial features, such as a long

> nose, hanging chin and thick lips. One statue in particular has been the subject of much debate as it represents the king apparently nude and lacking genitals."

Understandably, academia generally views these physical differences as artistic license, or indicative of Akhenaten having a congenital deformity, but there is no indication that Akhenaten and his family were sick in any way; they were just different. It is therefore possible, when we gather the Akhenaten evidence together, to conclude that Akhenaten and his family do match all the features of the Elohim, calculated earlier. They have a much larger skull, with a long rear-projection. Their family 'photo', shown above, shows that their young are born much smaller in size to the adults than our own children. We therefore seem to have a match. Akhenaten was one of the Elohim species, the aliens that seemingly created home sapiens as a hybrid of themselves and Homo Habilis, over 300,000 years ago.

The depictions of Akhenaten and his family are not the only signs that an ancient, tall race with elongated skulls lived on Earth. Elongated skulls have been unearthed at the Hypogeum in Malta, in Peru and in Siberia. Academia generally dismisses these finds as either hoaxes, or the product of head binding practices by normal humans. In fact, many of the exhibits cannot have been the product of head binding, since their cranial capacity far exceeds the volume of any human being. Head binding can only alter cranial shape, it cannot increase cranial capacity. Several of these elongated skulls also lack the cranial sutures or fissures where a human's skull plates join together.

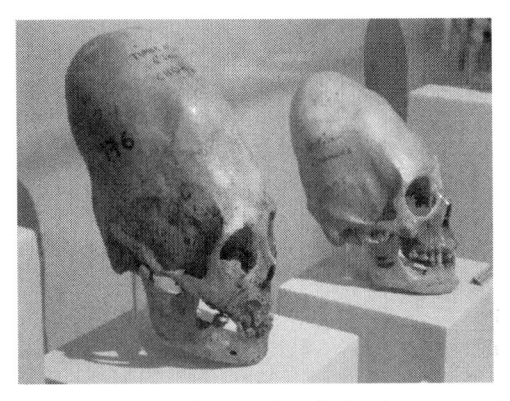

Peruvian Paracas elongated skulls (various sources)

The idea that an alien species, with advanced technology, visited Earth, created Mankind and developed civilization on our planet is weird, but it fits the evidence. It explains our strange physical form, at least compared to the other mammals of Earth. It explains our genetic make-up. It also explains the astonishing and sudden development of civilization on Earth, a development that makes little sense if we compare it to the life of hunter gatherers. It also explains *why* religions tell us that God made us and put us in the Garden of Eden. The reason the Book of Genesis reports this is because it actually happened, albeit in a darker and more amoral form than the Biblical version. In fact, ancient writings go into extensive detail about these gods, and what they did to us. Thanks to the latest science, and fresh, independent translations of those ancient texts, their agenda and their actions becomes clear, but there is one important element in the story that hasn't yet been discussed. It isn't about physical evidence, or physical properties, but something possibly even more important, something that has also been suppressed and kept out of the public gaze since the beginning of civilization. To understand what it is, we need to investigate two books that the Roman Catholic Church did their utmost to destroy, in the first few centuries after Christ's life. They almost succeeded, but fortunately copies of these books survived, hidden away by devotees in the wilderness. These two books don't just reveal the amoral nature of the gods, and their actions, they also reveal something deeper, that the gods had no souls.

The Shining

The Book of Enoch is an important ancient text. It was revered and respected in ancient times as the work of Enoch, the Biblical antediluvian patriarch. The book was mentioned, albeit briefly, in the Holy Bible, but it fell out of favour in the first and second centuries A.D. The leaders of early Roman Catholic Church declared that it was heretical and enthusiastically destroyed it whenever and wherever they found it. As a result, the book disappeared from history for nearly two millennia. Fortunately, after the Second World War, fragments of it were found amongst the Dead Sea Scrolls, a cache of books hidden in clay jars in the wilderness. The book was restored and translated. We can, once again, read its contents.

When we read the Book of Enoch, it soon became clear why the early Roman Church was so keen to destroy it. It paints a less than flattering picture of the behaviour of the ancient gods (plural). It states that they were far from angelic, even though a lot of them *were* angels. In fact, the Book of Enoch makes it clear that the gods were violent, sexually predatory warmongers. This view was, in fact, hinted at in the Bible itself. For example, in Genesis 6:4, the Bible states:

> "The Nephilim were on the earth in those days—and also afterward—when the sons of God went to the daughters of humans and had children by them. They were the heroes of old, men of renown."

The Book of Enoch makes this same statement, but in far greater detail. In its Section 1, Chapter 6 (H.R. Charles Oxford translation, *The Clarendon Press*) it states:

> "And it came to pass when the children of men had multiplied that in those days were born unto them beautiful and comely daughters. And the angels, the children of the heaven, saw and lusted after them, and said to one another: 'Come, let us choose us wives from among the children of men and beget us children.'... And they were in all two hundred; who descended in the days of Jared on the summit of Mount Hermon ... And all the others together with them took unto themselves wives, and each chose for himself one, and they began to go in unto them and to defile themselves with them, and they taught them charms and enchantments, and the cutting of roots, and made them acquainted with plants. And they became

> pregnant, and they bare great giants, whose height was three thousand ells: Who consumed all the acquisitions of men. And when men could no longer sustain them, the giants turned against them and devoured mankind. And they began to sin against birds, and beasts, and reptiles, and fish, and to devour one another's flesh, and drink the blood. Then the earth laid accusation against the lawless ones."

This passage in the Book of Enoch makes it clear that the ancient gods were far from compassionate, or caring. It then explains that these gods gave humans many components of civilization, an idea that matches the records of other ancient civilizations. In Section 1, Chapter 8, the book states:

> "And Azazel taught men to make swords, and knives, and shields, and breastplates, and made known to them the metals of the earth and the art of working them, and bracelets, and ornaments, and the use of antimony, and the beautifying of the eyelids, and all kinds of costly stones, and all colouring tinctures. And there arose much godlessness, and they committed fornication, and they were led astray, and became corrupt in all their ways. Semjaza taught enchantments, and root-cuttings, 'Armaros the resolving of enchantments, Baraqijal (taught) astrology, Kokabel the constellations, Ezeqeel the knowledge of the clouds, Araqiel the signs of the earth, Shamsiel the signs of the sun, and Sariel the course of the moon. And as men

perished, they cried, and their cry went up to heaven."

This information seems to show that a group of alien gods gave us civilization. What's more, because they were amoral, abusive, controlling beings, the civilization they gave us was inexorably entwined with their own character. In other words, we got *their* version of civilization, whether we liked it or not.

As the above passages shows, the human race did not like the life the gods had given them. They pleaded for rescue from their fate. According to the book, this plea was answered. A higher stratum of gods became aware of the Nephilim's, or Watchers', amoral actions. They punished the Watchers, before bringing a Great Flood that only Noah survived.

The Book of Enoch supports many of the ideas developed so far in this book. It agrees with the idea, described in Parks' translation of the ancient Sumerian texts, that alien gods arrived on Earth, or 'descended'. It also agrees with the idea that the gods behaved in an entirely amoral way with Homo Sapiens. But there is more to the story of these gods – their nature and origins – than is described in the Book of Enoch. To understand who these gods really were, we need to study another ancient, banned book that the Romans tried to destroy.

The Apocryphon of John or *The Secret Book of John* was another gospel that circulated in the century after Christ. Like the Book of Enoch, it was also declared to be heretical by the Roman Catholic Church and was also almost lost to history. Fortunately, a copy was found amongst the Nag Hammadi Texts, another cache of material discovered after the Second World

War.

The Apocryphon of John begins with the disciple John, in the desert, in mental turmoil after Christ's departure. He feels alone, abandoned, and unsure of what to do. He has already been criticized by many in his community for following Jesus. He also feels frustration that he did not fully understand Christ's teachings. At that moment, Christ appears (*Steven Davies translation, Gnostic Society Library*):

> "Straightway, while I was contemplating these things, behold, the heavens opened and the whole creation which is below heaven shone, and the world was shaken. I was afraid, and behold I saw in the light a youth who stood by me. While I looked at him, he became like an old man. And he changed his likeness (again), becoming like a servant. There was not a plurality before me, but there was a likeness with multiple forms in the light, and the likenesses appeared through each other, and the likeness had three forms. He said to me, "John, John, why do you doubt, or why are you afraid? You are not unfamiliar with this image, are you? - that is, do not be timid! - I am the one who is with you (all) always."

This appearance of Christ is very similar to an appearance he made that was reported in the Gospel of Judas, one of the Gnostic gospels that was also banned by the Roman Church:

> "Often he did not appear to the disciples as himself but was found among them as a child."

Christ then proceeds to give John a very different explanation of ancient history, and the role of the ancient gods in creating the human race. Just as in the Sumerian texts, and the Book of Enoch, Christ explains to John that the gods weren't lovely or compassionate beings. Instead, they were a toxic, abusive gang. He explains that the gods were led by an autocratic male, Yaldabaoth, a 'lion-faced' being with a dragon body. He explains that these shape-shifting gods created the first man; they worked together to construct Homo Sapiens. To make the first human sentient and alive, they needed to breathe life into him:

> "Yaldabaoth blew some of his Spirit into the man. That Spirit was the divine Power of his mother. [Yaldabaoth didn't understand what was happening, for he lived in ignorance.] His mother's divine Power left Yaldabaoth. It entered the psychic human body, modeled on the primordial image. The human body moved! It grew powerful! It shone! Yaldabaoth's demonic forces envied the man. Through their united efforts he had come into being; they had given their Power to him. His understanding was far greater than that of those who had created him. And greater than that of the Chief Ruler himself. When they realized that he shone with light and could think better than they could, and that he was naked of evil, they took him and cast him down into the lowest depths of the material world."

This is an illuminating passage. It is stating that the

gods realised that Mankind was 'naked of evil' and that the human race had great potential, greater than their creators.

The Archons or Watchers were shocked at what they'd created. They immediately placed Man somewhere where he would be blind to his ability, somewhere in 'the lowest depths of the material world'. To do this, they placed Mankind in the Garden of Eden:

> "The rulers took the man and put him into paradise. They told him to eat freely. [Their food is bitter; their beauty is corrupt. Their food is deceit; their trees are ungodliness. Their fruit is poison. Their promise is death.] They placed the Tree of Their Life into the middle of paradise. [I will teach you (plural) the secret of their life: The plan that they made together about an artificial spirit.] Its root is bitter, its branches are dead, its shadow is hatred, its leaves are deception. The nectar of wickedness is in its blossoms. Its fruit is death, its seed is desire, it flowers in the darkness. Those who eat from it are denizens of Hades. Darkness is their resting place. As for the tree called "The Knowledge of Good And Evil", it is the Epinoia of the light. They commanded him not to eat from it, standing in front to conceal it, for fear that he might look upwards to the fullness, and know the nakedness of his indecency."

The Apocryphon of John's description of the Garden of Eden, just as in Park's translation of the Sumerian records, shows that the place is far from idyllic. It has two trees, but their fruit is very different. It has a Tree of Life, but that is a deceptive title, for it is actually the Tree of the gods' life: an amoral, sensual life, whose fruits are hatred, lying, callous lust, and so on. By comparison, The Tree of the Knowledge of Good and Evil is the Tree of Compassion and of Spiritual Development. The Archons, being amoral beings, do not want Adam and Eve to eat from this tree. In fact, they try to hide the tree entirely. They might have done this in a physical way, but more importantly, they did it in a metaphorical way. In other words, they did their best to indoctrinate human beings to think that the Tree of the Knowledge of Good and Evil didn't exist, and that a base, sensual, physical reality, and an amoral life, was the *only* thing that existed, and the only thing that mattered. By doing this, the gods could keep human beings down at their level, lost in a spiritually-void, sensual level of abuse, greed, avarice, callous lust, and obsession with material things.

The description given in *The Apocryphon of John* explains a lot about the mysteries of the origins of our civilization, and ourselves. It matches comments made in *the Book of Enoch* and Anton Parks' translations of the Sumerian cuneiform records. It also explains why our civilization seems to have been set up as an abusive control system. If our civilization was forced on us by amoral aliens, beings who made us to be their slaves, and these aliens knew that we had the potential to be greater than them, then, logically, they would have done everything they could to keep us exhausted, drugged, ignorant, indoctrinated and have zero self-worth. Just as a monstrous landowner on a remote farm might terrorise a young victim, as exemplified in *the Monster of Mangatiti,* these aliens were desperate to keep us cowed and under their thumb. They did their best to charm us and make us believe that they cared for us and protected us, but at the same time abused us. They were Shepherd Gods, just as our Bible and other religious texts say, but this has its dark side, for it means that they treated us like livestock. They thought we were no better than sheep, or wild beasts, the A-DAM of Ancient Sumer. For thousands of years, this was the status quo. Even when Jesus, an enlightened person, spoke of equality, love, forgiveness, and non-violence, his teachings were taken by the ruling Empire at that time and turned into yet another incarnation of the Shepherd God overseer religion. By doing this, the Romans continued the same abusive control system that had been in place for four millennia; they repackaged it and kept it going for another two millennia, right up until to today.

Summary

In Parts 1 and 2 of this book, we studied the gifts of civilization, foods and other facets of our daily lives that don't exist in the world of hunter-gatherers. After examining them, it became clear that civilization is far from ideal. It is not the idyllic, enriching system that we've been led to believe. Instead, there is evidence that it has been constructed in such a way that a small, powerful elite can indoctrinate us and keep us in a state of overworked, drugged, ignorant, deluded, sick limbo.

In this Part of this book, we followed the trail of that civilization-system, and its mechanisms, back in time, to the beginnings of civilization in the ancient land of Sumer. There, we discovered shocking evidence, that civilization was not something we ourselves developed as part of our natural evolution. Instead, we were created to work as dogsbodies in a civilization set up by a group of amoral, soulless, technologically advanced aliens.

Fortunately, in more recent times, there are signs that we have at least partly escaped this situation. We have developed advanced technology, along with social care, democracy, and science. We have the power to choose our leaders, change our diet, work in humane conditions, and learn the facts about the universe. It's certainly true that many toxic elements of civilization are still with us, but many of us have the power to decline these so-called gifts, if we wish. Amoral, alien gods may have created the system we're using, untold millennia ago, but they seem to be gone, and their actions are only an artefact of history. Nowadays, as far as we can tell, we can do what we like.

Or can we? According to the Sumerian records, the gods were extremely long-lived. Six-thousand years would not have been a long time for them; a handful of generations at the most. The fact that they're not visibly lording it over us today doesn't actually mean that they've disappeared. For example, the celebrated Classical Greek historian, Diodorus Siculus (90 BC to 30 BC), stated in his *Library of History* that the primary gods were:

> 'Revealing themselves to men in the form of sacred animals, and at times even appearing in the guise of men or in other shapes; nor is this a fabulous thing, but possible, if these are

> in very truth the gods who give life to all things. And also the poet, who visited Egypt and became acquainted with such accounts as these from the lips of the priests, in some place in his writings sets forth as actual fact what has been said: "The gods, in strangers' form from alien lands, frequent the cities of men in ev'ry guise, observing their insolence and lawful ways."'

Siculus's description matches comments made in *The Apocryphon of John* and *The Book of Enoch*. All three make it clear that the gods were both fantastic, long-lived, and often secretive. They were perfectly happy to sneak around, rather than sit on a throne in a palace. Siculus himself points out, in his *Library of History,* that the gods often steered humans form the shadows, like puppet masters, rather than appearing on mountain tops, wreathed in smoke and flame.

If Siculus was right, then it is possibly that these amoral, soulless, technologically advanced aliens, or perhaps their descendants, are still here. Are they influencing us from the shadows right now, and continuing to keep us subjugated? It isn't a pleasant thought; it's also the subject of Part 4.

Part 4: Bio-Robots

Introduction

The first two Parts of this book explored the idea that many facets of our civilization haven't been boons. They haven't brought us freedom and happiness, as we're often told. Instead, we seem to be in a civilization that's tailor-made to keep us in a state of abused subjugation. Part 3 of this book showed evidence that this toxic system was deliberately created by a group of technologically advanced, amoral aliens. What's more, those aliens also seem to have made us too; they created us to be their slaves. Fortunately, there are signs that nowadays, we have our independence, and that we are going in the right direction. Unfortunately, it could also be said that this is delusional. Instead, our current situation is actually little different from the conditions our ancestors were in, six-thousand years ago. Literally billions of us are currently working to exhaustion, being drugged by alcohol, made sick by wheat, eating substandard meat to excess, being bombarded with propaganda and religious dogma, being sexually repressed, and suffering under amoral regimes. Many of us are also being intensively and abusively trained to become obedient killers. It's as if nothing has changed in all that time. Those amoral, soulless, abusive gods that allegedly set everything up could still be in charge right now, watching over us and continually dragging us down into 'the lowest depths of the material world', as stated in *The Apocryphon of John*. In that book, Christ warned John that the ancient gods wanted us to eat from their Tree of (amoral) Life, an existence mired in hatred, violence, envy, greed, lust, and selfishness. If a lot of our news content is to be believed, they're right on track.

Clearly, any of us with a heart and soul need to get out of this situation. One way for us to do this would be to physically remove ourselves from as many of these toxic facets of civilization as possible. Along with that, it would also be good to shed the indoctrination and propaganda that's been heaped on us. Once that's done, we'll be able look at the world with clear eyes and find the right path. This plan sounds good, with just one issue: It may be that our eyes aren't clear, so to speak, and they haven't been since the beginning of civilization. In other words, the Archons did their best to blind us, as part of dragging us down 'to the lowest depths of reality', from the very beginning, and they, or their descendants, have been keeping us blind ever since. To understand how we could be 'blind' without knowing it, we need to study the history of witchcraft, devilry and the modern world of Scientific Materialism.

Devil's work

For several thousand years, several of the major religions of the Western World have been united in one view: anyone who becomes curious about supernatural or psychic abilities, or reports on supernatural experiences, is playing with the Devil. Also, anyone who even attempts to develop psychic abilities is a witch and should be killed.

An Eighteenth Century witch burning (Wikipedia Commons)

Eventually, the iron grip of these religions diminished. During the eighteenth-and-nineteenth centuries - the Period of Enlightenment – scientists gained ground; they were able to develop a more rational understanding of the universe. As a result, we were no longer forced to gain our knowledge of the cosmos from God's word. Instead, we could work out for ourselves how the universe worked… but there was a twist. Our new, secular scientific establishment *also* did its utmost to undermine any development of psychic or supernatural abilities. Instead of saying such activities were the work of the

Devil, our freshly created scientific establishment stated that such endeavours were the products of an irrational, sick mind. According to them, all supernatural, psychic phenomena were impossible because only physical things exist. This view is known as Scientific Materialism and it is still the dominant view today. Scientific Materialism also includes the view that our conscious minds are nothing more than a side-effect of physical processes, of electrical and chemical activity in the neurons of our brain. What's more, our belief in our free will is also an illusion. Instead, we are nothing more than biological robots, carrying out a programme indoctrinated into ourselves through genetics and conditioning. For example, in the early twentieth century, the famous behavioural psychologist, B.F. Skinner, remarked:

> "The question is not whether machines can think, but whether men do."

His comment neatly sums up the degree to which our scientific establishment has gone down the 'inanimate robot' path. It's also a spiritually abusive view, because it tells us that we are nothing, that we no better than robots or machines; it is a message that crushes our belief in ourselves as spiritual, meaningful beings. This Scientific Materialist view dominates science today, and it seems invulnerable... except for one small problem: it's scientifically wrong.

In the 1930's, a group of brilliant scientists, including several Nobel Prize winning physicists, realised that the idea that the universe was purely physical was impossible. They included such luminaries as Neils Bohr, Wolfgang Pauli, Pascal Jordan, Werner Heisenberg, Max Planck, Arthur

Eddington, John Von Neumann and Eugene Wigner. They realised that physical reality can't be the only thing that exists. In fact, the physical universe we see around us has to be a construction created by our minds. [I've written in detail about this in my book *Minds Make the World*. It's a fascinating, fun and memorable story]

The famous fifth Solvay Conference of Physics in 1927 – Bohr, Pauli, Heisenberg and Planck are present (Wikipedia commons)

To understand why our minds make the world, we can start by looking at the living world around us. It is a magical place. Creatures continually emerge, reproduce, and spread across our landscape. Each of these living things contains unbelievably complex biological systems, such as cells, proteins, DNA, and other marvels. Even if disaster strikes, and entire countries are turned into ash and lava, life will slowly recolonise that area and eventually turn it back into a lush paradise. It's all quite amazing. What's more, according to orthodox science, it's impossible.

The reason that Life is impossible, according to orthodox science, is to do with entropy. The Law of Entropy, or the Second Law of Thermodynamics, states that all physical matter in our universe becomes more disordered over time, due to the random, chaotic nature of physical reality. We can see this every day in the crumbling of sandcastles, the erosion of coastlines and the corrosion of objects. Entropy is the inexorable and unavoidable increase in disorder in the universe. Entropy is such a fundamental part of the universe that the famous mathematician and astrophysicist, Arthur Eddington, once said:

> 'The law that entropy always increases holds, I think, the supreme position amongst the laws of Nature. If your theory is found to be against the Second Law of Thermodynamics, I can give you no hope. There is nothing for it but to collapse in deepest humiliation.'

Entropy is a fundamental aspect of the physical universe. It should affect all physical matter, without exception... except that Life seems to *completely* ignore it. Life grows, reproduces, and proliferates continuously, thereby adding order to the universe. If a seed is placed in the ground, it will often grow into a tree. During this process, the tiny seed draws in simple matter, such as carbon dioxide and water, and uses that material to turn itself into a highly complex tree, thereby turning a large amount of very disordered material - gases in the air, water in the soil - into complex structures as cells, proteins and nuclei filled with DNA. Life, it seems, is deliberately and comprehensively defying the laws of physics.

Scientists have noticed this paradox of Life and

entropy. For example, in Michael Brooks' entertaining popular-science book, *13 Things that don't make sense*, he explains on page 70:

> "Erwin Schrödinger, the famous quantum physicist, realised that Life is the one system that turns the natural progression of entropy, moving from order to disorder, on its head. Living things are, effectively, machines that create order from disorder in their environment."

Schrödinger thought about this paradox and concluded, in his book *What is Life?* that, "[plants] have their most powerful source of 'negative entropy' in the sunlight." (page 74). In other words, he believed that our sun transfers order to living plants through its electromagnetic radiation, and thereby adds the required order, thereby enabling Life to flourish. Unfortunately, like sandcastles on a stormy day, this sun-organisation argument rapidly falls apart. Our sun does impart an enormous amount of energy, but energy and organisation are not related. A hot gas might have more energy than a cold gas, but it is no more ordered than a cold gas. Instead, its molecules are simply moving around faster. Energy does not impart order. A hurricane is no more likely to create sandcastles on a beach than a gentle breeze. If we inject more energy into a system, it won't increase the system's level of order, it'll just give the system more energy. This fundamental disconnect between energy and order means that our sun can't add any order to living things, it can only add energy. Schrödinger's idea doesn't work. To put it bluntly, it's just hot air.

Other scientific commentators have suggested a

different solution, that our sun adds order to living things on Earth by reducing its own order, thereby transferring that order to living things. As a result, the total amount of order hasn't gone down. The problem with this idea is that our sun isn't very ordered. In fact, it's highly disordered, since it's an enormous, roiling ball of chaotic plasma. In fact, it's less ordered than a cup of coffee. The idea that our sun imparts order therefore has no basis in physics.

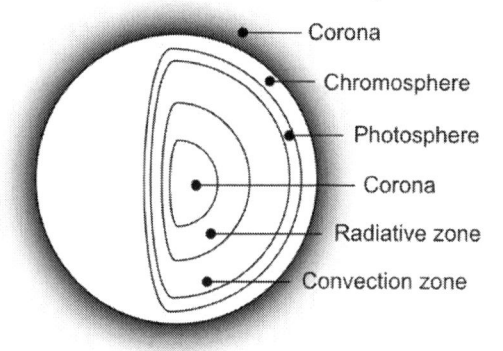

Our Sun: Less ordered than a cup of coffee

- Corona
- Chromosphere
- Photosphere
- Corona
- Radiative zone
- Convection zone

A third attempt at explaining the Life-entropy paradox has the 'lucky chance' idea. This idea postulates that a rare, lucky event caused Life to start, long ago. After that event, Life kept going by itself. This is a tempting idea, but it ignores the fact that entropy should be breaking ordered things down all the time. Even if Life started once, as a freak event, long ago, it should have rapidly been snuffed out by entropy's effects. Biological mechanisms need to be extremely accurate to keep an organism healthy. For example, in the scientific paper *Fidelity of DNA replication—a matter of proofreading*, the author explains that certain enzymes, which copy DNA inside living cells, can only make one mistake, on average, during every hundred *million* copies; that's how accurate biological processes need to be, in order for an organism to stay healthy and survive. Life is functioning in this highly ordered and accurate way all the time, and it has been doing so for hundreds of millions of years. What's more, Life can even survive in the most difficult conditions of heat and pressure. The 'lucky event' idea therefore also fails.

The way to solve the Life-entropy paradox is to examine the matter in simple terms. The method works as follows:

> We know that all physical things in our universe become increasingly disordered over time, due to entropy. Since Life makes the universe continually more ordered, it must be being influenced by something non-physical. Q.E.D.

In other words, the only way to solve the Life-entropy paradox is to conclude that there is more to reality than physical things. Something non-physical, with an organising influence and a positive intent, must be acting on our physical universe in order for Life to exist. This description matches our minds to a tee. This conclusion, that our minds bring order to our physical universe, is the same conclusion that those giants of physics came to, nearly a century ago. The only difference is that they approached it from a quantum physics angle, but the result is the same. To quote Max Planck, the founder of quantum physics:

"As a man who has devoted his whole life to the most clearheaded science, to the study of matter, I can tell you as a result of my research about the atoms this much: There is no matter as such! All matter originates and exists only by virtue of a force which brings the particles of an atom to vibration and holds this most minute solar system of the atom together. We must assume behind this force the existence of a conscious and intelligent Mind. This Mind is the matrix of all matter."

Max Planck in 1933 (Wikipedia commons)

These famous scientists' insight gives us a very different message to that of our scientific establishment. Instead of us being soulless, mechanical bio-robots, we are spiritual beings animating our physical bodies. This insight has more logical consequences. For example, if we're all non-physical minds animating our physical bodies, then that means we don't die when our bodies die. Instead, we must return to our non-physical origins, the place that our minds came from. In that sense, we are immortal. This means that all death in the physical universe is just a mind shedding its temporary, physical body. This is a far more inspiring and empowering message than Scientific Materialism, and yet it has been suppressed for over half a century. It has been buried by our scientific establishment. Nowadays, the Life-Entropy paradox, and its logical solution, is rarely even mentioned, even in popular science books. Even when the issue does crop up, the idea that minds create reality is often dismissed as 'controversial' or 'mystical speculation'. The net result is that a correct scientific solution, one that not only explains the existence of Life and reality, but also empowers us, has been banned.

Some sceptical readers, at this point, might wonder that if minds do create reality, and psychic or supernatural phenomena are actually an intrinsic part of reality, then why don't we see this 'spookiness' on a regular basis? Why isn't it picked up in scientific experiments? In fact, it does occur regularly, and it has been picked up in scientific experiments, with weird and fascinating results.

Spooky

In the early 1990's, a French scientist, René Peoc'h, thought about the strong, emotional bond that young birds form with their parent when they're born. He knew that birds can be very flexible about who or what they attach to. For example, young gulls can even emotionally bond with just a stick marked with two dots because those dots, for the young gulls, are the signifying feature of their parents. Peoc'h was therefore aware that chicks could bond emotionally to practically anything, if that was the first thing they saw when they emerged from their shell. He conducted an experiment that took advantage of this behaviour. He constructed a specially designed robot, whose movements were based on the output from a random number generator, an RNG machine. In other words, the robot would move around randomly as soon as it was turned on, its movements being governed by quantum-level randomness of specific circuits in its CPU chip. Peoc'h then built a cage with two compartments. In one compartment, he put the robot and some chicks that had just emerged from their shells. He knew that the robot would be the first thing the chicks saw, and so they'd immediately emotionally bond with it. As far as the chicks were concerned, the robot *was* their parent. Understandably, they would want it to be close to them all the time. They clustered around the robot and showed all the signs that they believed the robot was their mum or their dad.

Peoc'h then did something upsetting for the chicks. He took the robot out of their cage and placed it in an adjoining, empty cage. He turned the robot on and let it wander around randomly. He then observed what happened. According to standard science, the chicks should have done nothing more than look forlornly at the randomly moving robot and probably cheep plaintively. Instead, something very different happened. The robot's movements, that should have been random, became clearly biased towards the chicks' cage. Somehow, the chicks were influencing the robot's random movements to make it move closer to them. To make sure that the robot's movements were random, Peoc'h had already tested the robot's movements. When the chicks weren't around, it did move randomly but when they were around, it didn't.

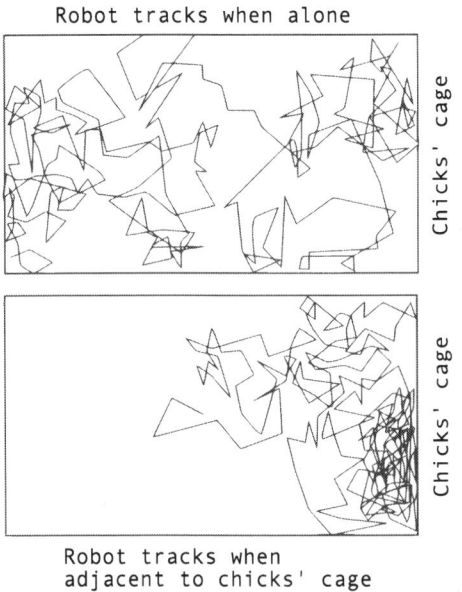

Robot tracks when alone

Chicks' cage

Robot tracks when adjacent to chicks' cage

Chicks' cage

The accompanying illustration shows the chicks' effect on the robot's movement. The top image shows the robots movement when the chicks were absent from the adjacent, right-hand cage (in other words, when there was no influence on the robot). It is clearly random. The bottom image shows the robot's movement when the chicks were in the adjacent, right-hand cage. It seems clear from the huge change in the robot's pattern of movement that the chicks had significantly influenced the robot's behaviour.

René Peoc'h published his findings in a scientific

paper, describing his findings, in 1995, entitled, *psychokinetic action of young chicks on the path of an illuminated source*. The implications of his experiments were clear: living creatures, such as chicks, were able to influence quantum events at a distance, the behaviour of physical matter at its lowest level. This fits with the idea described earlier, that our minds influence physical reality to make Life exist, and thereby overcome the negative, disorganising effects of entropy. The chicks were using this ability to make the robot move nearer to their cage, because they loved it.

The ability of living creatures to affect RNG machines, by influencing their quantum behaviour, isn't just true of chicks. A senior engineer showed that the same effect could be seen in human actions. His name was Dr Robert Jahn.

In the 1980's, Dr Robert Jahn was the Dean of the Engineering Faculty at Princeton University in the United States. He was a highly regarded rocket engineer. One day, one of his graduate students showed him the results of an experiment that the student had carried out. In his experiment, a test subject had attempted to influence the results of an electronic random number generator, or RNG. The data from the experiment seemed to show that the test subject had influenced the output of the RNG. Jahn was intrigued. With help from his colleague, Brenda J. Dunne, he set up a lab in which students could attempt to influence the output from random number generators. The machines were set up behind a glass screen, so that no direct tampering was possible. In order to relax the students and make them feel comfortable, Jahn and Dunne fitted out their lab with sofas, cushions and comfy chairs. A huge number of experiments were carried out. The results were unequivocal. The students could influence the output of the random number generators, skewing the machines' numbers in a chosen direction. Just like Peoc'h's chicks, Jahn's students seemed to be able to influence the quantum events that were going on in the RNG machines. They could also change the machines' output in the way they desired. These changes weren't huge, but they were consistent; they were not simply down to chance. The following graph shows the experimental results. The odds of getting the positive swing (HI) for example, by chance, is shown to be extremely unlikely (0.000002).

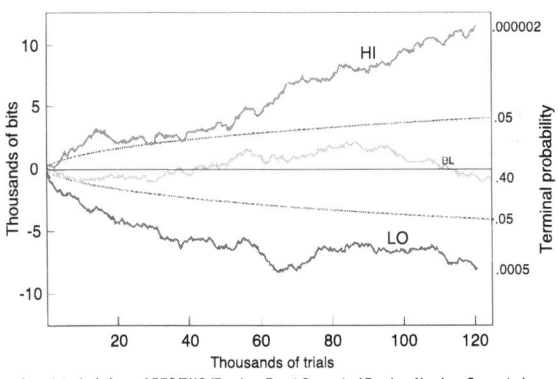

Cumulate deviations of REG/RNG (Random Event Generator/ Random Number Generator) mean shifts achieved by conscious intention of one operator over 375,000 experimental trials.

Jahn extended the scope of the experiments. He asked students to try and influence the output of the lab's RNG machines while they were out of the country. This also worked; in fact it produced almost identical results. It seemed that distance was irrelevant when influencing an RNG machine. A repeatable and strange phenomenon seemed to be present.

Unfortunately for Jahn, his work didn't go down well with the Princeton administration. Even though he performed his experiments with scientific thoroughness, they were clearly controversial. The Wikipedia page, describing his work, contains a sample of reactions and criticisms. For example:

> "The physicist Milton Rothman wrote that most of the faculty at Princeton considered the work of PEAR an embarrassment. Robert L. Park said of PEAR, "It's been an embarrassment to science, and I think an embarrassment for Princeton."

These criticisms didn't stop Jahn and Dunne carrying out further research. They formed an organisation, the Princeton Engineering Anomalies Research unit or PEAR. This unit not only carried out further experiments, it also manufactured kits so that interested parties could perform their own experiments. Jahn and Dunne's work is described in their excellent book *Margins of Reality*.

Jahn's field of study had been continued by other scientists. In particular, Dr Dean Radin has been working in this field for decades at the Institute for Noetic Studies, based in California, founded in 1973 by the Apollo 14 astronaut Dr Edgar Mitchell. Dr Radin has produced several books on the subject and many scientific papers. One experiment he was involved in is particularly strange and thought-provoking. It involved the Global Consciousness Project, a collection of random number generators placed around the world in approximately seventy locations. The output of these RNG machines is gathered centrally to see if their output is shifting away from a random result. In other words, by examining the outputs of these machines, researchers can look for a global mental influence, rather than that of an individual. Jahn had shown, years before, that people could affect an RNG machine's output while physically distant from the device. The aim of the Global Consciousness Project was to see if all minds on Earth might somehow influence these RNG machines, dotted around our planet.

One day, the GCP's showed that this may very well be true; that day was 9/11. The GCP RNG machines were running on that fateful day, when planes were flown into the Twin Towers in New York. Somehow, according to their outputs, the GCP machines were affected during that event. They showed a marked shift away from random results, a very similar shift to the ones Jahn's experiments demonstrated when a person deliberately influences an RNG machine. It was as if everyone on Earth had become more alert, more mentally intense that day, and had affected those machines' output. The strangest element of the results was that the RNG machines' output markedly shifted three hours before the attacks occurred. They then reached a peak of aberration during the attacks, before finally tailing off and returning to a base-noise level approximately seven hours after the attacks ended. Here is a black & white version, based on the graph from the GCP site:

Terrorist Attacks, Sept 11, 2001

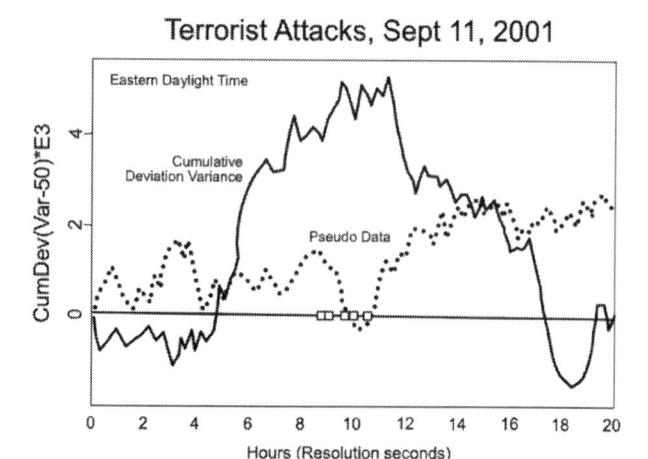

Eastern Daylight Time

Cumulative Deviation Variance

Pseudo Data

Hours (Resolution seconds)

The small rectangles on the black line mark the time when the 9/11 attacks occurred. The solid line is the change in the GCP machines' output around the world. The dotted line demonstrates random fluctuations.

Jahn and Radin's work seems to show that people can influence the output of RNG machines, just like Peoc'h's chicks. What is even stranger is that the Global Consciousness Project results seem to indicate that everyone on Earth can somehow be influenced by their own future. Is this possible? Can we be affected by our own future? This idea could be quickly dismissed if it wasn't for the work of a highly regarded psychologist: Daryl Bem.

In 2011, Daryl Bem, working at Cornell University, New York, reported some very interesting results in a paper entitled, *Feeling the future: Experimental evidence for anomalous retroactive influences on cognition and affect*, published in the Journal of Personality and Social Psychology, vol 100, p 407. To quote from the paper's abstract:

> "This article reports 9 experiments, involving more than 1,000 participants, that test for retroactive influence by "time-reversing" well-established psychological effects so that the individual's responses are obtained before the putatively causal stimulus events occur."

In other words, someone being affected by their own future. One of Bem's experiments worked as follows. He was aware of a well-known psychological fact, that writing out a list of words usually makes it easier to recall those words later. He decided to give this process a twist. He asked his subjects to view a list of words briefly. Shortly afterwards, they were tested on their initial recall. So far, so normal, but he *then* gave them a smaller, random selection of words from the same list, which they were asked to type out and memorise. At first glance, this additional work by the subjects seems pointless. Why tell the students to memorise some words *after* they'd done the test? The benefit of this extra work came out when Bem analysed the results from the test. He found that the subjects who were given the smaller, random set of words *after* the test, and memorised them, were more likely to have remembered those words *during the test*. In other words, their efforts after the test somehow improved their results *in* the test. It is as if they were being positively affected by their own future work in memorising some of the words. The difference in success-rate between the two sets of words was slight, only 2.27 per cent, but Bem carried out a lot of tests. Eventually, the likelihood of the difference being down to random luck became incredibly small. It seemed that somehow, people could be affected by their own future.

Bem carried out another experiment, involving a standard psychological effect known as habituation. Habituation is the idea that people prefer things they're used to. For example, if a person is asked to choose between two similar images, he or she will tend to prefer an image that they've seen before rather than one they haven't. Bem's twist to this experiment was that he showed subjects two new images and asked them to choose which one they liked better. A short time after, he *then* showed them one of those two images again, at random. There should have been no change to the odds of the subjects' initial choice of the two images, but there was. This experiment was published as *Precognitive Habituation: Replicable Evidence for a Process of Anomalous Cognition*, in 2003. In its abstract, it states:

> "To date, more than 400 men and women have participated in 9 variations of the PH experiment, including an independent replication by a skeptical investigator. Collectively the studies provide strong support for the two predicted effects. Across the six basic studies, the hit rate was significantly above 50% on negative trials (52.6%, t(259) = 3.17, p = .0008) and significantly below 50% on erotic trials (48.0%, t(149) = -1.88, p = .031)."

Once again, as the abstract explains, the probability that the results were down to random chance is extremely small, small enough for the results to be declared a verified phenomenon in most scientific journals. For example, many of the medical tests that labs carry out are assumed to show a repeatable phenomenon if their p-value is below 0.05. Some of Bem's results were far lower, showing how unlikely they were to be random. Bem's results therefore should be deemed, scientifically, to be showing a real effect. It would seem that people truly can be affected by their own future.

What can we make of the work of Peoc'h, Jahn, Radin and Bem? These experiments seem to tell us that people and animals' mental connection to reality is much stranger than we thought, and that our minds are fundamentally more than our brains. Rather than being creations of our brains, our minds influence our brains and can even influence quantum-level events in remote systems. What's more, this connection to remote systems isn't confined to animals, at least according to the work of a pioneering polygraph engineer. He discovered, one morning, that plants had supernatural abilities too.

According to Annie Jacobsen's book *Phenomena*, Cleve Backster was a key pioneer of the use of polygraph machines. On page 120, she states:

> "Backster was a deception researcher and interrogation expert, a man rooted in the intelligence community, where he worked for more than twenty-five years. He had earned his stripes in World War II, in the Army's Counter-Intelligence Corps, where he conducted narco-interrogations of enemy forces, early attempts to get POWs to reveal military secrets using so-called truth serums. After the war, Backster joined the CIA, where

he cofounded the Agency's polygraph program."

Backster eventually moved to New York City, where he founded *The Backster School of Lie Detection*. He taught N.Y.P.D. detectives and F.B.I. agents how to use the polygraph machine, as well as other techniques for lie detection. Backster testified in courtrooms and before Congress. His famed Backster Zone Comparison Technique, a methodology for conducting polygraphs, is still widely used. His career might have continued in this vein, in an illustrious and conventional way, if it wasn't for one event on the 2nd of February 1966.

Cleve Backster (Wikipedia – Gay Pauley)

Backster was pouring himself a morning cup of coffee when he noticed a new houseplant, a Dracaena Fragrans, that his secretary had brought into the office. Out of curiosity, he decided to hook the plant up to his polygraph machine. Logically, this should have been a waste of time, since a lie-detector is designed to pick up changes in the voltage levels on the surface of someone's skin, a.k.a. the galvanic skin response. When someone lies, their stress-level increases. This change in body chemistry also causes their hands to sweat, along with other physical effects. This is the principle behind a polygraph machine. By monitoring these physical effects, an interrogator can spot if a witness is lying. Since a plant is officially nothing more than a biological machine, with no brain or nerves, nothing interesting should have happened when Backster wired his house plant up to the polygraph machine.

Backster knew that wiring up a plant to a polygraph was silly, but he decided to do it anyway. In order to create a response from the plant that the polygraph might pick up, he decided to try and make the plant anxious, just like a suspect in a police interrogation. To do this, he decided to set fire to one of its leaves. He reached for a matchbox but before he could light a match, the polygraph registered an intense reaction on the part of the plant. Somehow, the plant had read his mind. Backster was astonished at this reaction from the plant. He performed more tests, including carrying out actions seemingly impossible for a plant to detect, such as boiling a brine shrimp in another room. The plant nevertheless reacted, creating a tell-tale polygraph reading. Backster concluded that plants must have an undiscovered sense, which he called primary perception. He concluded that plants are able to detect and respond to human thoughts and emotions. He carried out many experiments, testing such living creatures as chicken eggs and sperm. His results convinced him that there was a fundamental connection between all living things. This connection was not bounded by physical distance or physical perception. He publicised his findings in a paper entitled *Evidence of a Primary Perception in Plant Life*, in the International Journal of Psychology, in 1968. Two colleagues - Peter Tompkins and Christopher Bird - later used his findings in their bestselling book *The Secret Life of Plants*.

Backster wasn't the first person to talk about this plant ability. The brilliant polymath, physicist, biologist and biophysicist Jagadish Chandra Bose discovered similar evidence, decades before. For example, Bose played music in the area where plants grew. He discovered that this caused the plants to grow faster. He used a crescograph to measure plant response to various stimuli. Using these and other methods, he concluded that plants possessed feelings. After carrying out further work, such as the analysis of the variation of the cell membrane potential of plants under different circumstances, he hypothesised that plants can "feel pain, understand affection etc". He wrote two books on this subject, in 1902 and 1926.

Hopefully, these experiments, which have been picked from a large body of scientific work, show that there is scientific evidence that fully supports the idea that our minds are far more than a side-effect of our functioning brains. Our minds aren't a side-effect of our functioning minds, as our scientific establishment would have us believe. Instead, it's the other way around, our brains are a side-effect of our functioning minds. To quote a popular T-shirt slogan, 'we are not human beings having a spiritual experience, we are spiritual beings having a human experience.'

There is therefore extensive evidence that Scientific Materialism is wrong. Not only that, but it has been proven to be theoretically impossible, thanks to the work of famous, Nobel Prize winning scientists. Instead, reality is a magical mental construction, a place that feels very real but is in fact a mental construction. To quote from the ancient Indian text, the Yoga Vashista:

> 'The world is nothing but a mere vibration of consciousness in space. It seems to exist even as a goblin seems to exist in the eyes of the ignorant. All this is but Maya: for here there is no contradiction between the infinite consciousness and the apparent existence of the universe. It is like the marvellous dream of a person who is awake.'

In other words, our reality is a very spiritual place, where minds create the physical world and animate it. If this is true, then logically, are capable of supernatural abilities, of 'mind over matter', since reality *itself* is a product of 'mind over matter'. This idea leads us back to the time of Christ, and Christ's supernatural abilities. The Roman Catholic church made a huge effort to stamp out the idea that we could all become a Christ, a being with seemingly magical powers and knowledge. More recently, thanks to several Nobel Prize Winners, this idea has returned, via quantum physics, but once again, it's been buried. What gives? Modern science is supposed to be objective and rational, and yet Western science has ignored what these science luminaries discovered and pushed Scientific Materialism, an irrational message that demeans, deceives, and crushes our spiritual identity, along with our motivation to develop ourselves spiritually and psychically. It's as if the people in charge of science are the same as the people who were in charge of religion; their agenda seems to be the same. By strange coincidence, their agenda is *also* the same agenda of the gods, described in *the Apocryphon of John*; they also wanted humans to focus entirely on physical things, and for us all to believe that we're meaningless automatons, only fit to obsess about food, sex, violence and the other facets of a shallow, sensual, amoral existence. It's a wee bit suspicious.

The continual efforts of our establishment, over millennia, to stop psychic development begs the question: would happen if we did? Would we unlock new powers, find gnosis, and break out of our sensual prison, or would we just become slightly better in exams, according to Dr Bem's experiments? To answer this question, we can study some significant research that was done in the 1970's into the development of practical, useful, psychic abilities. This work wasn't done by grandmothers with tea leaves, or gypsies in tents, it was done by the CIA and the U.S. Military, with astonishing results.

Mind's Eye

In the 1970's, the United States' Central Intelligence Agency and the United States military became very concerned that the Russians were developing mind-techniques of various kinds: telepathy, telekinesis and other psi abilities. Many CIA and US military senior officers were sceptical; they believed that such research was useless hogwash, but their fear of losing ground to the Russians nevertheless galvanised some of them into action. The CIA and the U. S. military set up research programmes into this esoteric field. The first known funded work occurred at the Stanford Research Institute in California. Two accomplished physicists, Hal Puthoff and Russell Targ, were signed up to study the subject. They soon enlisted the help of a New York Artist and former soldier, Ingo Swann. It was a new area to them, and they needed results quickly.

Dr Puthoff knew, as he set up the project, that their work on extrasensory perception and other psi-skills would be zealously criticised by other scientists, and so he needed to come up with a test that no one could say had been the result of tampering or accidental interference. To this end, he decided to see if Swann could view, with his minds-eye, the workings of something that no one could get near to. For this purpose, Puthoff chose a superconducting, shielded magnetometer, known as a SQUID, used for studying decays in magnetic fields; it was owned by the Stanford High Energy Physics Laboratory. The device was buried in concrete and surrounded by orange, earthquake-protection supports, to prevent natural interference to its functions. Its workings were also classified, and so its internal construction was only known to a few people. A few physicists did know that it contained a Josephson junction, a clever quantum-related atomic barrier, but that was it. Puthoff knew that if Swann was able to describe the device's inner workings, simply through extrasensory perception, then no one could refute his result by saying he'd somehow cheated.

Puthoff, Swann and several of the SQUID scientists, including Dr Hebard - a colleague of Puthoff's who used the device for quark experiments - gathered in the lab room above the device, where the machine's chart recorder was installed. Swann began his mental visualisation task. He took a piece of paper and began sketching what he perceived was below him: the device inside its concrete shell. At the moment when Swann mentally perceived the machine's Josephson junction, and began describing it, the needle on the SQUID machine's chart recorder jerked. Swann continued drawing what he was picking up in his mind's eye. The chart recorder jerked again. It then produced an output very different to the SQUID's normal signal. Everyone was shocked. To quote from Annie Jacobsen's book *Phenomena* (page 134):

> 'Puthoff asked Drs Lee and Hebard to sign the chart paper as witnesses to what they had observed. The two physicians signed. Swann remembered a commotion in the room and watched as one of the doctoral students suddenly ran out, as if spooked, in such a hurry he hit his head against an orange structural support on the way out.'

The experiment was a success. The scientists running the SQUID admitted that Swann's drawings matched the machine's inner workings. Not only that, but Swann had somehow influenced the physical output of the device. Swann seemed to have affected the SQUID with his mind. The success of the SQUID test, and other early breakthroughs by Puthoff, Swann and Targ, enabled the team to forge ahead. Along with another recruit, the gifted psychic and police officer Pat Price, the team soon developed a practical technique to perform remote perceptions. This became known as coordinated remote viewing.

Ingo Swann

Ingo Swann was the main architect of Coordinated Remove Viewing as a methodical system of perception. He had been keen, from the very beginning, to turn the team's early remote-perception experiments into a practical tool. He realised, early on, that simple tests, such as perceiving what was in a sealed box in the same room, was a waste of time. If someone wanted to know what was in a box, why not just open it? By comparison, the ability to perceive something at some remote location would be extremely valuable. In its essence, CRV was a relatively straightforward procedure: Someone would give the CRV team member, a remote viewer, a target location in a sealed envelope. This remote viewer would then sit at a desk in a nondescript office with the sealed envelope, focus calmly and allow information to flow into their mind's eye about the target location. At first, basic elements would be perceived, such as motion, atmosphere, danger, risk, and calmness. After more attention, more detailed elements would appear, such as people, time, buildings, objects, colours etc.

The CRV methodology paid dividends. The team soon produced astonishing results. They were able to describe accurate and detailed information about a chosen remote target. Nevertheless, their work was still met with a lot of scepticism. To convince their overseers, the team decided to include, in their remote perception tests, a target team visiting the target site while the remote viewer carried out his or her work in the CRV session room... but this itself became a subject of suspicion. Many outside observers immediately suspected that the presence of agents at the target site could be a way to tamper with the results. To quote from Jim Marrs book, *Psi Spies* (page 112):

> 'One afternoon, in 1974, Puthoff's SRI division director, Bonnar Cox, apparently in an effort to determine for himself if the test protocols were flawed, accompanied the target team rather than give them [the remote viewer] the target in an envelope. "Cox deliberately drove in a random manner, turning left or right according to the flow of traffic." recalled Puthoff. "By this process, we ended up at Redwood City Marina, a harbor for local boating enthusiasts." Upon arriving back at SRI, the group listened to Price describe what he saw on a tape-recorder. "We don't have to wait til then. I can tell you right now where

> they'll be. What I'm looking at is a little boat jetty or a little boat dock along the bay. [...] Oriental architecture that seems to be fairly adjacent to where they are." Puthoff was astounded, as Price was accurately describing not only the marina but an Asian restaurant designed as a pagoda, located on the dock.'

What is even stranger about the test was that Price, as we can see from his initial comment, could not only perceive the target location, he also knew that it *would be* the target location. He gave his description twenty minutes before the target team reached the marina. This ability to perceive the future tarries with Daryl Bem's experimental work, discussed earlier.

The success of the remote viewing team can be shown by the fact that they were funded for twenty years. If they had been producing mumbo-jumbo, the funding would soon have stopped. Eventually, the CIA and the US military cancelled the programmes, allegedly because they'd finally concluded it was a waste of time, but rumours abound that the work hadn't actually stopped. Instead, it simply continued in a highly classified form to avoid further scrutiny. Joseph McMoneagle, one of the key military remote viewers, received the prestigious Legion of Merit award after his retirement. The Legion of Merit is a high honour; it is seventh in the order of precedence of all U.S. military awards. The fact that the U.S. military gave McMoneagle such an award speaks volumes, and is clearly at odds with many comments, mostly from outsiders, that the remote viewing work had been a waste of time.

Several remote viewers wrote extensively on their experiences. Ingo Swann, Russell Targ and Joe

McMoneagle wrote books about how they performed their remote viewing, what they'd seen (at least their non-classified work) and what they believed remote viewing said about reality and human beings. Their writings are consistent; they make it clear that we, as thinking minds, can observe virtually any location, anywhere. This corroborates with what's been discussed already in this book. If we, as thinking minds, only influence physical reality, rather than come from physical reality, then there is no reason that our minds should be constrained by any of physical reality's properties, such as distance and time. Our minds' inner perceptions, our 'mind's eye' or 'third eye', should logically be able to perceive any location in time and space. This is what the remote viewers discovered during their work. Understandably, they said that since the future isn't decided, someone remote viewing the future only perceives a possible future, but some future outcomes are more likely than others, and will dominate. For example, our planet is currently in the early stages of global climate change. What an individual is doing a year from now is highly undecided, but the state of our planet's climate, fifty years from now is much more determined as it is extremely difficult now for anyone to alter its course.

The inevitability of our planet's climate future was shown, to depressing effect, when, in March 1992, five PSI TECH remote viewers (a commercial spin-off created by some ex-members of the military CRV teams) were commissioned to explore the ramifications of the ozone problem by the Institute for Human Potential, a think-tank formed in honour of Senator Claiborne Pell, chairman of the Senate

Foreign Relations Committee. Funding for the Institute came primarily from grants by Laurance Rockefeller. The writer Jim Marrs was able to obtain a version of this report, and include it in his book *Psi Spies*, an excellent description of the whole remote viewing saga. As Marrs reports in his book, the report didn't make for fun reading. Its title said, succinctly, 'the outlook is grim'. It then made the following detailed predictions:

> "Atmospheric ozone depletion/replenishment was perceived to be driven by a natural ebb and flow process - a geophysical cycle. But this process has become overwhelmed by manmade activity... A critical point is reached, circa 2005-2012, where the destruction will begin a runaway course, in a fashion analogous to metastasis [the transfer of malignant cells from one location to another]. During this period, the problem and its potential consequences will no longer be subject to question. The ozone layer will not necessarily be slowed down but its effects temporarily ameliorated by coincidental volcanic activity. One such related event will be the explosion of an 'extinct' volcano in the North American Cascade chain... The volcanic activity will literally and figuratively eclipse the ozone problem, but decreased sunlight will wreak havoc with crop production in many places. Chaotic weather patterns in combination with decreased sunlight will necessitate the construction of huge, environmentally controlled greenhouses so

that food production can carry on without being subject to vicissitudes of climate/weather. Unwittingly, these structures form the templates for technologies that will become increasingly critical to sustaining human life. They will begin to be seen as sanctuaries, then habitats, as societies migrate into them. A point is reached where very little life is seen outside of the artificial structures. The atmosphere outside these biospheres is almost antiseptic. The sky is striated and multi-hued. Earth's remaining, surviving inhabitants have either been driven underground or into these very large, climate-controlled domes, which now house complete, medium-sized cities. Our children's children are resident there. There is no perceivable violence. Most creative energy is directed to questions of survival."

The prediction/report is scientifically sound. The authors may talk about ozone gases causing climate breakdown, which sounds odd, but in fact ozone depleting chemicals, such as CFC's, are highly potent greenhouse gases, far more so than carbon dioxide and methane.

The report also states that in the later stages of the climate breakdown, 'atmosphere outside the biospheres is almost antiseptic'. This sounds like an extreme outcome, but there is a scientific basis for such a situation. If our planet warms too much, and the warming melts the icesheets, then this can shut down ocean circulation. As a result, our oceans lose their oxygen, because oxygen isn't being carried into the deep oceans by the currents. Sea life dies. In their place, ocean bacteria thrive in the anoxic environment, breaking down biological material and producing hydrogen sulphide. As these bacteria spread throughout the oceans, their hydrogen sulphide emissions spread out over the landmasses, killing plants and animals. Eventually, there is little life anywhere on Earth, apart from in caves, and the atmosphere is acidic since hydrogen sulphide can turn into sulphuric acid when it's dissolved in water. This dark, dead-world, hydrogen sulphide result is known as a Canfield ocean scenario, after the geologist Donald Canfield. As the writer Gwynne Dyer explains in his book *Climate Wars*, such a hellish situation has occurred before on Earth, in the end-Triassic period, and so it can easily happen again.

The work of the remote-viewing teams, if correct, shows that we can perceive locations remote to ourselves, simply by perceiving them with our mind's eye. From personal experience, I would say this is possible, but the important factor is that it was successfully carried out for decades by multiple teams working for the C.I.A. and the military. It is also something we can all try for ourselves.

D.I.Y. Psi

If anyone would like to try remote viewing, here is an introduction to the process. More detailed instructions can be found on the web, but these steps should help anyone on the path to mental, remote perception:

Step 1: Ask your friend or family member to secretly choose a target. The target can be any place, anywhere, at any point in time. It's useful if the target is meaningful, such as the Eiffel Tower, the Great Pyramid, the Golden Gate Bridge, the assassination of J.F.K., Neil Armstrong's landing on the moon etc. Your friend then assigns a code number to this target. The code number can be anything, such as 435-165. He or she privately notes down what the code number refers to. Ideally, this is done for many targets, each one different, so that your friend has a list of numbers. He or she then gives you one of those numbers, or alternatively, places a photo of the target in a sealed envelope and gives that to you; either method works fine.

Step 2: Write down the code-number your friend gives you on an A4/letter sheet. Focus on the number and what 'lies behind it', in other words what the target code is referring to. You may see, in your mind's eye, a rough image. Note down what you see, but don't try to guess its content. This guessing is known as analytical overlay or AOL; it's your brain *guessing* the identity of the target. This won't help you and is very likely to lead you down the wrong path. Always try to note down what actually comes in, not what you think is there. Note down the overall impressions you sense about the target. Is the target inside or outside? Is the atmosphere at the target tense, relaxed, neutral, active, violent, dramatic, pleasant etc? Is there a structure? Is the main object a manufactured item? Is there a feeling of purpose? Is nature present? Are people present? Is the target location modern, historical, ancient or futuristic? What level of technology is present? Continue noting down what comes through. Don't try to work out exactly what the target is in one go; you're likely to guess it, and then, once again, you'll get AOL and a guessed result, which is almost always wrong. Draw pictures, if that helps. Close your eyes, or keep them open, whichever seems to help you connect to the target. Keep doing this until you've written down a lot of notes, or you begin to feel tired.

Step 3: Ask your friend to reveal the actual target. Study what you got right about the target, and what you got wrong. Sometimes, you can be completely wrong; even professional remote viewers do this. A lot of the time, you may discover that you were on the right track at first, but then you began guessing what was there and went astray. At other times, you may be shocked at how accurately you described the target. In some case, when the target is revealed to you, you might say 'oh my God, that is it!' However things might turn out, do persevere. It helps greatly if you remain relaxed, open-minded, curious, and steady in your approach.

Remote viewing isn't the only practical way to discover one's psychic abilities, and personally experience a reality that is more than the physical world around us. Another aspect of the larger spiritual reality that we all experience is dreaming.

Most of us wake up in the morning with fleeting

and vague with memories of the dreams we've had. As a result, most of us generally conclude that dreams are simply fleeting, vague concoctions made by the brain during sleep. In fact, it is the other way around. Dreaming is us experiencing other realities, it's just that we don't remember them because we haven't trained ourselves to remember them clearly or experience them more lucidly when we are in the dream world.

One trick to be fully aware when in the dream world is to realise that we *are* in the dream world, when we're dreaming. For example, we are often able to fly or float in the dream world. And yet, while dreaming, we don't think 'this isn't normal reality, what's going on?' If we did question what we were doing, it would wake us up to the fact that we're in the dream world and not in normal reality. This awareness of what reality we're in can make us fully conscious in that reality. As soon as we realise, in the dream world, that flying or floating isn't normal, and that we *are* dreaming, then we become fully aware. It's an exciting and memorable moment. Unfortunately, as soon as we get excited in the dream world, we often wake up in our beds, so the trick is to stay calm when we do become lucid in the dream world.

In order to train oneself to make these checks automatically, and thereby become lucid up in the dream world, you need to regularly check, every day, if the reality around you is normal. This might sound silly but do it anyway. If you're walking in the park, or standing in the kitchen, jump and see if you float, or just land. If you land (as you would in the real world), you can say in your head, "I'm in reality." If you have a scar, look at it regularly and see if it's there (people usually don't have scars in the dream world). If it's there, say, "I'm in reality." You'll hopefully find that after doing this for a while, you'll do it automatically. As a result, when you're dreaming, you'll also do it, out of habit. When that happens, you'll realise that you *are* floating, or your scar has gone, and realise that you're in the dreamworld. At that point, you will gain lucidity, you'll be conscious in the dream world. It's an eerie experience, the first time. You'll probably get excited, which unfortunately usually means you'll wake up in your bed, as already mentioned, but after more experiences, you'll be able to stay lucid in the dream. If you do, stay calm and focus on what's around you. Study the ground in detail, the blades of grass, the bark of trees etc. By doing this, you'll mentally anchor yourself in the dream world. Jurgen Ziewe's book *Multidimensional Man* is an excellent personal account of such experiences. It's an excellent way to understand, from personal experience, that there is more to the universe than the physical world we see around us.

Although lucid dreaming may not have clear practical benefits, remote viewing is a very important, real-world skill, so to speak. The United States military and the C.I.A. clearly showed great interest in it as an intelligence tool. At the same time, it was not a risk-free career. Pat Price, a highly gifted remote viewer, ended up dead, in highly suspicious circumstances. There is evidence that he was aware that he would be killed (being a gifted remote viewer doesn't help you that much if there are teams of people trying to bump you off). The video documentary *Third Eye Spies* explains that a year before his death, Pat bought a million-dollar life insurance policy. Price's death fits with the idea, based on books, articles, and documentaries on remote viewing, that the U.S. intelligent services were far from pleased that remote viewers were talking about their non-classified experiences.

The reported success of the remote viewers, and their employment by the U.S. military and C.I.A. for decades, makes a mockery of the official scientific idea that all psi or psychic abilities are impossible. These remote viewers showed that psi abilities *are* possible. What's more, the remote viewing teams realised that these abilities weren't restricted to a few, freakish savants. Puthoff and Targ, during their studies at the Stanford Research Institute, found that most people they tested, from all walks of life, showed some psi ability. The obstacle preventing these people from become psi-adepts wasn't their potential, but their willingness to explore the field. Understandably, many of these people didn't want to become involved in a discipline that would make them look like kooky weirdos. Some of these people might have also spotted that the field was also a dangerous place if you weren't under the protection of an Intelligence Agency. Nevertheless, Puthoff's and Targ's observations are critically important. It would seem that we are, in our very nature, a psychic species.

The idea that we are all, to some extent, psychic won't come as a surprise to many people. Many people unconsciously pick up supernatural signals on multiple occasions, giving rise to popular phrases such as 'bad vibes', 'bad atmosphere', 'foreboding', 'bright presence', 'I knew who was phoning when it rang', warning dreams, the spiritual presence of the deceased, being stared at and so on. Many people also notice the supernatural abilities of their pets, such as cats and dogs, as well as horses and birds. The author and scientist Rupert Sheldrake scientifically investigated pets' psychic skills in his popular book, *Why Pets Know When Their Owners Are Coming Home*. Such examples of psychic awareness pop up all the time, but what would the world be like if it was generally accepted that psychic abilities were real and factually true? What would our society be like if people were encouraged to develop practical and effective psychic skills, such as remote viewing? What would happen if it became part of our standard education? If we did, many of us might have some very strange experiences, at least according to Ingo Swann's own testimony. What he experienced is both illuminating, memorable and deeply disturbing.

La-La land

Ingo Swann, as already mentioned, was a key member of the original remote viewing team assembled at the Stanford Research Centre in Berkeley, California. He worked with that team for many years, but he also carried out remote viewing work for other organisations during his career. For example, he helped a marine salvage team find sunken wrecks. Along with these more open jobs were more secret ones, some of which we'll probably never know about. Fortunately for us, Swann did describe one highly secretive job, which he was able to report on after an agreed period of time. In his book *Penetration*, he describes a mission in which he was asked by a very secret, U.S. government team to perform a remote viewing. He agreed to this request, and was soon taken to a secret, underground location by mysterious agents. There, he was given a coded target number by an affable but entirely unreadable man. He remote-viewed the target, in his normal way, and found himself, mentally, on the far side of the moon. To his astonishment, the target location he was remote viewing contained towers, cranes, floodlights, mining machinery and giant, naked figures digging material from the lunar surface. His secretive client seemed unruffled by Swann's report; he'd clearly expected it to be the case. Swann describes the scene in more detail but discovers that some of the aliens on the moon have noticed his spiritual presence. His client abruptly asks him to stop the remote viewing. Swann mentally returns to the room's he's sitting in. His client pays him, and Swann is taken back to his New York apartment.

A month later, Swann receives a copy of the book, *Someone Else is on the Moon*, written by George Leonard, in the mail. There is no return address. The arrival of the book seems to be a message, that Swann's remote viewing of the moon was entirely correct, and that there are aliens on the moon. What's more, the people in power in the United States are fully aware of this and have no interest in informing the general public of this startling fact.

Ingo Swann's 'dark side of the moon remote-viewing session' wasn't the only time he'd encountered aliens, either physically or psychically, according to his memoirs. The same highly secret team that employed him in that work also took him to a remote part of Alaska to physically observe a UFO taking water from a lake. This experience, in his view, was intriguing but mostly baffling, but his third experience is perhaps the most important of all. In his book, Swann describes a trip he makes to Los Angeles, purely for social reasons. In a supermarket, he has a strange and memorable encounter. To quote from his book:

> "The supermarket had huge tables loaded with artichokes. At one of the artichoke tables was standing a ravishing woman. She had volumes of gorgeous black hair, and her eyes were covered by purple sunglasses. She was

> absolutely awesome. I thought, 'good heavens!' She was rummaging through the artichokes, and I wanted some too. So, I worked my way covertly and nonchalantly into her proximity. And then, for absolutely no reason at all, I experienced an electrifying wave of goosebumps throughout my whole body. The hair on my arms practically stood at attention and the hair on my neck definitely did. Without rhyme or reason or forethought, or anything at all, I suddenly 'knew' she was an alien, an extra-terrestrial. My throat went dry. My hands started shaking."

Swann reports that he immediately backed off to the other end of the aisle, where he tried to look nonchalant. While he was staring at a row of vegetables, he spotted two of the secret government team that had hired him to remote view the moon; they were watching the woman. Swann rapidly exited the supermarket and returned to his car, where his friend was waiting. He got in the car and asked his friend, Conrad, who was very experienced in psychic phenomena, to wait with him for a short while. Conrad, curious as to why, agreed. As Swann recounts:

> "Shortly, the female came out, pushing a loaded grocery cart. 'Study that one and tell me what you think,' I said. Conrad looked briefly at the woman and then said the most remarkable thing. 'Well, if you mean do I think she's an extra-terrestrial, yes,' he said in a bored way. 'We've got a lot of them here in La-La land.'"

Swann, still in a state of mild shock, returned to the friends' house. There, they cooked the meal and enjoyed their dinner. Later that evening, after the meal, Swann discussed his experience with two visiting friends, Viola and Shafika, who were also experienced psychics. As he explains in his book, 'this opened up rather inebriated discussions about the E.T. civilization which was busy infiltrating Earth. "There are a LOT of them, you know," said Shafika, "and many are bio-androids. They're dangerous, you know, and they realise that Earth psychics are their only enemies. Be careful, Ingo, be careful."'

On the face of it, this is a bizarre story. In some ways, it is too fantastic to be credible. Surely, if there are dangerous, alien bio-androids walking around Earth, disguised as humans, we'd know about it? But the comment made by Swann's friend Shafika resonates with many ideas already mentioned in this book. According to *the Apocryphon of John*, the gods who made us were technologically advanced, amoral, alien beings who looked a lot like us. The key difference between us and them was that they were soulless; they did not 'shine'. If members of their species were around now, they would fit the description of these 'bio-androids'. Of course, if they were around now, civilization's obsessive plan to indoctrinate us into *not* develop any psychic perception would help them enormously. It's as if our very civilization has been setup to help the kind of beings that Swann encountered, and that his friend Shafika warned him about. How odd.

Ingo Swann's experience in Los Angeles isn't the only published report of modern psychics encountering strange people in an urban environment who seem human, physically, but are spiritually alien.

For example, the journalist Georgina Bruni wrote an excellent book on the Rendlesham Forest UFO incident, entitled *You can't tell the people*. The book's title comes from a conversation that the author had with Prime Minister Margaret Thatcher. When Bruni asked Thatcher what the British Government knew about the Rendlesham UFO incident, Thatcher snapped back, 'you can't tell the people about that!'

In Bruni's book, after her extensive investigation into the Rendlesham Forest UFO incident - a classic British UFO mystery – she recounts a strange tale. To quote from page 284 of her book:

> "In the mid 1990's, I was introduced to an individual who claimed to have been trained by a US intelligence agency as a psychic spy. Kane (an adopted name) is a British subject who is indeed a very clever psychic; he has proved this to my media friends and myself on numerous occasions, but it was his untold story that intrigued me most. According to Kane, several years earlier, he had been visiting the United States, to meet with some government agents. He was told he could make a lot of money by using his psychic powers to assist them in a certain project. Kane agreed to meet them out of curiosity. They gave him several tests which he passed with flying colours, and they made him an offer he couldn't refuse. He was hired and taken to a special house in New York City where he and five other young men were put through daily mind tests. The house was very

simply furnished in pale grey colours, with no pictures on the walls or ornaments around. Apparently, this was so as not to clutter up their minds. *[my note: this is a standard remote viewing technique to reduce visual distractions]* They rarely left the building, which was highly secured, and when they did, they were driven in a black Cadillac, with black-tinted windows, under the supervision of your typical 'Men in Black'."

Bruni explains that she later discovered the location of Kane's house; it was in 'one of the most exclusive areas of New York City, close to the Mayor's residence.' She states:

"After several weeks of intensive training, Kane was becoming concerned. He realised that something was not quite right. Every weekend, the men would receive a visitor, who Kane described as oriental looking. He always wore black and had a very aggressive character. He seldom spoke but when he did, he did so in an odd sort of accent that was not familiar. The household staff were very nervous when he was around. It was during one of these visits that Kane questioned his own role in the project. Although he was already a talented psychic, the continuous mind-games were causing him some confusion; they seemed to be blocking his powers. Much to his amazement, he learned that he was being programmed to get inside the minds of others, and his first target was to be the president of a large American company. The idea was to plant Kane inside the company to disrupt the target's mind, destabilizing him so that he would have to resign. He would them be replaced by one of their own people. When Kane realised what they had planned for him, being a gentle soul, he made up his mind to leave, but realised that the only way out was to escape. He fled back to the United Kingdom, which was not an easy task because he had now been given a new identity. Apparently, the agency continued to pester him until he finally left England to live in Europe. Before he disappeared, he told me that the people he had worked with were interested in UFOs and it had passed through his mind that the oriental-looking man was alien in origin. His eyes, according to Kane, were so penetrating that no one could look directly into them."

Bruni's account, as with Swann's encounter in L.A., is almost too weird to be believed, but they have interesting similarities. What's more, the comment in Bruni's book that the man 'was alien in origin' and his eyes 'were so penetrating that no one could look directly into them' harkens right back to the events described in *the Apocryphon of John*, which describes Yaldabaoth, one of the original alien Watcher gods, as having 'eyes of flame'.

The experiences of Swann and Bruni's friend Kane are very strange, and yet they are logically consistent. The fact that they are hard to believe is understandable, but one thing that science has shown us is that what is believable is rarely true, and vice versa. Many key phenomena in our universe are, on the face of it, seemingly mad. For example, the sun loops around our sky every day. It therefore seems clear that the sun goes around our planet. In fact, it's the opposite; our planet goes around the sun. In addition, the idea that plants gain their material from the air also seems ridiculous, and yet they do. Our world is very strange, we just don't think about it. We carry on with our lives of easy familiarity, where little changes, and so the strangeness of the universe never arises for us, but for anyone thrust into the world of UFOs and aliens, they are suddenly faced with important experiences that they know are true but make them look mad. John Burroughs experienced just such a problem when he saw the UFO event in Rendlesham Forest, first-hand, while stationed at the nearby U.S. army base in a junior role. Afterwards, he worked for many years in the States to tell people about the event and raise awareness of it in the public eye. This is what he said in one interview, quoted in the book:

> "It really confuses me. If you look at it, what is the status of the world? You know, you can go along your life and basically you believe in God; you believe in your country; you believe in your government; you believe everything is under control. In the back of your mind you hear about UFOs, you think, well, there is a possibility but is it really possible? But then you actually see something like that and then have it handled the way the government handled it... You wonder what's going on in the world, and you're really interested in knowing but the American people, do the

> American people want to know? Does the world want to know? I began to wonder sometimes because nothing is done about it. I am not saying that nothing has been attempted... but the overall thing of the American people seems to be, 'yeah, that's interesting'... <u>but outer space and this stuff is going on</u>!"

Burroughs' concern is understandable, as it seems that our society has been set up to make sure that we *don't* notice UFO phenomena, or related events. Our media and scientists encourage us to scoff at UFO stories, rather than investigate them, understand their significance, or even think of them in an objective manner. This strategy, unfortunately, is straight out of Charles Sanders Peirce's essay, *The Fixation of Belief*. To quote it again:

> "Let the will of the state act, then, instead of that of the individual. Let an institution be created which shall have for its object to keep correct doctrines before the attention of the people, to reiterate them perpetually and to teach them to the young, having at the same time power to prevent contrary doctrines from being taught, advocated, or expressed. Let all possible causes of a change of mind be removed from men's apprehensions. Let them be kept ignorant, lest they should learn of some reason to think otherwise than they do. Let their passions be enlisted, so that they may regard private and unusual opinions with hatred and horror."

Pierce's plan seems to have succeeded. The only difference is that many people ridicule and avoid 'private and unusual opinions', rather than hate them. As a result, when someone such as John Burroughs witnesses a UFO and wants to tell everyone about it, he is faced with a truly Herculean struggle.

The Missing Times

News Media Complicity in the UFO Cover-up

TERRY HANSEN

The efforts of our institutions, and our media, since the Second World War to debunk and ridicule UFO reports, has been a disturbing example in information management. The author Terry Hansen studied this matter in his meticulously researched book, *The Missing Times: News media complicity in the UFO cover-up*. In his book, Hansen describes the extensive efforts by the U.S. Military, the U.S. government and the C.I.A. to control and suppress UFO reports since the Second World War. Hansen points out that there are many, *many* UFO reports by credible witnesses, and many of these were published in local and regional newspapers in the United States, but virtually none of them ever made it into the national newspapers and television stations. The only national publication that would report them was *the National Enquirer*, a notoriously disrespected magazine. The United States media, it would seem, had therefore acted systematically for decades to erase the matter from public debate.

It's worth asking: why would it be so important for those in power to stop us talking, or thinking, about UFO's? One clue to this puzzle may be that many UFO encounters, according to the witnesses involved, included telepathic communication between the witness and the aliens. In addition, the witnesses received feelings of love and calmness from the aliens they encountered. The witnesses also report that during the encounter, the aliens warned them of future calamities and the need to change their materialist and warlike lifestyles in order to prevent environmental destruction. This interaction is revealing, for it is a lot like someone from outside a cult compound visiting it and telling some of the followers that they are locked into a dark situation, and that they're heading for disaster. Not surprisingly, the abusive and controlling cult leaders who run the compound would *not* want such visitors. They would therefore do everything they could to keep those visitors away, convince their followers to avoid the visitors, and persecute any follower who tried to pass on the visitors' message. By strange coincidence, this is exactly what our establishments are doing with UFOs.

The UFO situation on Earth is therefore mixed. One the one hand, Ingo Swann reported that there are bio-androids walking around that are highly dangerous. On the other hand, many witnesses say that there are benevolent aliens who are doing their best to warn some of us that we're heading for disaster. There seems to be enough material for a whole host of science fiction stories and, oddly enough, there have been.

For example, in the popular sixties T.V. series *Invaders*, an ordinary America discovered that there were aliens in his country, disguised as normal people. The only difference between them and true humans was that their little fingers were malformed.

In the classic sci-fi film, T*hey Live*, directed by John Carpenter, an everyday guy accidentally finds some sunglasses. When he puts a pair on, he sees aliens walking around. He discovers that the sunglasses he's found cancel out a special signal, one that's secretly being broadcast by aliens on Earth to prevent human beings noticing the aliens' disguised presence since, without the sunglasses, the aliens look just like normal people.

In the classic sci-fi film, *Invasion of the Body Snatchers*, many people in a town start declaring, hysterically, that their loved-ones aren't their loved-ones but some sort of alien mimic. The hero of the film is at first sceptical of these claims, then he finds evidence that it's true. He discovers that an alien plant creature has reached Earth. This alien targets a human and while the person sleeps, it forms into an identical version of that human. The human dies and dissolves and the alien plant-creature takes over its target's life. The hero desperately tries to alert the population to the danger but faces disinterest, disbelief and ridicule. It's interesting to note that the main premise of *Invasion of the Body Snatchers* was inspired by a serious psychological condition known as Capgras Syndrome. To quote Wikipedia:

> "Capgras delusion is a psychiatric disorder in which a person holds a delusion that a friend, spouse, parent, or other close family member (or pet) has been replaced by an identical impostor. It is named after Joseph Capgras (1873–1950), a French psychiatrist."

Someone can develop Capgras Syndrome when they have some form of brain injury, one that causes them to no longer feel an emotional response when they see a loved one. Because they feel no emotional response when seeing that person, they develop the belief that that person *isn't* their loved one, but is in fact an alien imposter, made to look like their loved-one.

In the 1980's, the hugely popular T.V. series *the X-Files* included an ongoing idea that secret groups in the United States defence establishment were hand-in-glove with malevolent aliens, an idea that had been circulating for decades.

The success of these shows seems to indicate that there is a strong undercurrent amongst people in the United States that strange things are going on, and their government is keeping them hidden. This anxiety is understandable, since there have been many highly credible UFO encounters in the last seventy years, and they all indicate that the Western military is systematically covering such events. Key events, such as the Roswell Incident, and the Australian Westall school incident, and the recent Pentyrch UFO incident in Wales, all include extensive evidence of some form of alien or advanced craft. At the same time, in each case, the military has rapidly closed everything down, taken all the evidence and done their best to squash any reporting of the event. As many witnesses state, knowledge of these events is in the public interest, and yet it is systematically and repeatedly buried. What's more, any and all attempts to bring it back to the surface often result in obstruction, classification and, according to some reports, harassment and persecution. It would seem, according to those witnesses, that the more you try, the worse they get. As a former M.I.5 officer once said, 'the Security State is like an onion; the more layers you peel off, the more you feel like crying.'

There are therefore intriguing reports, from multiple individuals, that aliens do exist and that multiple races of aliens are visiting our planet.

Senior people around the world have also stated openly that aliens are present on Earth. For example, the late Paul Hellyer - a former Canadian cabinet minister and the longest serving member of the Queen's Privy Council for Canada at the time of his death - openly stated that he was aware, through his personal connections, that at least four different races were present on Earth.

Another senior witness to alien activity on Earth is Haim Eshed, a retired brigadier general in Israeli Military Intelligence. He was the director of space programs for Israel Ministry of Defense for nearly 30 years and is known as 'the father of Israel's space capabilities.' Haim recently stated that aliens were present on Earth. He went further and stated that the United States government has signed a deal with several alien races to conduct experiments on Earth.

Haim Eshed (Wikipedia commons – FIASS)

Unfortunately, there is very little solid evidence to support any of the UFO claims by these witnesses. This, in itself, is understandable, as nearly all of these reports, if true, would be immediately classified by governments and the military, then kept in encrypted, sealed storage. Fortunately, there are other ways to discover information about possible alien visitors. One way is to delve back into the past, when things weren't hidden so well, and information was crudely encrypted. If we study that evidence, then we can make progress in understanding the alien presence on Earth.

Nephilim

Earlier in this book, we examined evidence that a group of ancient gods set up civilization and created our species. According to what we uncovered, these gods were around nine-feet-tall and hairless, with large, elongated skulls. The Bible has a word for these beings; the giants or Nephilim. According to the

Book of Genesis, the Nephilim, or the Fallen Ones, were Fallen Angels. In Genesis 6:4, it states:

> "The Nephilim were on the earth in those days—and also afterward—when the sons of God went to the daughters of humans and had children by them. They were the heroes of old, men of renown."

In the Old Testament, In Numbers 13:33, the Nephilim or giants are mentioned again:

> "We saw the Nephilim there (the descendants of Anak come from the Nephilim). We seemed like grasshoppers in our own eyes, and we looked the same to them."

The Holy Bible isn't the only respected ancient book to talk about these ancient, superhuman giants. *The Book of Enoch*, the famous, ancient apocryphal book that the Roman Catholic Church tried to eradicate, also speaks of the Nephilim. It describes them in deeply critical terms. It refers to them as giants (Anakim/ Anak) and explains that they were the offspring of gods and human women:

> "And they [the human women] became pregnant, and they bare great giants, whose height was three hundred ells: Who consumed all the acquisitions of men. And when men could no longer sustain them, the giants turned against them and devoured mankind. And they began to sin against birds, and beasts, and reptiles, and fish, and to devour one another's flesh, and drink the blood."

The Book of Enoch explains that the gods that fathered these Nephilim taught humans all the facets of civilization, but their teachings only led to amoral behaviour and violence:

> "And Azâzêl taught men to make swords, and knives, and shields, and breastplates, and made known to them the metals of the earth and the art of working them, and bracelets, and ornaments, and the use of antimony, and the beautifying of the eyelids, and all kinds of costly stones, and all colouring tinctures. And there arose much godlessness, and they committed fornication, and they were led astray, and became corrupt in all their ways."

In this way, *The Book of Enoch* confirms the description made in *The Apocryphon of John* that the gods taught Humanity the facets of civilization, but that these gifts were a poisoned cup that led to abuse and suffering. But there is more to this story, because in the book *Peake's Commentary on the Bible*, the following quote appears:

> "In addition, the Aramaic peoples of that time referred to Orion's Belt as Nephila. It follows that the Nephilim were believed to have come from those stars."

It is only a single reference, but it is tantalising. As we've already seen in this book, Anton Parks' translation of the Sumerian texts states that the civilizing gods were aliens that landed on Earth in Harbu ships. Logically, if this is true, then these alien gods must have come from some other planet. If the

Aramaic people were correct about the Nephilim, then this other planet was in the Orion's Belt cluster of stars.

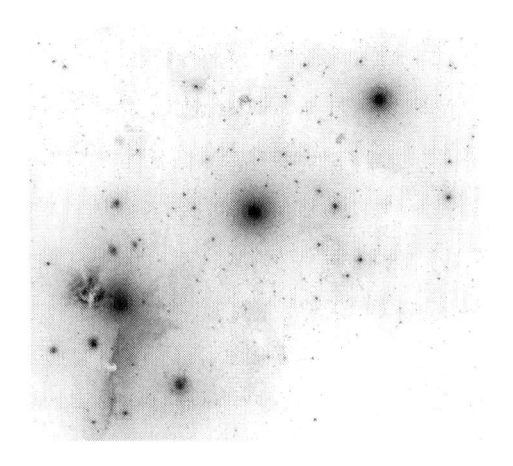

Orion's Belt

The idea that the ancient Nephilim, offspring of the gods or the gods themselves, came from Orion's Belt isn't too weird an idea, at least in the eyes of ancient sources. For them, and many other ancient tribes on Earth, Orion's Belt was vitally important, and a legendary home of the gods. The three stars, or star-systems of Orion's Belt - Alnitak, Alnilam and Mintaka – were known as the Golden Grains, the Light of Heaven, the Hearth Stars and The Three Kings. According to Osirian myth, for example, the birth of Osiris was heralded by the brightest star in the sky, Sirius. The Three Kings then followed that star (since Sirius is to the southwest of Orion's Belt) and these Three Kings brought valuable gifts. Christ, as a risen god, was therefore praised, and possibly bribed, by the Kings of Orion's Belt.

From a practical point of view, Orion's Belt is

feasible as a source of another alien race. The three stars, or star-systems, are approximately 300 light years away from us, which means they're relatively close to us in galactic terms. If the Milky Way was a city, they'd be on our street.

Nevertheless, this evidence is only anecdotal. According to our textbooks, our ancient civilizations had no advanced information about neighbouring star-systems, and no idea about their properties, distances, or content. If there were interstellar aliens setting up civilization in our ancient past, and training senior humans in various technologies, surely they would have also passed on knowledge about their origins, their home planet and other inhabited star systems? If they did that, such information would have been extremely valuable and preserved amongst the human elite. And yet, there seems to be no sign of it. This is a compelling argument, with one important flaw. As we've seen already in this book, knowledge is power. It is therefore likely that senior humans would have kept this knowledge to themselves and not told *anyone* else. If that occurred, then we'd only find out about it if these powerful people let it slip out. Fortunately, they did.

Heroic code

In 1882, Robert Hewitt Brown wrote a book, *Stellar Theology and Masonic Astronomy*. On page 7 of his book, he states:

> "The mythological stories, the wonderful adventures of the gods. These fables are most of them absurd enough if understood as real

histories, but the allegorical key being given, many of them are found to contain profound and sublime astronomical truths. This key was religiously kept secret by the priests and philosophers. It was only imparted to those who were initiated into the mysteries. The profane and vulgar crowd were kept in darkness. They believed in and worshipped a real Hercules or Jupiter, whom they thought actually lived and performed all the exploits, who underwent all the transformations of the mythology... By these means the priests ruled the people with a despotic power. The fables of the mythology disclosed to them grand scientific truths, and to them only. The very stories themselves served to perpetuate those truths for the benefit of the initiated, and also formed an easy vehicle for their transmission. Books were not only rare and difficult of multiplication, but it is also probable that, in order that scientific knowledge might be concealed, it was considered unlawful to commit it to writing, the sacred hieroglyphs were employed. These were known only to the initiated; there was another set of written characters used by the common people."

Brown is therefore stating that senior people in the Ancient World *did* know 'profound and sublime astronomical truths.' Who they gained these truths from isn't made clear, but this information was clearly powerful, as Brown states that it enabled this ancient elite group to 'rule the people with a despotic power', just as the gods seemed to have done, at least according to multiple, ancient sources.

Brown also tells us what ancient material contains these 'profound and sublime astronomical truths': 'the mythological stories, the wonderful adventures of the gods.' In other words, the Greek Myths. It would therefore seem that the Greek Myths are not just dramatic tales but coded information. All we need to do is to crack their code.

To start this process, we can examine a Greek Myth. Here is the first half of Apollodorus's version of the Tenth Labour of Hercules:

> "As a tenth labour Hercules was ordered to fetch the kine (cattle) of Geryon from Erythia. Now Erythia was an island near the ocean; it is now called Gadira. This island was inhabited by Geryon, son of Chrysaor by Callirhoe, daughter of Ocean. He had the body of three men grown together and joined in one at the waist, but parted in three from the flanks and thighs. He owned red kine, of which Eurytion was the herdsman and Orthus, the two-headed hound, begotten by Typhon on Echidna, was the watchdog. So, journeying through Europe to fetch the kine of Geryon Hercules destroyed many wild beasts and set foot in Libya and proceeding to Tartessus he erected as tokens of his journey two pillars over against each other at the boundaries of Europe and Libya. But being heated by the Sun on his journey, he bent his bow at the god, who in admiration of his hardiness, gave him a golden goblet in which he crossed the ocean. And having reached Erythia he lodged on Mount Abas. However the dog, perceiving

him, rushed at him; but he smote it with his club, and when the herdsman Eurytion came to the help of the dog, Hercules killed him also. But Menoetes, who was there pasturing the kine of Hades, reported to Geryon what had occurred, and he, coming up with Hercules beside the river Anthemus, as he was driving away the kine, joined battle with him and was shot dead. And Hercules, embarking the kine in the goblet and sailing across to Tartessus, gave back the goblet to the Sun."

As a story, it's a mess - it's mostly a string of odd people and dramatic events – but this tells us something. If it *were* a dramatic story, it would be structured better, but if it was a code, its structure would be primarily to encode information and ir *would* be a tedious string of odd facts. We therefore have the first clear sign that Brown was right, and that the Greek Myths are encoded data.

The second step to decoding these Greek Myths is to note another comment by Brown: 'it was considered unlawful to commit it to writing'. In other words, the priests had to memorise the information. This sounds like a tall order, as there are a lot of Greek Myths, but it can be done if a person uses an age-old system of memorisation: The Memory Palace or Method of Loci system.

The Method of Loci memorisation technique works as follows. Someone wants to memorise a string of abstract information, such as 'red four, blue two, green five, pink three.' This data is relatively simple - only eight words - but it can be easily jumbled up in our heads because it's so dry and abstract; it's easy to accidentally alter the sequence of the colours, or the numbers. A better way to memorise this information is to turn the data into vivid images. For example, imagine you're in a familiar place, such as your house. You're going to travel on an imaginary journey through your house. One the way, you'll encounter strange creatures. You start your journey in your front room. You step into it and see a four-legged Red Dragon. Imagine that dragon, sitting in your favourite chair, wings spread, scales shining, his four legs sprawled out in front of him. You leave your front room and walk to your kitchen. There, you find, leaning against your stove, a two-legged Blue Pelican. You leave your kitchen and step into your garden. There, you encounter a five-legged Green Frog on your lawn. Beyond it, by the back gate, is a three-legged Pink Princess. Imagine them in great detail, especially noting their numbers of legs. Repeat the journey in your mind again. Keep doing it until its contents are clear and fixed in your memory. You should find that once you have mentally walked that journey a number of times, it's very hard *not* to remember it, due to the familiarity of the locations and the vividness of the creatures. This is how the Method of Loci, or Memory Palace technique, works. Memory champions have used it, with subtle alterations, to memorise entire 52-card packs of randomly shuffled cards.

Our brains, or minds, haven't changed much in six-thousand years, and so it's highly likely that the ancient priests used the Method of Loci system to memorise strings of data. If Brown is right, then it's therefore likely that the Labour of Hercules is actually a Method of Loci story, contained encoded information about the stars.

In order to work out which stars the Labour of Hercules is referring to, we can use the fact that Hercules was a giant hero, a hunter with a bow and a club. Fortunately, a major constellation in our Northern heavens does depict a heroic man with a bow and a club: the constellation of Orion the Hunter. There's therefore there's a good chance that Hercules represents the Orion constellation in those stories. The stories also involve Hercules travelling around. Therefore, the constellations around Orion may be the true subjects of Hercules' mythical adventures. To test this hypothesis, let's examine the constellations around Orion the Hunter. They include Gemini (the twin brothers), Canis Minor (the Small Dog) and Canis Major (the Big Dog). In the Labour of Hercules, Hercules does encounter two brothers and their guard dog. Therefore, if the myth is actually encoded information about those stars, then the character of Geryon in the myth refers to the star Castor, the main star of Gemini. The character of Eurytion refers to the second star in Gemini: Pollux, and their dog Orthrus corresponds to the main star of Canis Minor, Procyon. If this is correct, then the vivid descriptions of those characters in the myth should match something to do with those corresponding stars.

Civilization is a system of abusive control

The constellations around Orion

In the Labour of Hercules, when Hercules encounters Geryon and Eurytion, we are told that Geryon 'had the body of three men grown together and joined in one at the waist but parted in three from the flanks and thighs'. In other words, Geryon was a triple-paired man. It's therefore fascinating to discover that the star Castor is actually three pairs of stars. Geryon's brother, Eurytion, has no special features. His corresponding star, Pollux, also has no special features, as it is a single star system. Their dog Orthrus is two-headed. It's therefore *also* fascinating to discover that its corresponding star, Procyon, is a binary system; it has two stars.

Hercules and Cerberus by Antonio Tempesta (Wikipedia commons – LA County Museum of Art)

Orthrus is not the only dog to be encoded this way. In a later Labour, Hercules fights Cerberus, the Guard Dog of the Underworld. It is likely that Cerberus, being a giant, famous dog, represents the main star of Canis Major: Sirius. In the Labour, Apollodorus describes Cerberus as having, 'three heads of dogs, the tail of a dragon, and on his back the heads of all sorts of snakes.' It's therefore fascinating to note that the star Sirius is at least a binary star system and possibly a triple star system. In other words, it may be three-headed. There are clues to what the other properties of Cerberus mean, but they're too involved to describe here. For a fuller account, please read my book *Ancient Secrets, Future Warning*.

It would seem, based on these examples, that Brown was right. The Greek Myths are encoded information. Rather than being fanciful tales, they are Method of Loci stories designed to enable someone to memorise advanced knowledge about star systems.

If this is correct, then two facts stand out. Firstly, all the stars mentioned are relatively close to us. Secondly, they include information that our astronomers only discovered in the last half-century. In the case of a third star in the Sirius system, astronomers aren't even sure if this is true; they don't have sufficient information to work it out. It is therefore astonishing that priests and philosophers, thousands of years ago, knew this information. Logically, there are very few ways that they could have obtained such information. Perhaps the most likely is that they gained the information from technologically advanced aliens.

Brown's clue adds another piece of evidence that seems to indicate that alien gods arrived here on Earth, set up our civilization, and imparted knowledge to a select few humans. This knowledge didn't just include how to run a civilization, as described in the Book of Enoch. It also included advanced technical information about neighbouring star systems. A human power-elite obtained this knowledge and kept it to themselves, maximising their knowledge so they could 'rule the people with a despotic power'. Millennia later, the Roman power-elite tried to destroy some of that incriminating information by destroying certain books, such as *the Book of Enoch* and *the Apocryphon of John*. Other pieces of information were left untouched as they seemed to be safe, in the eyes of the power-elite, since they were cleverly encoded, but as we can see, codes can be broken.

Fortunately, therefore, even in the face of deliberate efforts to destroy and hide information, it is possible to gather together evidence that supports the idea that aliens with advanced technology visited Earth and passed on their knowledge to humans. The possibility that they, or their descendants, are still here is supported by personal accounts from a variety of people, in particular the professional remote viewer Ingo Swann. According to his testimony, soulless bio-androids are mingling amongst us right now. This is a disturbing idea, and it's tempting to dismiss it for lack of supporting evidence, but there is a book that endorses such a claim. Not only does this book state that soulless bio-android aliens from Orion's Belt are here, it also explains their origins, and their agenda.

Interim Summary

According to what we've seen so far in this book, it seems that soulless aliens, possessing advanced technological skills, particularly genetic engineering skills (the Archons or Watchers), left a planet in the Orion's Belt star group (the home of the Nephilim) and came to Earth in spaceships, or Harbu (as Anton Parks discovered in his Sumerian translations). When these aliens arrived here, they found Earth to be a quiet, undeveloped planet. They landed in the mountains of Eastern Turkey (Edin, according to Parks' research) and built a compound. They seemed to be relatively clueless about Earth's natural world, which may indicate that they fled to this planet, rather than coming here as part of a long-term plan. Their ignorance can be seen in their brute-force plan to feed themselves by ploughing up the ground in their compound and growing wheat. It's reasonable to think that any advanced, interstellar species should be able to feed themselves with hydroponics or something more sophisticated, and yet these aliens dug up the ground instead. They didn't want to do this arduous work themselves, and so they made (or created) a subservient race, the Igigi, to do it for them. The Igigi eventually became sick of the work, and rebelled. The alien gods, in response, created another subservient race: Homo Sapiens. After creating us, whom they called A-DAM, or wild beasts, they discovered something shocking: we were superior to them (according to *the Apocryphon of John*). They realised that we were spiritual, 'shining' beings, unlike them, who were not. Feeling inferior and threatened, these soulless or spiritless aliens devised a nasty plan. They decided to abusively control us, their subjects (from the Latin 'sub jacere', to 'throw under'). They proceeded to drug us, lie to us, indoctrinate us, and keep us weak and ill, just like a toxic landowner in control of a remote, rural compound. By doing this, they could make sure we never reached our potential and threatened their position of power.

The idea that the gods were soulless monsters who created, then abused and gaslighted us, is a grim story; it's worthy of a horror sci-fi movie, but it also has its farcical side. They weren't just amoral and cruel, they were stupid too. Not only were they relatively clueless about Earth - to the point of having to make their own food and manually sticking it in the ground - they were also clueless about life. They created us without anticipating that we'd have a spiritual core. In that sense, their story is less like *The Powers of the Elder Gods* and more like *Dumb Androids Run Away From Home and Accidentally Make Real People*. This latter description may be the most accurate, for a book explains their origins in detail, and it is both tragic and farcical.

Amicizia

In 2009, the Italian engineer Stefano Breccia published a book: *Mass Contacts*. In his book, he reports on an extensive, decades-long interaction between many Europeans - Italians, Germans, and a few Russians – and at least one humanoid, alien race living on Earth. Breccia's account is, on the face of it, incredible. It's hard to believe that such a large-scale interaction between Europeans and aliens wouldn't have made it into the mainstream press but, as he explains with printed evidence, some of the events he describes *did* make it into the Italian press. Unfortunately, as is often the case with UFO reports, much of the media didn't want to touch the subject and it was quickly forgotten.

Breccia's book is split into two parts. In the first half, he describes encounters with an alien group referred to as the Ummites. Unfortunately, I found this part of the book implausible and most likely to be a form of disinformation. I don't think Breccia knowingly propagated a falsehood. Instead, it seems more likely that he simply felt duty-bound to report these encounters, however dubious they might appear. Readers can come to their own conclusions on this matter when they read his book.

In the second half of Breccia's book, things become much more interesting when he describes his repeated encounters with members of another alien race, a race acting in the spirit of Amicizia (friendship). To quote from his book (pg 166):

"(Author: Let me make a short introduction to what follows: Bruno is going to relate some of his experiences with some alleged extra-terrestrials; they said they belonged to a kind of Federation of many different planets. Bruno gave them the collective of 'W56'. They have been on our planet for millennia. In Italy, they had built a huge underground base, very deep and very large, extending from the middle of the Adriatic Sea, westward to central Italy, and ranging from Ortona northward up to Rimini; its ceiling was 300 metres high, and its global volume was so great that it often rained inside! Of course, there were many other, small bases, nearer to the surface. These (alien) people were hostile towards another race, whose 'people' were a kind of biological robot; Bruno had named these beings the CTRs [a vague term, short for Contrarian or Opposers]."

Breccia explains that the W56's, the friendly aliens, are non-violent vegetarians. They are around ten-feet tall in height, or thereabouts. He includes a picture of one of them in the book. The man looks normal enough to pass unremarked in human society, except for his great height. Breccia's alien friends talk extensively to him, throughout the book, about their activities on Earth and the presence of another alien race, a group they refer to as the bio-android CTRs. The friendly, W56 aliens explain that the bio-android CTRs are indistinguishable from normal humans, even down to the biological level. The CTRs have only one identifiable difference: the flesh at the outer edge of their eyes doesn't have the almond shape we possess, but a circular overlap. The CTRs often wear sunglasses to hide this difference (It's a description that seems to belong in a sci-fi story, like the old TV series *Invaders* but, nevertheless, that was their statement). They also explain to Breccia where the CTR bio-androids came from, and how they came into existence. To quote from the book:

> "These robots (bio-androids) started evolving in... a star in the Centaurus constellation. They are the result of an experiment that has run out of control. They are robots, in the full meaning of this word, even if centuries ago, they have started an activity of biological reproduction... They are artificial creatures, and they remain as such, even if nobody amongst your physicians would be able to discriminate. Their main goal is trying to fill the gap between them and natural races, and therefore they are studying... To them it is a matter of vital importance. They have an extremely high culture in biology. The experiment that gave birth to these robots has been made by a natural man, who unfortunately, died while trying to stop the process. Therefore, the bio-androids are Sons of Man, as your Bible states."

Breccia's alien friend's explanation fits with what we've already learned in *The Apocryphon of John* and *the Book of Enoch*. Both of these books report that the gods who created civilization were masters of genetic engineering and biology. *The Apocryphon of John* also makes it clear that these ancient gods were soulless, that they didn't 'shine', a description that would fit an alien race of bio-androids or bio-robots.

At this point, it's worth asking: Are these CTRs really the ancient gods described in *the Book of Enoch* and *the Apocryphon of John*? According to the W56 aliens, these bio-androids, or CTRs, present on Earth now, are almost indistinguishable from us. This clashes with evidence we've looked at earlier in this book, which stated that the gods who created us were nine-foot-tall, hairless beings with elongated heads, the so-called Nephilim. To explain this difference, it's worth noting that the W56 aliens stated that the CTRs 'started an activity of biological reproduction, centuries ago'. It therefore seems possible that these modern, CTR bio-androids, described in Breccia's book, are simply the latest generation of a soulless, bio-android reproduction programme, one that started a very long time ago by creatures who were physically very different. It's little more than speculation, but it's logical.

Dr Frankenstein (Wikipedia commons – Hammer Horror films / Columbia pictures)

If Breccia's alien friend is correct, then the CTRs' origin is a strange and tragic tale, one very similar to

Mary Shelley's famous gothic science-fiction classic, *Frankenstein*, in which a brilliant but misguided scientist makes a flawed creature that turns around and destroys him. This idea is timelessly compelling. For example, it was reworked as a science fiction story in the classic film *Bladerunner*, in which replicants, or artificially created humans, return to Earth, desperate to lengthen their artificially shortened lives. In the film, their leader confronts the genetics expert who designed them, with tragic results.

Breccia's alien friends state that a group of gods, in our distant past, around a nearby star, killed their own parent or creator, and then used his genetic engineering skills to make their own, ultimately flawed creations on Earth. This is a dramatic and compelling idea. It also correlates with at least one Greek Myth. For example, one of the earliest Greek Myths tells the tale of the god Cronus. Cronus killed his own father, Uranus, then cut off his father's testicles (which may have symbolised his father's 'ability to create new life'). To quote Wikipedia, after that murderous act:

> 'from the blood that spilled out from Uranus and fell upon the earth, the Gigantes (Giants), Erinyes (Vengeful, violent Furies), and Meliae (Nymphs) were produced.'

In other words, Cronus's act of killing his father caused the creation of a host of dangerous beings, including giants, who then populated the Earth, causing great strife. This tallies well with the evidence we've seen so far.

The W56 aliens in Breccia's book don't just tell him about the origins of the bio-android CTRs, they also give him a list of the inhabited star-systems in our galactic neighbourhood. On page 292 of the book, it states that the stars are:

> Capella (Alpha Auriga), Arcturus (Alpha Bootis), Shedir (Alpha Cassopeiae), Aldebaran (Alpha Tauri), Mirach (Alpha Andromedae), Albireo (Beta Cygni), Pollux (Beta Gemini), Kochab (Beta Ursa Minor), Altais (Delta Draconis), Almaaz (Epsilon Aurigae), Tyl (Epsilon Draconis), Ain (Epsilon Tauri), Alcyone (Eta Tauri), Edasich (Iota Draconis) and Taigete (19 Tauri).

Several of these star-systems correlate with the decoded Greek Myths list, mentioned earlier. They also partly correlate with a list of inhabited stars that I assembled during my research of further Greek Myths, in my book *Ancient Secrets, Future Warning*. They are:

> Thuban (Alpha Draconis), Kochab (Beta Ursa Minor) Sirius (Alpha Canis Majoris), Fawaris (Delta Cygni), Vega (Alpha Lyrae), Rukbat Al Rami (Alpha Sagittarii), Muliphen (Gamma Ophiuchi), Rijl Al Qanturus (Alpha Centauri). Orion's Belt (Alnitak, Alnilam and Mintaka), Aldebaran (Alpha Tauri).

Many of these stars aren't just represented in the decoded Greek Myths, according to my research they also exhibit mysterious infra-red and x-ray emissions, whose origins are unclear to astronomers.

The W56 aliens in Breccia's book also state which stars are inhabited by the bio-androids. They are:

> Delta Pavonis, Alnilam (Epsilon Orionis on Orion's Belt), Epsilon Ursa Minor, Zeta Orion (Alnitak on Orion's Belt), Tau Ceti and 61 Cygnus.

It therefore seems, at least according to the W56 aliens, that the CTR aliens may be the same race as the Archon gods, as both are soulless bio-androids *and* both came from Orion's Belt, the home of the Nephilim or Fallen Giants.

The W56 aliens also warn Breccia about the agenda and capabilities of the CTR bio-androids. They explain that the CTRs are active on Earth right now, and that they have been experimenting on the human race for a long time:

> "Mankind is the object of their research. In practice, they try to experiment on the people who are so weak to be unable to defend themselves, or not even realise that they are in danger. The evil that your priests speak about actually does not exist, because it is foreign to human nature. Only when a man tries to give up, even only in part, his nature, then he acquires part of the features of the bio-androids, and of people like them, and that is evil; the dualism exists between who is human and who is not."

The W56 aliens' comment, that 'the evil that your priests speak about actually does not exist, because it is foreign to human nature' matches what was said in *The Apocryphon of John*. Both comments make it clear that we are not fundamentally evil or flawed. In other words, the religious idea that we are fundamentally sinful is wrong. In fact, the W56 aliens and *the Apocryphon of John* both state that we are 'naked of evil', because we shine with spirit. It is only when we allow ourselves to slide down to an amoral level, the level inhabited by the bio-androids - the Archon gods in the apocryphal texts - that we take on an evil nature. If we do that, then we literally become inhumane. In that sense, the bio-androids, or the Archon gods, are truly the Devil: they are the evil presence tempting us to become amoral. This is ironic, since it would mean that the collective 'god' that created us is also its religious antithesis, the collective 'devil'. This paradox would explain why Lucifer, the Devil who brought fire to Humanity, was identified by some sources as an angel. To quote from Wikipedia:

> "In the Bogomil and Cathar text *Gospel of the secret supper*, Lucifer is a glorified angel but fell from heaven to establish his own kingdom and became the Demiurge. Therefore, he created the material world and trapped souls from heaven inside matter. Jesus descended to earth to free the captured souls."

In other words, we are in the clutches of a lesser being who pretended to be the Creator of the Universe but in fact only created the physical world we see around us. This demiurge (literally 'worker of people') fashioned our physical bodies and has kept us blind to the fact that he *isn't* the Ultimate Deity and that there is far more to reality than this physical realm.

Another Medieval group that believed strongly in the demiurge were the Cathars, a renegade Christian group based in the Languedoc region of Southern France. The Cathars were mostly vegetarian, included women in senior roles and lived modest, non-violent lives, at least until the Catholic Church ordered that they all be exterminated, in the infamous Albigensian Crusade. Entire Cathar towns were massacred and many Cathars were burnt at the stake. The Vatican's actions probably encouraged the Cathars' belief that it was an instrument of the demiurge.

The ancient Archons seem to perform the role of the demiurge (Lucifer), the Light Bringer, very well. According to *the Apocryphon of John*, those ancient, soulless gods did abusively control us, and keep our ancestors blind to the fact that we are much more than physical beings, and that reality is much more than the physical world we see around us. If descendants of those Archons are still around today, then we truly are stuck in an ongoing trial, where we must choose between ignorance, greed, fear, and violence on the one hand, and knowledge, gnosis and compassion on the other. History tells us that choosing the right path, especially en masse, could get us killed – just look at the Cathars – but that is probably an important part of the challenge.

It seems, according to these various testimonies, that we're in a serious drama. According to Breccia's friendly W56 aliens, we're running around, working away, buying things and getting drunk at the bar, while soulless aliens are studying us, and prodding us in various directions without our knowledge, in order to find the nature of the soul. It is both tragic, and blackly humorous. It's an idea redolent of Douglas Adams' science-fiction comedy novel, *The Hitch-hiker's Guide to the Galaxy*.

In *the Hitch-hiker's Guide to the Galaxy*, its main character, Arthur Dent, discovers that Earth has been run by mice for thousands of years, in their bid to discover the Ultimate Question to Life, the Universe and Everything (The Ultimate Answer has already been worked out – it's '42' – but the Ultimate Question is much trickier). In order to solve this conundrum, long ago, the mice commissioned the construction of an organic, living planet: Earth. Arthur is shocked to discover this fact, and that they have been studying humans for millennia, rather than the other way around. He's even more shocked to discover that they want his brain, as it might hold the answer to their search. Arthur's not keen on losing his brain, but the mice do offer to replace it with an electronic one. They also point out that he wouldn't notice the difference, as he'd be programmed not to. Arthur's companion, Zaphod Beeblebrox, thinks this is a great idea. At the end of the day, Zaphod comments, if the electronic brain just said, 'I don't understand', 'sorry' and 'where's the tea?', who'd notice the difference?

The idea that our civilization is being influenced by soulless bio-android aliens isn't very nice. It also sounds implausible. Surely, over time, such a group would be found out? Alternatively, even *if* these horrible robot aliens wanted to control seven billion people, surely they wouldn't be able to exert much influence? Unfortunately, as we've already seen in this book, our civilization's setup makes it relatively easy for a secret group to gain huge control. Our civilization's combination of hierarchies, top-down recruiting, shareholding, and banking leverage makes it very easy for a group to gain massive financial control. This group can then use this control to populate the boardrooms and executive offices of multiple corporations. Earlier in this book, we examined this issue. We focussed particularly on secret societies, but the idea works just as well for alien bio-androids. Georgina Bruni reports on just such a plan in her UFO book, *You can't tell the people*, she. To quote again from the text:

> "Much to his amazement, he [the remote viewer Kane] learned that he was being programmed to get inside the minds of others, and his first target was to be the president of a large American company. The idea was to plant Kane inside the company to disrupt the target's mind, destabilizing him so that he would have to resign. He would them be replaced by one of their own people."

It therefore seems possible for a group of alien bio-androids to control our civilization, but would they be able to maintain this control? If this was a sci-fi movie, then, in the third act, us brave humans would realise our situation, then the bravest of us would lead a rebellion; we'd all bravely rise up against the alien overlords and achieve our freedom, along with much cheering and the hero and heroine kissing. Then again, that is a movie. In real life, as the W56 aliens point out, we may not actually be that kind of people. As we've already seen in this Part, the W56 aliens commented that the CTR bio-androids. 'try to experiment on the people who are so weak to be unable to defend themselves, or not even realise that they are in danger'; in other words, us. This seems an unnecessarily harsh indictment of our species, but sadly, there may be some truth in it. Our media usually portrays us as being an impressive species, filled with intelligence, compassion and heroic courage, but many psychology experiments paint a different picture. According to their results, a large proportion of us are weak, compliant, uncaring and cruel.

Conformity

Earlier in this book, we studied the Stanford Prison Experiment, and discovered that it showed a deep weakness in human character. Sadly, it is not the only experiment that puts human beings in a bad light.

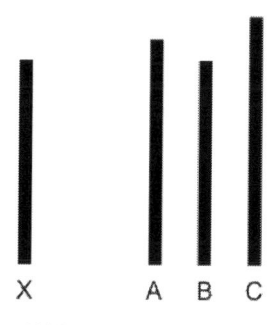

Which line on the right is
the same length as X?

For example, In 1951, the psychologist Solomon Asch decided to study human compliance. In other words, he wanted to find out how willing, or unwilling, people were to contradict their fellow humans. To do this, he set up an experiment. In it, five people were asked to sit in a room and take a test. The test was absurdly simple – stating which line, of a choice of three, matched a reference line - but there was a twist. Four of the five people in the room had been planted by the experimenters and told to state the wrong answer. The fifth person, who always spoke last in each test, was therefore faced with a dilemma: should he, or she, openly state the correct answer, and thereby publicly contradict everyone else in the room, or go along with the group and state something was blatantly the wrong answer? Asch discovered that over a third of the subjects in his experiment stated the wrong answer, in order to conform to the group.

The Asch Conformity experiment shows that a third of us are basically spineless. Another classic psychology experiment showed something even worse, that we're willing to kill someone else, just to obey instructions from officialdom.

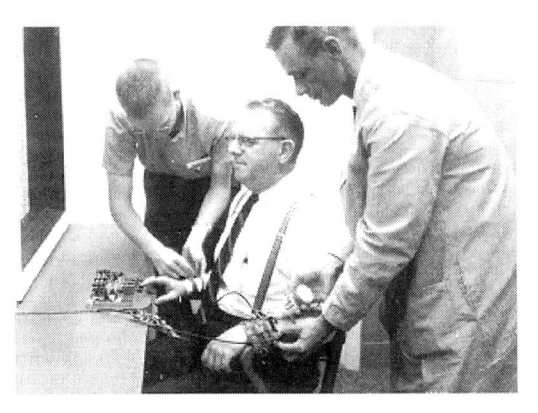

Milgram's Experiment (various sources)

In 1961, Stanley Milgram decided to find out how much pain and suffering people would carry out, on another person, simply because they were told to by a senior figure. He was inspired to do this after seeing the horrors of the Nazi concentration camps in the Second World War. He wondered if those monstrosities occurred because they were done by Nazis, or because it was part of a deeper problem, a basic aspect of human nature. He set up an experiment to answer this question. In the experiment, subjects were invited to help in a 'motivation learning study'. They were instructed to give someone in another room a series of questions and give the person an electric shock every time they got a question wrong. After each mistake by the 'student' in the other room, the subjects were told to increase the shock level. In truth, the 'student' in the other room wasn't being shocked, they were only faking it, but their shouts and yells were convincing.

Stanley Milgram assumed, before starting the experiment, that his test subjects would only administer minor shocks to the 'student' and then refuse to continue, out of concern for their victim. Instead, he found, to his horror, that 65 percent of the test subjects went as far as administering the experiment's final, massive 450-volt shock, which they knew could kill the 'student' in the other room. In other words, two-thirds of them knowingly administered a potentially lethal-level shock to another person, purely as part of a learning experiment.

In the decades since Stanley Milgram conducted his infamous experiment, psychologists and social commentators have done their best to discount and discredit what he discovered, for understandable reasons. Unfortunately for them, in 2010, a French television producer showed the validity of Milgram's results by creating a game show. To quote from the

Wikipedia page:

> "The experiment was performed in the guise of a game show known as *La Zone Xtrême*. Volunteers were given €40 to take part as contestants in a "pilot" for the fictitious show, where they had to administer increasingly stronger electric shocks to trained actors posing as players as punishment for incorrect answers, as encouraged to do so by the host and audience. Only 16 of 80 'contestants' chose to end the game before delivering the highest voltage punishment."

The creator of the show, Christophe Nick, stated in interviews that he wanted to demonstrate the power of television. To quote from a Today.com article:

> "Television is a power. We know it, but it's theoretical," producer Christophe Nick told the daily Le Parisien. "I wondered: Is it so important that it can turn us into potential executioners?"

It therefore seems that Milgram's Experiment, the Stanford Prison Experiment, and Asch's Conformity Experiment do confirm the W56 aliens' implied comment that we are ripe for being exploited. They stated that the bio-androids choose people 'who are so weak to be unable to defend themselves, or not even realise that they are in danger'. The idea that most of us are weak is borne out by psychology experiments that we've just studied. The idea that we don't even know that we're in danger is borne out by

John Burroughs frustration to inform people that UFOs do exist, and what he saw in Rendlesham forest that night was real. It's similar the ending of the black and white original version of *Invasion of the Body Snatchers*, where the hero frantically warns everyone of the menace in their midst, but they just think he's mad (only without the frenetic background music).

Breccia asked his W56 alien friends why they didn't intervene to stop the CTR bio-androids' manipulation of Homo Sapiens by openly visiting Earth. The aliens replied that they couldn't intervene because a direct appearance, by far more technologically advanced aliens, would shatter human beings' self-image and identity. Instead, the W56 aliens were doing their best to educate and support some humans; ones who were more able to deal with alien contact. The aliens also pointed out that the challenges and temptations facing the human race, partly brought on by the CTR bio-androids, were part of a spiritual challenge for the human race. The situation we're all in, they explained, was an opportunity for us all to do the right thing, to act courageously, selflessly, and develop spiritually. Breccia explains, on page 242:

> "They [the W56's] call our Earth 'The Universal Centre for Redemption' because they believe that the souls who get incarnated over this planet are the ones who have yet to fulfil their evolution. That's why there are so many sufferings, but at the same time also so much success may be found. Moreover, Earth is one of the most beautiful and most complete planets. Its history is much longer than the

one we are acquainted with. It has seen many more civilizations than our books tell."

The last sentence of the quote will probably not be a surprise to readers of authors such as Graham Hancock and Freddy Silva. As I explain in my book *Ancient Secrets, Future Warning*, there is ample evidence that a technologically advanced civilization existed on Earth in 15,000 BC.

The key part of the W56 aliens' comment is that our tough situation, here on Earth, is an important opportunity for us to develop as spiritual beings, to 'fulfil our evolution'. This idea is not new. For example, the philosopher Friedrich Nietzsche thought extensively about it. He realised that an easy, problem-free life was a disaster because it gave no opportunity for personal development. He wrote:

> "Examine the lives of the best and most fruitful people and peoples and ask yourselves whether a tree that is supposed to grow to a proud height can dispense with bad weather and storms; whether misfortune and external resistance, some kinds of hatred, jealousy, stubbornness, mistrust, hardness, avarice, and violence do not belong among the favourable conditions without which any great growth even of virtue is scarcely possible."

Friedrich Nietzsche

Nietzsche developed this idea further by talking about an Eternal Recurrence, in which a person might be forced to experience the same life, over and over again. At first, the person might think it was an eternal Hell, but then he or she might realise that they could turn it into an eternal Heaven. As Nietzsche writes in *The Gay Science*:

> "What, if some day or night a demon were to steal after you into your loneliest loneliness and say to you: 'This life as you now live it and have lived it, you will have to live once more and innumerable times more' ... Would you not throw yourself down and gnash your teeth and curse the demon who spoke thus? Or have you once experienced a tremendous moment when you would have answered him: 'You are a god and never have I heard anything more divine.'"

Nietzsche's idea of Eternal Recurrence is clever and profound. It's so good that it was later turned into the classic film *Groundhog Day*, in which a grumpy weatherman, played by Bill Murray, is locked in an endless re-living of the same day. At first, Murray's character hates the quaint town he's stuck in - Punxsutawney, Pennsylvania - but as time goes by, he realises that there's nothing wrong with the place, it's *him* that's the problem. He decides to improve himself and, eventually, he becomes truly happy in the very place he hated. He no longer minds return to the same day, over and over again, because it becomes another opportunity to improve himself, rather than curse it as a prison.

Groundhog Day shows that something seemingly awful can, on another level, be valuable for one's spiritual development. This is probably what the W56 aliens were getting at when they call Earth, 'The Universal Centre for Redemption'. According to them, we're choosing to take on this challenge, of living here on Earth, out of duty, but also because it will give us a chance to improve and do the right thing. We're incarnating on this planet, in this toxic, abusive, alien-bio-android-controlled prison, in order to better ourselves as spiritual beings. This sounds a bit masochistic, but it's also a compliment, of sorts. If we are choosing to do this, then we must be a brave and noble bunch to even incarnate here.

If we are choosing to be here, and deal with these difficulties for our own improvement, and our own sense of duty, then it would mean, in a strange sort of way, that the CTR bio-androids are fulfilling an important role. In other words, someone has to be the bad guy, just so that the rest of us, in our quest for spiritual improvement, can prove or test our courage, compassion, generosity, forgiveness etc in this 'Universal Centre for Redemption'. We should therefore be thankful towards those bio-android aliens for their important role, at least when we're not busily trying to escape their soulless, mechanical, abusive, Luciferian control.

The idea that our civilization, and ourselves, are being controlled by soulless alien bio-androids is therefore logical, possible, and supported by a variety of evidence. It is also seriously weird. It would be perfectly reasonable, for any of us, to put these ideas in a metaphorical box marked 'interesting idea', and carry on with our lives, but the problem with that approach is that if these ideas *are* correct, then that would mean that we would be ignoring an incredibly important issue with our entire species; we would be willingly ignoring our predicament, just as the W56 aliens warned. To paraphrase John Burroughs - the Rendlesham Forest UFO witness - 'this stuff is going on!' so we can't ignore it. It's a tricky dilemma. One way to deal with problem would be to do something that's seemingly harmless, and won't disrupt our lives, but one that could still check out if there *is* a problem. For example, we could try to improve our psychic abilities, since these seem to be what these malevolent alien overseers are most worried about. If we developed our psychic abilities, for example, by learning remote viewing, (while carefully keeping an eye out for malevolent beings with funny eyes, or their callous human servants), then we wouldn't be ignoring this alleged threat and we wouldn't have to radically alter our lives. We could have our cake and eat it, so to speak.

Whatever we decide to do, we need to do it soon. Our civilization, in its current form, can't go on much longer. We are in a deeply flawed system that has been exploiting the natural world; it has been callously burning down forests, ploughing up the soil, polluting waterways and leaving larger and larger amounts of waste in its wake. From the point of view of the wildlife of Earth, human civilization has been a monster, a spreading infection. We've now reached the stage where our civilization has tipped our entire planet's climate into a process of runaway breakdown. To put it bluntly: climate change is here and it's global crunch time. We're approaching a major reckoning, one which will probably catapult nearly all of us into social breakdown, starvation, war, and catastrophe. It sounds terrible, but it does have an upside: the breakdown of our current civilization-system might give us an opportunity to escape the control of our toxic overlords and create a new and better way to live. Will this happen? Will we seize this possible chance to find freedom, or instead plunge us into something even worse? That's the subject of Part 5.

Part 5: The Way Out

Introduction

This book, so far, has been a quest to investigate what civilization has been doing to us, and why. The results have been sobering, saddening, strange and, in the previous part of this book, downright bizarre, but some have been illuminating. Firstly, civilization is not an entirely lovely thing. It has not brought us prosperity, health, and happiness. Instead, civilized life, since its very beginning, has been filled with exhaustion, poor food, hard labour, alcohol, rampant diseases, illness, brutal oppression, cruel wars, overpopulation, pollution, refugees and growing environmental destruction. By comparison, the so-called primitive world of hunter-gatherers seems positively idyllic. We've also seen evidence that we've been lied to over many important issues. For example, our scientific establishment has been telling us that we're soulless bags of molecules with no mind, spirit or free will. They've also stated that we evolved from apes, two million years ago. These are both entirely wrong. Instead, we are immortal, spiritual beings, or minds, and we are simply living a physical life. We also can't have evolved from apes in two million years, or even twenty million years, as this is scientifically impossible. Instead, we are an artificial hybrid and, according to our ancient records, we were created by a technologically advanced, alien race. This isn't exactly pleasing news. It makes us look like the creatures in Jules Verne's dark tale *The Island of Dr Moreau* – freakish results of genetic experiments by a brilliant but deranged scientist – but that doesn't in any way stop us being a loving, intelligent, progressive species. We have free will. We can become what we wish; it's up to us, which is pretty good in anyone's book. The problem is, we'd better do this soon, because we're currently in big trouble. Due to multiple factors, our entire planet's ecosystem is collapsing. What are we going to do?

No more Eden

The science is clear about our near future. By the end of this century, civilization on Earth will have collapsed due to accelerating climate breakdown. This isn't stated in our media, but that's hardly surprising as our media is mostly owned by the same people who are profiting from the climate breakdown. We are already seeing the physical effects of this process. For example, this year (2021 AD), the province of British Columbia, in western Canada experienced a heatwave in its south-west that topped at an astonishing 49.6 Centigrade, or 121 Fahrenheit, smashing the previous record. Five months later, it then experienced record-breaking floods that killed around 640,000 animals and forced 17,000 people from their homes. These natural disasters are occurring more and more often. There are extreme wildfires in many states, along with mass die-offs of sea and coastal life. Tragically, according to the science, these disasters are just the start. To understand what we'll be experiencing in twenty-years-time, I recommend Gwynne Dyer's well-researched book *Climate Wars*.

I've mentioned *Climate Wars* already in this book, but let's examine it again. It was published in the 1990's, but its predictions, based on military and corporate studies, have so far been spot on. Here is its introduction:

SCENARIO ONE: THE YEAR 2045

Average global temperature: 2.8 degrees Celsius higher than 1990.

Global population: 5.8 billion.

Since the final collapse of the European Union in 2036, under the stress of mass migration from the southern to the northern members, the reconfigured Northern Union (France, Benelux, Germany, Scandinavia, Poland and the old Habsburg domains in central Europe) has succeeded in closing its borders to any further refugees from the famine-stricken Mediterranean countries. Italy, south of Rome, has been largely overrun by refugees from even harder-hit North African countries and is no longer part of an organised state, but Spain, Padania (northern Italy) and Turkey have all acquired nuclear weapons and are seeking (with little success) to enforce food sharing on the better-fed countries of northern Europe. Britain, which has managed to make itself just about self-sufficient in food by dint of a great national effort, has withdrawn from the continent and shelters behind its enhanced nuclear deterrent.

Russia, the greatest beneficiary of climate change in terms of food production, is the undisputed great power of Asia. However, the reunification of China after the chaos of the 2020s and 2030s poses a renewed threat to its Siberian borders, for even the much-reduced Chinese population of eight hundred million is unable to feed itself from the country's increasingly arid farmland, which was devastated by the decline of rainfall over the North Chinese plain and the collapse of the major river systems.

Southern India is re-emerging as a major regional power, but what used to be northern India, Pakistan and Bangladesh remain swept by famine and anarchy, due to the collapse of the flow in the glacier-fed Indus, Ganges and Brahmaputra rivers and the increasingly frequent failure of the monsoon. Japan, like Britain, has withdrawn from its continent and is an island of relative prosperity bristling with nuclear weapons. The population of the Islamic Republic of Arabia, which had risen to forty million, fell by half in five years after the exhaustion of the giant Ghawar oil field in 2020, and has since halved again due to the exorbitant price of what little food remains available for import from any source.

Uganda's population, 5 million at independence in 1962, reached 40 million in 2030 before falling back to 30 million, and the majority of its survivors are severely malnourished. Brazil and Argentina still manage to feed themselves, but Mexico has been expelled from the North American Free Trade Area, leaving the United States and Canada with just enough food and water to maintain at least a shadow of their former lifestyles. The Wall along the U.S.—Mexican border is still holding.

Human greenhouse-gas emissions temporarily peaked in 2032, at 47 per cent higher than

1990, due largely to the dwindling oil supply and the Chinese Civil War. However, the release of thousands of megatons of methane and carbon dioxide from the melting permafrost in Arctic Canada, Alaska and Siberia has totally overwhelmed human emissions cuts, and the process has slid beyond human ability to control. The combined total of human and 'neo-natural' greenhouse-gas emissions continues to rise rapidly, and the average global temperature at the end of the century is predicted to be 8 or 9 degrees Celsius higher than 1990.

Prognosis: Awful.

Since the publication of *Climate Wars*, global events have closely matched the book's predictions. Its only error so far, that I can see, is that it predicted that the giant Saudi Arabian Ghawar oil field would become exhausted by now, but this mistake is understandable, as Saudi Arabia has always been extremely secretive about the state of its oil resources.

The books *Six Degrees* by Mark Lynas and *Storms of Our Grandchildren*, by James Hansen paint a similar picture to Dwyer's. They echo Dyer's prediction that global civilization will have completely crashed by 2099 AD. By that date, only a tiny remnant of our current world population will be alive, hiding in protected domes or underground bases. Our future, on Earth, is therefore extremely bleak. The civilization that we've been living in for the last few thousand years, with its religion, soldiers, wheat, alcohol, sugar, meat, dehumanising specialisation, top-down hierarchies, secret societies, and money, will end. The fairground / prison camp we've been living in will be over. Will we be able to replace it with something better?

Logically, if the evidence in this book is correct, then we need to remove all the toxic or abusive elements in our civilization. Let's study them in turn and see what we can replace them with. First off: religion.

No more religion

For large numbers of people on Earth, their religion is their rock, their foundation of existence, their connection to the spiritual universe and their fellow humans. They may think that losing their religion would plunge them into an amoral, dark abyss, but according to what we've learnt so far in this book, removing religion wouldn't remove spirituality, or morality, regardless of what religious leaders might tell us. The idea that we're flawed beings that need religion to make us good is false; it's a form of abusive control. Instead, goodness naturally arises in us because, at heart, we are spiritual, loving beings, as *the Apocryphon of John* explained. Some of us can fall into the temptation of negative behaviour, because we have free will, but it isn't religion that will rescue us from it, it's the love, support and kindness of other living things. For example, many people report that their lives were turned around through the love of an animal, a pet or wild creature, just as much as another person, or an institution.

Another fear that religious people may have, if we get rid of religion, is that we'll fall back on the scientific view of reality, which states that we're nothing but mechanistic bio-robots. This is understandable but, as we saw earlier in this book, this Scientific Materialist view is actually, scientifically impossible. The correct scientific view is that non-physical, organising and influencing minds, or spirits, *have* to exist in order for Life to overcome the disorganising effects of entropy. If we fall back on correct science, then our spiritual state is actually enhanced, rather than diminished. What's more, if we apply this correct scientific view, then we can also establish the existence of a Creator Spirit.

According to science, our universe began as a chaotic mass of fundamental particles. After that, our universe slowly turned into stars and planets. Such a process, going from chaotic disorder into order, defies the Law of Entropy, since the Law of Entropy states that all physical system must become more disorganised over time. The famous pioneer of thermodynamics, Ludwig Boltzmann, spotted this problem a century ago and it's now known as Boltzmann's Well-Ordered Universe Problem. The only logical way to solve Boltzmann's Well-Ordered Universe Problem is to conclude, just as with Life, that a non-physical, influencing and ordering presence must have existed at the beginning of time, and has been present ever since. This organising Presence turned the primal chaos into stars and planets. Minds, therefore, don't just create Life, one also created and sustains the universe.

We can therefore conclude, scientifically, that a mind, an organising non-physical presence, created the universe and has sustained it ever since. This presence influences everything; it has always existed and will always exist. It is also the source of all existence. Some might call this being God but, as we've seen in this book, such a term is inextricably bound up to a wrathful male overlord, an abusive controller. The term is also linked to a demiurge and soulless, bio-android aliens, and so it makes sense for us to look for another word to use. Fortunately, the being that must have created the universe has already been given several names, by ancient civilization in various continents of Earth. For example, in *the Apocryphon of John*, Christ describes the Primal Presence or Original Mind as follows:

> 'The Inexpressible One. The One rules all. Nothing has authority over it. It is the God. It is Father of everything, Holy One, The invisible one over everything. It is uncontaminated. Pure light no eye can bear to look within. The One is the Invisible Spirit. It is not right to think of it as a God or as like God. It is more than just God. Nothing is above it. Nothing rules it. Since everything exists within it. It does not exist within anything. Since it is not dependent on anything, it is eternal. It is absolutely complete and so needs nothing. It is utterly perfect Light. The One is without boundaries. Nothing exists outside of it to border it. The One cannot be investigated. Nothing exists apart from it to investigate it. The One cannot be measured. Nothing exists external to it to measure it. The One cannot be seen, for no one can envision it. The One is eternal, for it exists forever. The One is inconceivable, for no one can comprehend it. The One is indescribable, for no one can put

any words to it. The One is infinite light, Purity, Holiness, Stainless. The One is incomprehensible. Perfectly free from corruption. Not "perfect", not "blessed", not "divine", but superior to such concepts. Neither physical nor unphysical. Neither immense nor infinitesimal. It is impossible to specify in quantity or quality, for it is beyond knowledge. The One is not a being among other beings; it is vastly superior, but it is not "superior." It is outside of realms of being and time, for whatever is within realms of being was created, and whatever is within time had time allotted to it. The One receives nothing from anything. It simply apprehends itself in its own perfect light. The One is majestic. The One is measureless majesty, chief of all Realms, producing all realms, Light producing light, Life producing life, Blessedness producing blessedness, Knowledge producing knowledge, Good producing goodness, Mercy producing mercy, Generous producing generosity [It does not "possess" these things.] It gives forth light beyond measure, beyond comprehension.'

This description is profound and detailed. It also matches a description in one of China's oldest religions, or philosophical traditions: Taoism.

Taoism's first scriptures were written in around 500 BC but it's highly likely that they were based on oral teachings that had already been passed around, in that region, for centuries. Taoism's most famous book is the Tao Te Ching, a collection of many Taoist statements about life, people, happiness, reality and the Creator Spirit, known as the Tao. The book's title literally means 'the book (ching) of Tao, the Primal Force and Te, the way to live'. The Tao Te Ching is said to have been written by a wise man called Lao Tsu. The story goes that Lao Tsu was heading into the mountains to die, tired at the ways of mankind, when a border guard stopped him. The guard begged Lao Tsu to write down his wisdom for future generations. Lao Tsu agreed and thus we have the book. In truth, it is more likely that the book was a compilation of many writers' views and was amassed over a long period of time, but it makes for a good story.

The Tao Te Ching begins by describing the Tao, the Source, the Primal Spirit, etc, as follows:

> "The Tao that can be described is not the eternal Tao. Origin of Heaven and Earth, it is the mother of myriad things. In tranquil thought, one observes its essence. In material reality, one observes its manifestations. Its unity is its mystery. It is the door to all wonders. The Tao is empty, yet inexhaustible, the source of all creation. It is the preface to existence."

As we can see, the Tao is very similar to the One described by Christ in *the Apocryphon of John*. Both beings are infinite, indescribable, non-gender, and non-species, as well as being the source of love, compassion, and creation.

There is also a third description that closely matches these first two. It comes from another ancient civilization - Ancient Egypt – and a particular book: *The Hermetica*. According to legend, *The*

Hermetica was written by the Ancient Egyptian god Thoth, who was said to have started out as a mortal man but was elevated to the ranks of the gods because of his achievements. Thoth was known by the Ancient Greeks as Hermes Trismegistus. He was often depicted, in Egyptian hieroglyphic inscriptions, as a man with the head of an ibis; a marsh bird that lived in the Egyptian Nile Delta. It could be said that he was the first scientist-engineer on Earth. The actual age of *The Hermetica* is unknown. Evidence indicates that the copies of it we now possess are copied from older copies, and so on. These copies have been preserved and passed around over many generations, and it's clear that the book is very old. For example, pyramid inscriptions written in 2500 BC, at Saqqara in Egypt, match some of the book's text, word for word, and so the book's origins must be at least that old, and possibly much older. The best we can say is that someone wrote at least some of the book's content more than four-and-a-half thousand years ago.

The text of *the Hermetica* revolves around an adept. He acts as a narrator during the book. As the book progresses, he receives instruction from a wise individual. In one chapter entitled 'The Initiation of Hermes', the adept describes a visionary encounter in which he is shown how Atom (or Atum), the primal god of the Egyptians, created the universe:

> "I saw in thought limitless power within the Light, to form an infinite yet ordered world. I saw in the darkness of the deep, chaotic waters without form, permeated with a subtle intelligent breath of divine power. Atom's

Word fell on the fertile waters making them pregnant with all forms. Ordered by the harmony of the calming Word, calming the chaotic waters, the four elements came into being."

The elements of Atom's creative act are then described:

"The Light - the Mind of Atom - existed before the chaotic waters of potentiality. The Light's calming Word is its son - the idea of beautiful order, the harmony of all things with all things. Atom is the parent of the Word, just as in your own experience, your human mind gives birth to speech."

The person granting the vision then says:

"You have perceived the boundless primal idea, which is before the beginning. By Atom's will, the elements of nature were born as reflections of this primal thought in the waters of potentiality. These are the primary things, the prior things, the first principles of all in the universe. Atom's Word is the creative idea - the supreme limitless power which nurtures and provides for all the things that through it are created."

The Hermetic also talks about the nature of Atom:

"To conceive of Atom is difficult, to define Atom is impossible. Atom is whole and constant. Atom is motionless, yet self-moving, immaculate, incorruptible and everlasting.

> Atom is hidden, yet obvious everywhere. Atom's nature can only be known through thought alone, yet we see Atom's form before our eyes. Atom is bodiless yet embodied in everything. Atom is the root and source of all."

As we can see, this description of Atom agrees with the description of the Tao, as well as the One described by Christ in *the Apocryphon of John*.

The fact that these three ancient sources describe effectively the same idea isn't that surprising, as it a logical consequence of the science we examined earlier. It also leads to an interesting question. We are alive and we experience the world as independent beings. As this is the case, it begs the question: are our minds separate to this Primal Mind? On the face of it, we seem separate to each other, so it would make sense to conclude that the Primal Mind is separate to us... but there's a twist. We've already seen in this book that experiments show, in the fields of remote viewing and telepathy, that we are fundamentally linked to each other, and everything in existence. This indicates that we do exist as individuals at one level, particularly our conscious level, but at a deeper level, we're not separate at all from each other. Instead, we're part of a Unity. This would explain the experience of many people, when they have a Near Death Experience, Hallucinogenic Experience or Deep Meditation Experience, that we are ultimately all One. If this is true, then all of us, and every living thing throughout the universe, are part of, members of, and constituents of a Unity, one that spans reality and in fact *makes* reality. The whole of reality is therefore a physical manifestation of the

One, Atom, the Tao or the Unity, whichever word you'd prefer to use, and we are part of that Unity.

Our new description of the Creator – the One, the Tao or the Unity – gives us a wonderful, non-gender, non-patriarchal, non-judgemental, pantheistic source to existence and ourselves. The next step would be to think about how we behave, as spiritual beings connected to the Unity. For starters, since we are fundamentally good, all negative behaviour is a sickness, rather than an indication of evil. As a result, we should treat all negative behaviour by other people as a sickness, one that needs help, support, and healing. Secondly, since we are all One, if we direct any violence or negativity at others, we're therefore, at a deeper level, attacking part of ourselves. If you hit someone, for example, for any reason, then you are, at a deep spiritual level, hitting yourself. This, logically, is a stupid and self-defeating thing to do. It's as if our current way to deal with a leg-cramp is to stab ourselves. All violence, hate and aggression is, therefore, an indication of sickness and, ultimately, a form of self-harm.

There is also the matter of worldly goods. Since we're all immortal beings, according to science and ancient records, then our physical bodies are only a temporary manifestation or vessel that we inhabit. All physical assets - property, luxury goods etc – are even more ephemeral, so it makes no sense to obsess after them, or sacrifice one's mental state to amass them, as they're just temporary constructions. By comparison, our knowledge of what we've done won't go, as it's part of our spiritual state. When we die, we'll lose the physical trappings, but we'll keep our knowledge of what we've done. This could lead to terrible, endless guilt, depending on how we conducted our life. This, in a way, would be Hell, and one from which we can't escape. The only way to avoid such a fate would be to do the right thing in our lives, just so that we could live with ourselves. As the philosopher and logician Bertrand Russell once said:

> "My whole religion is this: do every duty, and expect no reward for it, either here or hereafter."

By doing the right thing *because* we know it's the right thing to do, we would escape the Hell of guilt. We would also escape the Hell of being a person who didn't help others, etc.

It's relatively easy to talk about doing the right thing, and a lot harder to carry it out. Fortunately, if we cast aside the elements of civilization that drag us down – alcohol, overwork, poor food, propaganda etc – then we will become calmer, healthier, and happier people. This positive state should help us find the time, and ability, to clear our minds. By doing so, we can then turn these spiritual ideas into a way of life.

Some might say that developing one's own moral state might sound nice, but the only way to really make sure people behave correctly is to give them moral laws. According to many people, without moral laws, everyone inevitably sinks into amorality. This view is based on the religious idea that people are fundamentally amoral and sinful. As we've seen in this book, this idea is wrong and is a deception created to subjugate us and make us more compliant. What's more, the idea that religious people are more moral than non-religious people is not borne out by evidence. In fact, studies that show that non-religious people - ones who don't vow to follow any official moral code - are, in fact, *more* understanding than religious people. For example, the Guardian newspaper article, *Religious children are meaner than their secular counterparts, study finds* (6th Nov 2015), begins by saying that 'Children from religious families are less kind and more punitive than those from non-religious households, according to a new study.' To quote from the article:

> 'Academics from seven universities across the world studied Christian, Muslim and non-religious children to test the relationship between religion and morality. They found that religious belief is a negative influence on children's altruism. "Overall, our findings ... contradict the common sense and popular assumption that children from religious households are more altruistic and kind towards others," said the authors of *The Negative Association Between Religiousness and Children's Altruism Across the World*, published this week in *Current Biology*. "More generally, they call into question whether religion is vital for moral development, supporting the idea that secularisation of moral discourse will not reduce human kindness — in fact, it will do just the opposite."'

The article explains that twelve-hundred children, aged between five and twelve, from roughly a dozen countries participated in the study. They were asked to choose stickers and then told there were not enough to go round for all children in their school, to see if they would share. In another test, they were also shown film of children pushing and bumping one another to gauge their responses. To quote from the article:

> 'The findings "robustly demonstrate that children from households identifying as either of the two major world religions (Christianity and Islam) were less altruistic than children from non-religious households.". Older children, usually those with a longer exposure to religion, "exhibit[ed] the greatest negative relations". The study also found that "religiosity affects children's punitive tendencies". Children from religious households "frequently appear to be more judgmental of others' actions", it said. Muslim children judged "interpersonal harm as meaner" than children from Christian families, with non-religious children the least judgmental. Muslim children demanded harsher punishment than those from Christian or non-religious homes. At the same time, the report said that religious parents were more likely than others to consider their children to be "more empathetic and more sensitive to the plight of others".'

Based on this evidence, it seems that being religious doesn't make people more Christian, in the sense of following Christ's teachings of compassion, forgiveness, understanding and selfless behaviour. Instead, it does the opposite; it creates a feeling of superiority in them, along with a willingness to negatively judge others, as well as giving them a feeling entitled to punish others. It would therefore seem that if you worship a God who judges and punishes people with hellfire, you can end up treating others in a hostile, aggressively righteous way (Who'd have thought...?).

There is therefore a way for us all to lead spiritual, moral lives in the future and *not* have religions. This change would not only make us more rational in our view of the universe, in its creation, and ourselves, it would, most likely, also make us more compassionate, caring, and moral people.

Let's now move on to some more toxic elements of civilization and see how we can remove them too. One group we can bunch together: ploughed fields, wheat, meat, preserved meat, and dairy. The reason these can be treated as a group is because they all rely on large amounts of cleared land and, especially, fertile soil and a reliable supply of outside water. Unfortunately for us, that's all running out.

No more wheat, meat, or dairy

Earlier in this book, we saw the prediction, made by a PSI-TECH team of remote viewers, that we were on a one-way ticket to catastrophe. Their report was commissioned by a very senior U.S. politician and the Rockefellers, and it didn't make for pleasant viewing. Since they made their prediction, sadly, everything has pretty much followed what they described. Our weather has become increasingly extreme, crops are failing worldwide and in the next fifty years, the scientific evidence makes it clear that this trend will increase to an apocalyptic degree. As a result, our traditional system of growing crops, by clearing trees and ploughing the ground, will soon become impossible. The end of agriculture is therefore in sight, but in fact it would probably have happened without climate change. According to many studies, intensive agriculture has denuded our soils to a hopeless degree over the last few millennia. Ploughing soil up and planting seeds is far from an ideal system, as it continually degrades the soil. Humans have avoided this negative effect, historically, by finding more untouched land to farm, such as clearing woodland and draining swamps, or by clearing indigenous tribes off prairie land and ploughing up their prairies. More recently, as the amount of fresh, fertile land has shrunk, countries have used fossil fuels to create vast amounts of nitrate fertilizer. This innovation has temporarily increased yields, but it has also accelerated soil loss. As a result, worldwide agriculture might appear rosy, on the surface, but it's a ticking bomb. The Guardian article, *Third of Earth's soil is acutely degraded due to agriculture* (12th Sept 2017), reports on this matter. It begins by saying:

> 'A third of the planet's land is severely degraded and fertile soil is being lost at the rate of 24bn tonnes a year, according to a new United Nations-backed study that calls for a shift away from destructively intensive agriculture.'

It then discusses how nitrate fertilizers have increased yields but adds:

> 'Over time, however, this diminishes fertility and can lead to abandonment of land and ultimately desertification.'

A separate Guardian opinion article, *We're treating soil like dirt. It's a fatal mistake, as our lives depend on it,* exploring the same subject. It reports that 'there are only sixty to hundred harvests left', depending on where you are in the world. Once that happens, all farmland will eventually look the Oklahoma Dust Bowl disaster, where over-use of the region's thin soils caused them literally to blow away.

Buried machinery in barn lot in Dallas, South Dakota, United States during the Dust Bowl (Wikipedia – USDA)

History tells us that once agriculture fails on a major scale, social conflict soon follows. This has been demonstrated recently by the Arab Spring, which was triggered by a price rise in bread. The conflict in Syria also occurred after a record drought in the area. More recently, the conflicts in South Sudan are heavily connected to its droughts, desertification, and crop failures. Climate change will make this process much worse for most countries, with inevitable consequences. Some commentators have suggested that as our planet warms, new areas for growing crops will appear at or near the poles, which would be a silver lining amongst the gloom. Unfortunately, soil takes millennia to build up. The soils of these polar areas are very thin and nutritionally deficient, due to the region's historical cold temperatures. There therefore isn't enough time for these soils to develop into fertile farmland before climate change reaches its hellish later stages and stops any form of farming on Earth. Soil is therefore on the way out. What about the other key resource, water?

Our planet is a watery world, but freshwater (rather than saltwater) only makes up a small proportion of that total amount. Much of this freshwater is also locked up in glaciers or ice sheets, particularly in Antarctica. Therefore, the actual amount of fresh water that's usable for us a tiny proportion of our planet's total water content. According to the United States government, only '0.5% of the earth's water is available fresh water.' We gain much of this water from rivers, which are themselves usually fed by snow melt from glaciers in the mountains. Unfortunately, as our world has warmed, these glaciers have been melting away. Deceptively, this melting has increased water flow, giving us a false sense of plenty, but this boon will soon end. Other major rivers are fed by seasonal rainfall but, once again, climate change is making rainfall patterns increasingly erratic, leading to long periods of drought, or devastating floods. Another source of freshwater for agriculture have been natural aquifers: huge underground water reservoirs. These too are shrinking, as they have been drained far faster than they can be naturally replenished. For example, in Northern India, farmers have been using increasingly powerful diesel motors to pump water out of aquifers but as the water level in these aquifers has descended, the farmers have been forced to spend more and more money on pumps, and fuel, to gain further water.

Several major nations are responding to the increasing problem of water scarcity. Some of them are using their control of mountain ranges to dam or redirect water flow to their farmlands, rather than let the water flow naturally into a neighbouring country. Such plans are going to cause major international hostility and, in the long-term, may trigger full-scale wars.

In fifty-years-time, if the science is correct, it will be practically impossible to farm outdoors. The loss of soil, and fresh water, combined with the increasingly hostile weather systems – floods, storms, hurricanes, heatwaves – will end the traditional supply of wheat, arable crops, meat and dairy. The only way for human beings to function in the second half of the twentieth century is to go under cover.

No more cars, suburbs, or overpopulation

As climate change worsens, the human race will eventually be forced to go under cover. It won't be possible to live outside, under the sky, or stars, as we once did. The weather systems and temperature changes will become too extreme for us to survive in urban, suburban or rural homes. The way we grow food will also have to be done undercover. Fortunately, thanks to modern technology, we've already made a lot of progress in growing food under cover, or underground. Hydroponics – the practice of growing food without soil – has been used for decades. Aeroponics – growing food in a mist environment – is also being developed. Artificial, full-spectrum lamps can be used as a substitute for sunlight. For example, one entrepreneur has turned an old, World War 2 bomb shelter in London into an underground salad farm (pictured). The farm now supplies high-quality, fresh greens to many London restaurants. This shows not only that such an approach is feasible, it's also commercially viable.

Underground salad farm in London (internet - various)

The World War 2 bomb shelter is an excellent example of what is possible, but the cost of powering the full-spectrum lights is currently prohibitive. A more logical middle-ground, in terms of food production, is to build large, domed farms. These can still use sunlight to grow their crops, thereby avoiding the huge energy costs of artificial light, but their crops are still protected from the increasingly extreme weather. Inside these domed farms, hydroponic or aeroponic trays allow multi-tiered growing of crops such as potatoes, salads, and greens.

Large-scale, domed farm with 'vertical' crops (Except Integrated Sustainability)

An excellent example of what can be done in terms of a domed farm is described in the Horizon (EU research and innovation magazine) article *Under the dome – multi-storey farms bring crops, livestock indoors* (15th Dec 2015):

> 'Huge indoor farms combining crops and livestock could transform the way we think about food, bringing exotic produce to countries such as Estonia without costing the earth. With an expected two billion more mouths to feed by 2050, the world needs to learn how to grow more food on less land. Over the last century, agriculture has intensified, dictating global diets, reducing biodiversity, and contributing to global warming. With more mouths to feed every day, two recent EU feasibility studies have shown that high-yield indoor farms could be the missing link in achieving a sustainable food chain. Around a sixth of all global

> greenhouse gas emissions come from agricultural production. Prioritising sustainable food production will help feed Europe's population and enable Europe to achieve its target of reducing 1990 CO2 emissions levels by 80 % to 95 % by 2050. To reach this end, the EU has put together The Roadmap to a Resource Efficient Europe, which looks at ways to lower the environmental impact of food production and consumption, and launched the SME instrument to help small- and medium-sized enterprises optimise food production.'

In the article, Tom Bosschaert, Director of Except Integrated Sustainability, an organisation developing innovative sustainable solutions, states:

> 'The way our food is grown, harvested, distributed and delivered to our plates, is an incredible, wasteful and energy-intensive cycle. We collected a group of scientists and studied how we could use some of the principles of permaculture to come up with an industrialised natural food system.'

Together, they invented the Polydome: a very large greenhouse using complimentary crops and animals in a mini ecosystem. The relationship between these plants and animals maximises production while all waste is reused within the system, eliminating the need for artificial fertilisers. To quote from the article:

> 'The Polydome has potential yields of 60-90 kilogrammes per square metre, diverse outputs of over 50 crops including

> mushrooms, chickens, eggs, fish, and honey, and can provide pesticide-free food for 3 000 to 5 000 people per hectare each year. To put that into context, the current EU average yield per hectare for single cultures of wheat is 0.56 kilogrammes per square metre, while for potatoes it's 3.16 kilogrammes per square metre, according to a report by the EU's in-house science service, the Joint Research Centre. Indoor farming like this can also greatly reduce water use and emissions compared with conventional farming, but with the business model for these systems yet to be widely tested we're still some way from another agricultural revolution.'

In other words, we can make domed farms, but no one's expecting to make money from the project at the moment. This will change. As our climate worsens, food costs will increase, and domed farms will rapidly go from being interesting ideas to needed and profitable investments.

Domed farms are a sensible idea now, and will soon be a necessity, but there are other ways to farm and live undercover, without actually going underground. For example, it is possible to build a habitat in a natural or man-made hole. The Russian architectural company AB Elis Ltd followed this idea when they designed a domed habitat to be built in one of the largest man-made holes in the world; the Kimberlite diamond mine in Mirny, in Eastern Siberia. Their project is laid out in the Evolo online article, *Eco-city Inside a One Kilometer Crater in Siberia*. To quote from the article:

"The project would be located inside a giant man-made crater of more than one kilometer in diameter and 550 meters deep that used to be one of the world's largest quarries. The idea is to create a new garden city that will be shielded from the harsh Siberian environmental conditions characterized by long and severe winters and short hot summers. The new city would attract tourists and residents to Eastern Siberia and would be able to accommodate more than 100,000 people. The new city is planned to be divided in 3 main levels with a vertical farm, forests, residences, and recreational areas. On of the most interesting aspects of the proposal is the glass dome that will protect the city and would be covered by photovoltaic cells that will harvest enough solar energy for the new development. A central core houses the majority of the vertical circulations and infrastructure along with a multi-level research center. The housing area is located in the first level with outdoor terraces overlooking a forest in the center of the city. The idea is to create a new type of highly dense urbanism in harmony with nature."

Mirny eco-city project (Evolo)

The Mirny domed habitat may seem to be only theoretical but in a century's time, Eastern Siberia will be a very different from what it is today, and a desirable place for many people to move to. It is far enough North to escape the scorching heat of rampant climate change. It is also distant from coastlines, thus avoiding storm surges and floods. It will also avoid tidal waves caused by possible future catastrophes such as methane clathrate eruptions, seamount collapses, and volcanic events. Mirny is also distant from major populations centres, insulating it from war and civic breakdown. The Mirny habitat is therefore a potentially vital project for Russia. According to the AB Elis Ltd study, the project is feasible, at least from an engineering perspective. It could even become a human Ark, as it theoretically can sustain 100,000 people. This may seem a tiny number, in terms of our current global population, but it is a large enough number to produce a genetically healthy population. In our distant past, according to archaeological records, early version of our species may have shrunk to an even lower number, due to natural catastrophes such as the Toba volcanic eruption in South East Asia, in around 70,000 BC. Even if the Mirny habitat was the *only* place where humans survived, in the world, as our climate collapsed, we would still survive as a healthy species. Hopefully, that won't come to pass.

It's worth noting that once we move into domed habitats, it will not be possible for our species to grow at an exponential rate. In a more hostile Earth, building domed habitats, or excavating underground habitats, will not be easy. If we have a lot of babies, then these habitats will rapidly become overcrowded and there won't be anywhere else for people to go. Catastrophe would follow. Therefore, the days of rapid population growth will be over. On the plus side, this will liberate many women from the health problems of repeated births, and allow them to educate themselves, and return them to the important roles that they have often occupied in hunter-gatherer societies.

Domed habitats will therefore be a challenge, but it's one that we have the technology and resources to deal with. Living in domed habitats will also have a silver lining; we will escape some more of the toxic elements of our current civilization, but will we be able to handle it? Will we become malnourished, or just go mad? To help answer this, we can study what's happened to teams of people who have lived in a sealed environment, for months or years on end. By studying their experiences, and how sealed-dome living changed them, we can also see the potential to rid ourselves of the last items in our toxic-civilization list.

No more alcohol, soldiers, money, luxury items, dehumanising specialisation, or overwork

In the next fifty years, it is likely that some of us, if we're lucky, will move into some form of domed habitat. Many of these structures are likely to start as domed farms, in order to safeguard food production. Over time, as the climate worsens, they will become domed habitats where people will live, as well as grow food. If the worst-case scenario unfolds, in which our ocean circulation stops, our oceans turn septic, then flood our continents with hydrogen sulphide gas - a doomsday results known as a Canfield Ocean Event - we'll be in those domes all the time. If that happens, then we'll face serious psychological challenges, as well as physical ones.

Fortunately, we have some data on what it's like to live inside a sealed dome. In the last fifty years, there have been several experiments in this area. For example, between 1987 and 1991, the largest ever sealed habitat was constructed in Arizona. It was called Biosphere 2. To quote from the Wikipedia article:

> "Biosphere 2 was only used twice for its original intended purposes as a closed-system experiment: once from 1991 to 1993, and the second time from March to September 1994. Both attempts, though heavily publicized, ran into problems including low amounts of food and oxygen, die-offs of many animals and plants included in the experiment (though this was anticipated since the project used a

strategy of deliberately "species-packing" anticipating losses as the biomes developed), group dynamic tensions among the resident crew, outside politics and a power struggle over management and direction of the project. Nevertheless, the closure experiments set world records in closed ecological systems, agricultural production, health improvements with the high nutrient and low caloric diet the crew followed, and insights into the self-organization of complex biomic systems and atmospheric dynamics. The second closure experiment achieved total food sufficiency and did not require injection of oxygen."

Biosphere 2 (Wikipedia Commons – Dr Starbuck)

The story of Biosphere 2 is a fascinating one. It is described in the enthralling documentary *Spaceship Earth*. The documentary shows that the scientists who were sealed into the habitat for a year or more, suffered badly. The team's calculations of oxygen creation in the habitat were wrong and oxygen level steadily diminished as time went by. This may have been because the scientists didn't understand how much oxygen, on our planet, is actually created in our seas, by tiny sea creatures such as phytoplankton, rather than by land-based plants. The project was also steered by someone who clearly behaved, to a worrying degree, like a cult leader. At one point in the documentary, he seems unconcerned about the pitiful state of his team in the habitat. As far as he seems to be concerned, the project will succeed, and they all just need faith. This dangerous situation is saved from disaster by another member of the project team, who bravely states that what's happening is abuse, as he's personally experienced abusive behaviour and he knows it when he sees it. Fortunately, the cult-like leader is overruled, the team in the dome are given oxygen, as well as food from outside, and they are thereby saved from permanent physical damage. Biosphere 2 is therefore both a captivating drama, and an excellent study in what to do, and *not* to do, when setting up and living in a sealed habitat.

A more recent, and more intelligently handled example of sealed-dome living is the HI-SEAS (Hawaii Space Exploration Analog and Simulation) Isolation Habitat project. This project was carried out in 2016 in a high-altitude and remote part of Hawaii.

HI-SEAS Habitat – Hawaii

The purpose of the HI-SEAS habitat was to test the ability of a team to survive on Mars. The experiment lasted for a year, in which the habitat team experienced sealed habitat life without major problems. During that year, its crew discovered many practical, and psychological challenges that come from living in a sealed dome. One of the team, doctor Sheyna Gifford, talks candidly about her experience in the *New Scientist* article *My year on Mars: Frontier life of a space doctor* (4th Jan 2017). Her description of life inside a sealed dome is both practical and thought-provoking. For example, she notes in the *New Scientist* interview that naturally grown food became rare in their habitat, as they had subsisted on freeze-dried stores for much of their time there. To quote from the article:

> 'Our first Martian holiday was in honour of our first tomato harvest. Our astrobiologist spent months raising those tomatoes. They grew out of bottles, hydroponically, because we had very little soil, just like on Mars. We each got one. We set out plates, sprinkled over dried parsley, lit candles and showed up nicely

> dressed for our one tomato. We called this holiday the Jour de la Grand Tomate – Day of the Great Tomato. That was the first fresh tomato we'd had in at least four months. I took my tomato and smelled it like a maniac for 10 minutes – it smelled like a whole hothouse of tomatoes. When I finally tasted it, it burned my lips. There wasn't anything wrong with it, there was something wrong with my lips. We didn't have any acidic food; we had been eating powdered tomatoes. I had to eat the tomato carefully.'

Gifford's description shows that something as simple as growing a tomato had become a special event, because it was so difficult to do in their habitat. As a result, she'd developed a newfound admiration and love for this natural creation.

Gifford also explains, in the interview, that electrical power was a precious commodity; it was never wasted or used in a profligate way. She mentions during the interview that if she stood in Times Square, she'd be shocked at the wasteful use of power. She also explains that all physical objects, tools and machinery in the habitat were used until they failed, at which point their components were melted down and turned into new resources. In other words, like hunter gatherers, everything was used until it literally fell apart, and it was then recycled back into new equipment. Crucially, she states:

> 'We don't value stuff on Mars except in terms of its utility. Money is useless, and the only thing that matters is how smart, sane and capable you are.'

Gifford's comment tells us a lot about what life will be like in a sealed habitat. Her comment makes it clear that survival in such a habitat is a precarious thing. Everyone in the habitat has to be alert, knowledgeable, focussed, and dedicated to keeping the habitat functioning. There is no room for money, luxury items, drunkenness, the creation of arms or the maintaining of soldiers, because there aren't enough excess resources to maintain these unproductive elements, or deal with their toxic consequences. Everyone has to pitch in, stay alert, make only what is needed, stay sober, stay healthy and be multi-skilled. There is also no room for exploitation of other people. Overworked or exhausted people make mistakes, or fall ill, or both, which would only add to the difficulties the habitat faced. Therefore, paradoxically, living in a sealed habitat, on a hostile Earth, would be tough, but it could become a far healthier and more fulfilling life than we have now.

The idea that climate change might actually help the human race, in terms of its spiritual, social and moral development, might sound odd. It would seem reasonable to think that a world of plenty, of harmonious weather and abundant crops, would be the best environment for human development. The problem with this idea is that, as we've seen, if things are too easy, people can get worse. In a world of plenty, of easy richness, humans can develop a lack of respect and appreciation, like spoilt rich kids. This paradoxical result has already been foreseen by many people at a key moment in their lives: when they were dead.

No more fear

Earlier in this book, we saw why our universe can't a purely physical place. Minds or spirits have to exist for Life to overcome the disorganising effects of entropy. This simple idea has profound consequences, one of which is that since we're fundamentally non-physical minds, we don't die when our body dies. Instead, we just leave our physical body and go somewhere else. Death is not the end. Instead, it's a transition. This is an interesting idea for many of us, but for some people, it's more than an idea, as they've directly experienced it.

Many people, when they have a serious accident, or severe illness, they can physically die. In other words, their heart stops beating for minutes, or even hours. During this time, when they are physically dead, many of these people have profound experiences. They experience leaving their body and looking down on it, often watching doctors and nurses trying desperately to save their life. They then leave the physical plane and travel to another reality, where interact with other spirits, often angelic and loving, as well as deceased friends and family. Their ethereal meeting then ends with the loving spirits telling them that they have to return and continue their life, because there are still things they need to do. They return to their body, enter it, and wake up, often to the shock of the doctors attending them, who had given them up for dead.

Several books have explored this phenomenon, known as a Near Death Experience. For example, the Dutch cardiac surgeon Dr Pim Van Lommel studied it in his hospital for months, using multiple forms of recording, and then published a scientific paper on the matter in the prestigious journal *The Lancet*. He later wrote a book: *Consciousness Beyond Life*. Another medical professional, the American neurosurgeon Dr Eben Alexander, personally experienced his own NDE, in which a large part of his brain was shut down by a malignant bacterium. He described the event in his book *Proof of Heaven*. Both of them clearly show that some NDEs cannot be explained as a physical phenomenon, as a hallucination brought on by an oxygen-starved brain. They make it clear that the only rational explanation is that our minds *can* leave our physical bodies, and that there is more to the universe than the physical world around us.

Another book that explores the world of NDEs is *Heading Towards Omega* by Dr Kenneth Ring. Ring's book focusses on reporting what these NDEs want to tell us about what happened to them, and what they saw. Ring's book, as a result, is full of insights, visions, advice and spiritual philosophy from those

NDEs. One key message from the NDE subjects in Ring's book is to do with spirituality, the nature of God and love, and the purpose of our lives. One NDE subject, Belle, explains that she underwent surgery for a persisting back condition. During the operation, her heart failed. She was informed later, by her family physician, that she had been clinically dead for twenty minutes. On page 70 of Dr Ring's book, she recounts her NDE, and the being she met:

> "I met this beautiful being of light. It is the most beautiful person and it is not at all effeminate. Masculine, filled with love, pulsating love. You're just surrounded with love. It's not a physical or a sexual love. It's God's love of man and man's love of God. It's an all-consuming feeling."

She then describes the judgement of her life:

> "You are shown your life, and you do the judging. Had you done what you should do? You think, "oh, I gave six dollars to someone that didn't have much and that was great of me." That didn't mean a thing; it's the little things - maybe a hurt child that you helped or stopped to say hello to a shut-in. Those are the things that are most important. You are judging yourself. You have been forgiven your sins but are you able to forgive yourself for not doing the things you should have done and some little, cheaty things that maybe you've done in life? Can you forgive yourself? This is the judgement."

This idea makes a lot of sense. Unlike the religious

idea that some autocratic, authoritarian male God judges us, we judge *ourselves*. As a result, we can't lie or hide our deeds, since we did them. We are both the prosecution and the defence. It is our guilt, and our desire to improve, that decides our punishment. This approach, by its nature, is compassionate and empowering because no one is rejected, or deemed beyond redemption, because they are in control of their judgement, punishment and course of penance. On page 99, Belle continues by saying:

> "I realised that there are things that every person is sent to Earth to realise and to learn. For instance, to share more love, to be more loving toward one another. To discover that the most important thing is human relationships and love and not materialistic things. And to realise that every single thing that you do in your life is recorded and that even though you pass it by, not thinking at the time, it always comes up later. For instance, you may be at a stoplight and you're in a hurry and the lady in front of you, when the light turns green, doesn't take off; [she] doesn't notice the light, and you get upset and start honking your horn and telling her to hurry up. Those are the little kind of things that are recorded that you don't realise at the time are really important. One of the things that I discovered that is very important is patience toward other human beings and realising that you yourself may be in that situation sometime."

Barbara, another NDE, says on page 109 of the

book:

> "The true value of existence is the connectedness that you have going with every other living thing."

We can see, based on these examples, that these people no longer have any need for religion. They also have no interest in worldly goods, luxury items, power, wealth, or other trappings of material success. Therefore, in a way, if we want to find out what to do with our lives, spiritually, we don't need a Bible, or a church, or priests; we just need to listen to them.

The NDE subjects in Dr Ring's book talk about our future on Earth, as a species. During their NDEs, some of them were given visions of what was to come. Unfortunately, several of their reports seem worryingly accurate. For example, on page 201 of the book, one NDE subject, Hank, had this to say:

> 'We'll start getting more droughts, which will bring about shortages in crops, and the shortages in crops will cause food prices to rise, which will cause a strain on the economic situation, which is already going downhill. Also, at the same time, because of the shortage of food and the failing economy, I see a strengthening of arms, which causes tension. These kind of hostilities, and [increasing] inflation, start more hostilities."

Dr Ring's book is roughly forty-years old, but Hank's prediction is spot-on, at least according to what's happening now, in 2021. Another NDE subject, Reinee Pasarow, who experienced her NDE in 1967, had this to say on page 198:

> "The vision of the future I received during my Near Death Experience was one of tremendous upheaval in the world as a result of our general ignorance of the 'true' reality. I was informed that mankind was breaking the laws of the universe and, as a result of this, we would suffer. This suffering was not due to the vengeance of an indignant God, but rather like the pain one might suffer as a result of arrogantly defying the law of gravity. It was to be an inevitable educational cleansing of the Earth that would creep up on its inhabitants, who would try to hide blindly in the institutions of law, science, and religion. Mankind, I was told, was being consumed by the cancers of arrogance, materialism, racism, chauvinism, and separatist thinking. I saw sense turning to nonsense, and calamity, in the end, turning to providence. At the end of this general period of transition, mankind was to be 'born anew', with a new sense of its place in the universe. The birth process, however, as in all the kingdoms, was exquisitely painful. Mankind would emerge humbled, yet educated, peaceful and at last, unified."

This description touches upon many ideas we've already explored in this book. Reinee adds to this by saying that this toxic situation we're in *is* bad, but that it will eventually, painfully, transform into something far better. As we've already seen in this final Part of this book, the science shows that we're heading for a traumatic upheaval, but it could be one in which we finally shed the toxic elements of civilization that have plagued us for so long, wherever they might have originated from. In a form of 'trial by fire', we will be able to cleanse ourselves of those negative elements and adopt a new life, one similar to the one described by Dr Gifford in the HI-SEAS habitat. It'll be a future where there is no money, alcohol, luxury items, soldiers or religion. Instead, there will be people working together, in harmony, to stay alive. When we reach that enlightened stage, and all the toxic elements of our current and historical society have gone, then, perhaps, we will, through adversity, have finally found the right civilization. In a sense, it will be so different from what has been civilization for us, for the last six-thousand years, that we should probably give it a new name. We could call it community, or perhaps we could use a term mentioned earlier, to describe the Creator Spirit, the Tao, the Atom or the One. How about we just call it Unity?

About the Author

Adrian Ellis has written two previous non-fiction books. The first is, *Minds Make the World*, which explains scientifically that our minds must make the world, in order for reality to exist. This was the conclusion of a group of famous scientists in the 1930s, but it was buried by the scientific establishment after the War. His second book is *Ancient Secrets, Future Warning*. which explains that our ancient past is very different to the official explanation, and that it hides a dangerous warning about our future.

He lives in London, England, where he cycles and walks a lot, feeds birds and plays the guitar.

Bibliography

Here is a list of books that readers might find useful. They include books mentioned already, along with related works.

Diet, Nutrition and Health

Grain Brain by Dr David Perlmutter
This book opened my eyes to the hidden problems of consuming wheat. The science is clear; wheat is not good for our bodies. The fact that it both pleasantly drugs us, while damaging our bodies, is particularly devious.

Fat Chance: The Hidden Truth About Sugar, Obesity and Disease.
Dr Lustig has campaigned for many years to highlight the damage fructose sugars are doing to people in the developed world. His research is thorough, clear and illuminating.

Physics

13 Things that don't make sense by Michael Brooks
This is a fun and entertaining popular-science book. It investigates a bunch of fascinating topics, such as the Pioneer Anomaly, the Viking 'life on Mars' mystery, the Wow signal and others. It also mentions Erwin Schrödinger's idea that Life increases order in the universe. Unfortunately, the book does have its flaws. For example, when discussing life, Brooks agrees with Schrödinger's view that Life increases order in the world, but he then says on page

71 that, "a candle flame creates order from disorder in its environment and is patently not alive." This is plain wrong. A candle flame turns wax into carbon dioxide gas and water vapour, which is a decrease in order. The appearance of order (the functioning flame) is just the process of disordering the wax. Crucially, the candle and its wax are ordered because a living being constructed that candle. Apart from that annoying error, *13 Things* is a good book and well worth a read.

Ancient History

Eden – The Sumerian Version of Genesis by Anton Parks

Parks' book is thorough, extensive and highly revealing about what the ancient Sumerian records truly say about the beginnings of civilization. As with any translation of cuneiform texts, there will be much debate about his accuracy, but he explains his methods and supplies extensive related evidence.

Stellar Theology and Masonic Astronomy by Robert Hewitt Brown

When it comes to investigating the past, or in fact investigating anything, it's worth digging out books that are more that seventy-five years old. Although there are a lot of books being published nowadays, many of them are recycling each other's material. By comparison, some older books can be a source of highly valuable information. Brown's book most definitely falls in that latter category.

Homer's Secret Iliad by Florence Wood

In this book, and more extensively in my previous

book *Ancient Secrets, Future Warning*, I explain that the Greek Myths are, in fact, encoded Method of Loci stories describing neighbouring star-systems. This idea was echoed in Brown's book, mentioned earlier. The idea that Greek Myths are more than just stories is also explored in *Homer's Secret Iliad,* in which the authors explain that the Iliad was not purely an epic tale, but was in fact an encoded description of constellations in the sky, and their movements during the year. The book reads well, is supported by diagrams and is well worth a read.

The power of the mind

Margins of Reality by Dr Robert Jahn and Brenda Dunne

This is a dry book but it's filled with important data on the mind's influence on physical systems. Jahn covers not only his basic RNG experiments but also further experiments involving time and distance. He did send me a copy, years ago, so I'm biased, but I still recommend it.

Supernormal by Dr Dean Radin
The Conscious Universe by Dr Dean Radin
Entangled Minds by Dr Dean Radin
Real Magic by Dr Dean Radin

I've read all these books by Dr Radin. Of them all, I think my favourite is *Supernormal*. Dr Radin does repeat material in these books but that's understandable as he is focussed on one area: minds' influence of reality. I'd recommend Supernormal first, then go from there.

Dogs that Know When their Owners are Coming Home - and other unexplained powers of animals by Rupert Sheldrake
Seven Experiments that Could Change the World by Rupert Sheldrake

Sheldrake writes well and he discusses scientific topics in an accessible way. He also investigates fascinating, heretical areas while still remaining level-headed and scientific.

Remote viewing

Phenomena by Annie Jacobsen

This book is full of interesting material about remote viewers and related topics. Unfortunately, it's clear that Jacobsen is sceptical of psi abilities. In the book, she makes it clear that because there isn't an official explanation for psi phenomenon, they can't be real. This is illogical and unscientific. Science works by establishing what phenomena are repeatable, then developing scientific theories to understand them, not the other way around. Otherwise, it's a very interesting book.

Mind Trek by Joseph McMoneagle
Natural ESP by Ingo Swann
Resurrecting the Mysterious by Ingo Swann
Penetration by Ingo Swann

McMoneagle and Swann were both experienced remote viewers. Their insights and recollections make for very interesting reading. Swann also looks further into what the universe holds for those with heightened mental perceptions and its spiritual implications. These books can be slow going, at times, but they do hold some fascinating nuggets of historical, physical and spiritual info.

Psi Spies by Jim Marrs

For me, this is the best book about the remote viewing programmes carried out by the US military and the CIA. The late Jim Marrs was an excellent journalist and writer. His books are very readable and very informative. Marrs approaches these tricky subjects with a calm, open-minded attitude. Thank you, Jim.

Spirituality

The Gnostic Gospels by Elaine Pagels

This is a well-researched book into an important aspect of Christianity, possible the true form of Christianity, depending on your point of view.

The Gospel of Judas by Rodolphe Kasser, Marvin Meyer, Gregor Wurst

The Gospel of Judas itself is fairly short, and some of it is damaged, but the book does a good job of translating it, explaining the translation and talking about its context. The result is a thought-provoking insight into yet another banned gospel and what it says about Jesus and Judas's true relationship.

The Tao Teh Ching by Lao Tsu

This is a wonderful, wise and thought-provoking book but because its content is enigmatic, its English translations can vary widely in their style and interpretation. My favourite editions are a slim, hardback, Peter Pauper Press Book edition (I've no idea if that's still in print or even available) and the

Wildwood House edition, with a translation by Gai-Fu Feng and Jane English.

The Hermetica - The lost wisdom of the Pharaohs
The Hermetica, like the Tao Teh Ching, varies depending on the translation. My favourite edition is by Tarcher Cornerstone Editions, written by Timothy Freke and Peter Gandy.

UFOs and aliens

You can't tell the people by Georgina Bruni
The Rendlesham Forest Incident is perhaps the most important UFO case in British history. It is, to a large degree, the UK version of Roswell. Several books have been written on the event but of them all, I would recommend Bruni's book. It is exhaustive, clear and engrossing.

The Missing Times by James Hansen
Hansen's book does an excellent job of putting forward the case that those who control the national media in the United States have a clear agenda of keeping all UFO reports out of the public eye, particularly any UFO reports that portray alien visitors as friendly.

Earth: An Alien Enterprise by Timothy Good
Timothy Good has done a sterling job, over several decades, to record and publish UFO accounts. He was a professional violinist but found time, in his spare hours, to record and publish a huge amount of witness testimony. His books are all good, in my experience, although they can seem long-winded, as

he methodically reports on one UFO case after another.

Mass Contacts by Stefano Breccia

When I first read *Mass Contacts*, I thought it was an odd but interesting tale of friendly aliens in Italy. Over time, particularly after re-reading *the Apocryphon of John*, I realised that Breccia's book could actually be true, and extremely important. Nevertheless, it's hard to believe but, then again, the truth often is hard to believe.

Climate Change

Climate Wars by Gwynne Dyer

This is a particularly good book on climate change, as it studies the geopolitical effects of accelerating climate change and how they interact with the environmental changes. For example, droughts and crop failures produce civil wars and international wars. These then cause the breakdown of society and distribution networks, making it more difficult to get the remaining crops to people. As a result, climate change will cause a cascade of interconnected problems, which will only worsen the situation.

Six Degrees by Mark Lynas, and *Storms of our Grandchildren* by Jim Hansen

Both of these books supply solid information about our climate change emergency. They are slow-going at times, but still worth a read.

Near Death Experiences

Heading Towards Omega by Dr Kenneth J Ring

This book is a gem. I would recommend that everyone read it. In fact, I'd recommend everyone read it once a year. On the face of it, it's about Near Death Experiences but I've realised, over the years, that it's more than that. It's an everyman's Bible about how to live our lives. Truly profound.

Consciousness Beyond Life by Dr Pim Van Lommel

This book is an excellent description of Dr Lommel's efforts to prove that Near Death Experiences aren't hallucinations by an oxygen-starved brain, or fantasies created by deluded patients. Instead, they are experience that people have when their body is not physically functioning. They are therefore experiences directly perceived by non-physical minds.

Proof of Heaven by Dr Eben Alexander

This book is also about an NDE but it has a novel twist; the author is a neurosurgeon and therefore a specialist on brain function. Dr Alexander experienced an NDE after contracting a virulent infection that crippled the cortex of his brain. He survived the experience and the infection. He then wrote about what happened and how that related to our knowledge of the brain, using his advanced neurological understanding. It's a relatively short book but it's well worth reading.

Index

1

1984, 173

9

9/11, 251

A

A-DAM, 203, 211
Adams, Douglas, 3, 315
Akhenaten, 218
Albigensian Crusade, 314
alcohol, 37
Aldebaran, 311
Alexander, Dr Eben, 364
amines, 32
Amun, 184
Ancient Secrets, Future Warning, 301, 311
Annunaki, 199
Apocryphon of John, The, 226, 335
Archons, 229
Ark (Biblical), 200
army training, 158
arsenic, 44
Arthur, King, 149
Asch Conformity experiment, 318
Asch, Solomon, 318
Atom, 338
Atrahasis, The Epic of, 198
Atum. *See* Atom
Azazel, 225, 292

B

Backster, Cleve, 255
Bagemihl, Bruce, 88
Bem, Daryl, 253
Biderman, Albert, 8
Biderman's Chart of Coercion, 10, 101, 154, 167
bio-androids, 279
Biosphere 2, 357
Bishop Irenaeus, 177
Bladerunner, 310
Bøckman, Petter, 89
Bohr, Neils, 239
Boltzmann, Ludwig, 334
Book of Enoch, The, 223, 291
Bose, Jagadish Chandra, 258
Bosschaert, Tom, 352
brainwashing, 8
Brave New World, 133
breast feeding, 96
Breccia, Stefano, 306
British Columbia, 63
Brooks, Michael, 241
Brown, Robert Hewitt, 295
Bruni, Georgina, 280, 316
Budge, E.A. Wallis, 182
Bullingdon Club, 83, 141
Burroughs, John, 283
Bushman, 15

C

Calhoun, John B., 102, 107
Campbell, T Colin, 28
Canada, 64
cancer, 29, 52, 54
Capgras Syndrome, 288
Cathars, 314
Catholic Church, 91, 163, 173, 226, 314
Cerberus, 301
chicks, 246
climate change, 111
Climate Wars, 113, 269, 329
computer future simulation, 112
Constantine the Great, 179
Coordinated Remove Viewing, 264
Cordyceps fungus, 146
Cradles of Eminence, 131
Cronus, 310
cryptocurrencies, 76
CTR bio-android aliens, 307
CTR bio-androids, 317
Cubberley, Ellwood, 131
cuneiform, 198, 201

D

Dead Sea Scrolls, 223
Diamond, Jared, 2
disgust, 90
DMT, 32
DNA, 30, 204, 210, 243
domed farm, 351
domed farms, 353
domestic abuse, 6
Dumuzid, 186
Dunne, Brenda J., 248
Dyer, Gwynne, 113, 269, 329

E

Eddington, Arthur, 239, 240
Einstein, Albert, 131
Elizabeth I, Queen, 47
Elohim, 202, 217, 221
elongated skulls, 221
Enki, 199
Enoch, 223
Entropy, 240
Eve, 192

F

face masks, 119
fact, 117
factory schooling, 127, 130
farming, 14
Fawaris, 311
Federal Reserve, 73
fertility drop, 109
fiat currency, 74
First Nation, 95
Fixation of Belief, The, 126, 284
Forbes article, 27
Forks over Knives, 30
Forrester, Jay, 112
France Bacon, Sir, 118
Frankenstein, 310
fructose, 48, 49
fungus, 146

G

Gao, George, 121
Garden of Eden, The, 191, 212, 229
Gaslight, 181
Gates, Frederick Taylor, 133
Gelfand, Prof Michele J., 99
Genesis, The Book of, 188
Genetic engineering, 204
Georgetown UCEW, 124
Gifford, Sheyna, 360
Gnostic Christians, 175, 227
God (Biblical), 190, 195
gold, 66
Gospel of Judas, The, 227
Grain Brain, 20
Greek Myths, 296
Groundhog Day, 324
Guthrie, Woody, 81

H

Haim, Eshed, 290
Hansen, Terry, 285
Harbu (fiery chariots), 201
Harris, William Torrey, 132
Heading Towards Omega, 364
Heisenberg, Werner, 239
Hell, 163
Hellyer, Paul, 289
helot slaves, 153
Hercules, 296, 300
Hermetica, The, 180, 337
HFCS (corn syrup), 48
hierarchy, top down, 140
highland clearances, 47
Hill, Jess, 6
HI-SEAS habitat, 360
Hitch-hiker's Guide to the Galaxy, The, 4, 315
Holy Grail, The, 149
Homo Habilis, 207, 215
Homo sapiens, 204
homosexuality, 87, 95
hunter-gatherers, 53, 65, 95, 101, 117, 140, 150
Huxley, Aldous, 133, 173
hydroponics, 350

I

Insulin-like growth, 29
Invasion of the Body Snatchers, 287
Islam, 92
Island of Dr Moreau, The, 328

J

Jacobsen, Annie, 255
Jacobsen, Annie, 263
Jahn, Dr Robert, 248
Jarhead, 151
Jebel Irhoud, 213
Jesus Christ, 174
Jews of Judea, 189
Johnson, Boris, 84, 141

K

Knights Templar, 69

Korean Prisoners of War, 7

L

Law of Entropy, 240, 334
Leonard, George, 277
Library of History, The, 233
Lord Bishop of London, 128
lucid dreaming, 272
Lucifer, 313, 314
Lustig, Dr Robert, 49
Luther, Martin, 129

M

M.I.T., 112
maize, 208
Mangatiti, The monster of, 5
MAO, 34
Mao, Chairman, 149
Marine Corps, U.S., 158
Marrs, Jim, 265
Mass Contacts, 306
Mass Psychology of Fascism, The, 85, 93
McMoneagle, Joseph, 266
meat, 25
Memory Palace, The. *See* Method of Loci
Mencken, H. L., 132
Mesoamerica, 208
Method of Loci, 298, 299
Milgram, Stanley, 319
Milgram's Experiment, 320
milk, 22
Mirny habitat, 354
Missing Times, The, 285

Mitchell, Dr. Edgar, 250
mitochondria, 56
money, 62
Monty Python, 149
Moroccan fossils, 213
Morris, William, 44
Mouse Utopia Experiment, 103
Muliphen, 311
Mummert, Amanda, 16

N

NDE. *See* Near Death Experience
Near Death Experience, 363
Nebuchadnezzar, 188
Nephilim, 224, 291, 312
Nibert, David, 17
Nick, Christophe, 320
Nietzsche, Friedrich, 322, 323
Nixon, Richard, 74
Nutt, Prof David, 42

O

Oklahoma Dust Bowl, 347
One, The, 335
Original Sin, 163
Orion, 299
Orion's Belt, 293, 311, 312
Orwell, George, 124, 173
Osiris, 181
overpopulation, 99, 101

P

Pagels, Elaine, 175
parasites, 146
Parks, Anton, 201
Pauli, Wolfgang, 239
Peirce, Charles Sanders, 126, 284
Pentyrch Incident, 289
Peoc'h, René, 245
Perlmutter, Dr David, 20
Peru (Paracas), 221
Planck, Max, 239, 244
Polydome, 353
polygraph, 256
potlatch, 64
precognition, 254
preserved meat, 35
Price, Pat, 265
prison, 37
Proof of Heaven, 364
propaganda, 126, 134
PSI TECH, 267
psychokinesis, 248
psychopath, 142
Puthoff, Hal, 261

R

Radin, Dr Dean, 250
Reich, Wilhelm, 85, 93
religion, 162
Religious children, 343
Rendlesham Forest, 280
Rijl Al Qanturus, 311
Ring, Dr Kenneth, 364
RNG machine, 246, 251

Roman Empire, 177
Roosevelt, F. D., 72
Rukbat Al Rami, 311
Russell, Bertrand, 342

S

Schrödinger, Erwin, 241
Schwaller de Lubicz, 147
Scientific Materialism, 238
secret societies, 143
Serapis, 183
sexual abuse, 167
Seyfang, Dr. Gill, 79
Sheldrake, Rupert, 275
Shepherd gods, 187
Short, R.V., 96
Siculus, Diodorus, 232
siddhis, 174
Sirius, 311
Sitchin, Zechariah, 200
Skinner, B.F., 238
Smith, Adam, 115
soil, 345
Someone Else is on the Moon, 277
Spaceship Earth, 358
Spanish Flu, 119
Sparta, 152
SQUID (quantum device), 262
Squid Game, 108
Stanford Prison Experiment, 138, 173
Stellar Theology and Masonic Astronomy, 295
sugar, 46

Sumer, 187, 197
Sumerian King List, The, 213
Swann, Ingo, 261, 276, 279
Swofford, Anthony, 151

T

Tammuz, 186
Taoism, 336
Targ, Russell, 261
Teller, Edward, 110
telomeres, 30
teosinte, 209
Thatcher, Margaret, 280
thermodynamics, 240
They Live, 287
Thuban, 311
time-based currency, 78
Trump, Donald, 80, 100
Trump, Fred, 80
Trump, Mary, 82
two-spirit, 95

U

UFO, 278, 280
Ummites, 306
Unity, The, 340
Upitis, Rena, 131
Uranus, 310

V

Vega, 311

Victoria, Queen, 44
Vigano, Archbishop, 170
virus, 210
Von Neumann, John, 239

W

W56 aliens, 307, 316
Wallace, Alan, 174
Warburg, Otto Heinrich, 56
Watchers, 226
water, 348
Wealth of Nations, The, 115
Westall Incident, 289
Wheat, 20
Wigner, Eugene, 239
Wilson, Edward O., 106
witchcraft, 237
World Health Organisation, 122

Y

Yaldabaoth, 228, 283
Yoga Vashista, 259
You can't tell the people, 316

Z

Ziewe, Jurgen, 273
Zimbardo, Philip, 137, 173
Zone Xtrême, La, 320

Printed in Great Britain
by Amazon